Choura

THE MEMOIRS OF
ALEXANDRA DANILOVA

To Diani
Happy Easter
'93

Choura

THE MEMOIRS OF

Alexandra Danilova

Fromm International Publishing Corporation

New York

Published in 1988 by Fromm International Publishing Corporation
560 Lexington Avenue, New York, NY 10022 by arrangement
with Alfred A. Knopf, Inc.

Library of Congress Cataloging-in-Publication Data
Danilova, Alexandra, date
   Choura : the memoirs of Alexandra Danilova.
   1. Danilova, Alexandra, date   .   2. Ballet
dancers—Russian S.F.S.R.—Biography.   I. Title.
GV1785.D24A3   1988   792.8′0924 [B]   87-27496
ISBN 0-88064-103-7

Photographic Credits

Cover—from Alexandra Danilova's private collection

Photographs follow pages 56, 120, and 184.

Following page 56:
Pages 5, 8, 9, 10, 11, 14, 15, 16—Ballet Society
pages 12, 13—Dance Collection, The New York Public Library
Following page 120:
Page 13—Maurice Seymour (from the Dance Collection, The New York Public Library)
Following page 184:
Pages 2, 3, 4, 5, 8—Maurice Seymour (from the author's private collection)
Pages 1, 9 (above), 11—Dance Collection, The New York Public Library
All pictures not otherwise credited are from Alexandra Danilova's private collection.
Special thanks to Nancy LaSalle and Jane Emerson of Ballet Society.
   Monica Mosley of The New York Public Library's Dance
   Collection, and to Clement Crisp.

Printed in the United States of America

To my pupils

ACKNOWLEDGMENTS

These memoirs came about through the generous efforts of many people. I am grateful to Dame Alicia Markova, Irina Baronova, Leon Danielian, Doris Brett, Eugene Fraccia, and Bobby Lindgren, my friends who helped to jog my memory.

To Mary Clarke, for her suggestions; Jane Emerson of Ballet Society, for her help in locating pictures of me; Clement Crisp and Arthur Hammond, for photographs in their possession; and Simon Barnes, for his support.

To Charles France, with whom I undertook this project; and Robert Cornfield and Amanda Urban, who have represented it.

To Lewis Ufland, my manager, for his encouragement and sustaining conviction that this book should be written; to Bob Gottlieb, my editor, for his extraordinary patience and guidance; and to Holly Brubach, for her compassion and skill in helping to translate my recollections into print.

Thank you all very much.

A. D.

THE MEMOIRS OF
ALEXANDRA DANILOVA

One

HEN I WAS BORN, my city was called St. Petersburg. While I was in school, it was called Petrograd. By the time I left Russia, in 1924, it was called Leningrad. My childhood was full of commotion.

I have no idea what my father did for a living. I know only that he was out hunting and caught cold—that was the story. The cold got worse, and my mother looked after him. Then he died. My mother came down with the same disease, and soon she died, too.

All of this must have taken place in Peterhof, because I once saw my birth certificate and that was the place written on it. Peterhof, which was near St. Petersburg, consisted only of the tsar's palaces, the people who served in them, and the regiments stationed there, so I suspect that my parents must have been connected in some way with the court.

After my parents' deaths, my sister, Elena, and I went to live with our grandmother—Babushka, we called her. Her first name was Anastasia, but I don't know her last name. I don't even know whether she was my mother's or my father's mother. Babushka had only one leg and walked with crutches. We all lived together in a very modest house—

one big room. Elena, or Lenochka, who was two years older than I, slept on the divan. Because I was the smaller one, I slept with Babushka.

I remember one day when I was four years old, going to play with Lenochka in the courtyard of our house in Peterhof. (Most apartment buildings in Russia were built around a square court. The servants' entrances and doors to the kitchens all opened onto this courtyard, and it was there that children played, because it was quite safe, well protected by the building.) It was the deep of winter, and Lenochka and I were sledding, squealing with pleasure. Suddenly, we were interrupted by our grandmother, calling to us in a stern tone of voice, telling us to come home immediately. "Which of you two broke my cup?" she asked.

Without a moment's hesitation, I said, "Not me, Grandmother—it must have been Lenochka."

"Ah!" she said. "So it was Lenochka?"

Poor Lenochka started to cry. Suddenly, Babushka lost her temper, picked me up and put me over her knee, and spanked me hard. I started to cry, too. How did she know that I was the one who had broken her cup? "Very simple," she explained. "I can read your eyes, and I knew straightaway that it was you."

So I went to the mirror and studied myself. I looked at my eyes and wondered: What is written in them? How is it that the way I look can overrule what I say? How can someone's appearance be so convincing?

Soon after this episode, I awakened one morning and, to my surprise, saw my grandmother still asleep. I thought: Why didn't Babushka wake me up? Where is my tea? And I jumped out of bed and began to shake her. "Get up, dear Babushka! Get up! You've overslept!" Suddenly, I understood that something terrible had happened, that she would never awaken. The next thing I remember is a room full of people, everybody talking at once, all of them sorry for me and my sister. From their talk, I understood that I would be taken to live with our uncle. But Babushka had always told us that our uncle was no good, an alcoholic. So, very definitely, I said, "I don't want to go to my uncle!" For the next few days, people I didn't know, had never seen, came and went, saying: "Poor little orphans, they have nobody—this is terrible!" Yes, I thought, it's true.

Instead of our uncle, our godmother, Mme Molvo, took us. She lived on the outskirts of St. Petersburg, in a large, very pretty house.

Her children showed us their own rooms first—nursery rooms, decorated with animals, dolls, all kinds of toys. "And where will *we* sleep?" I asked.

"You also have a room," her daughter told me. "It's there, next to the kitchen."

Next to the kitchen? I thought. But why can't I sleep in this beautiful nursery? The daughter showed us our room, which was dark and narrow. Our meals were always brought into that room—our morning tea, our dinner. Lenochka and I ate by ourselves, but every afternoon we played together with Mme Molvo's children in their garden.

One day, the children came to fetch me and took me to the drawing room, where my godmother and a lady I'd never seen before were sitting together. "Look how very tiny she is," my godmother told this woman, "and what beautiful big eyes she has!" And then Mme Molvo turned to me and said, "Here is your new aunt." I didn't understand what was happening. I turned and looked at the lady, who replied to my godmother, "Yes, I like her. I will take her tomorrow."

How wonderful to leave this place, I thought. "And Lenochka, will she go with me?" I asked my godmother.

"No, Lenochka will be taken by another lady. Only you, Chourochka, are very lucky—your new aunt is rich, and you will be happy with her." I was glad to know that I would have a nice life but sorry to leave Lenochka.

The next day, my new "aunt," Lidia Mstislavna Gototsova, née Nestroeva, came for me and took me to her home. I learned later that she had adopted me to take the place of her own daughter, who had just died. The butler took my coat at the entrance, then picked me up and carried me into the drawing room, where Aunt Lidia was talking with a gentleman. "Look—you see how tiny she is, exactly like my Lidochka." The gentleman, as it turned out, was my new "uncle." And my room in this new home was the billiard room.

The big table covered with green felt, the cues on the wall—all this was new to me, and very interesting. I took down one of the cues and pushed the balls around the table until, suddenly, I heard my uncle's voice: "Never, never touch these things—billiards is not for little children!" Why, I thought, it's my room, I sleep here, but I can't even touch anything in it! I was offended but didn't say a word.

Eventually, I got used to the new life—I liked everything, especially the five dogs who ate their dinner with us, in the dining room, and the horses. In the evening, the three of us—my uncle, my aunt, and I—would go to the stables. My uncle carried me on his shoulders—that, I loved very much—and I learned how to give the horses sugar, right out of the palm of my hand.

How long we lived like that, I don't know. But for a time, life settled into a pattern, very comfortable.

Then one morning, I was awakened by my aunt kneeling beside my bed, crying. "Very soon, we will go away from here, Chourochka," she whispered.

"But why?" I asked.

"If you want to stay with Uncle, you stay, but I must go."

"No, no, I'll go with you," I said. "But what about the dogs, the horses?"

"I'm sorry, but we can't take them with us."

It seems that my uncle drank a lot and engaged in affairs with other women. So Aunt Lidia divorced him, and she and I moved to another quarter of St. Petersburg, not nearly so chic as where we lived before. We no longer had a house but an apartment, rather small. The street on which we lived was noisy. My aunt decided that I should have a governess and hired a German lady, a real tyrant. These changes seemed to me for the worse, but I resigned myself to them.

My aunt Lidia was a member of St. Petersburg society. On Thursdays, her day to "receive," the drawing room would always be full of people drinking tea and chattering. She walked with a limp—one leg was shorter than the other from birth—but she had a very pretty face. There were always men surrounding her, courting her. She wore beautiful clothes, and perfume—I loved to watch her get dressed. With me, she was generous and sometimes extravagant. When summer arrived, she announced that we would go to the Caucasus. "But I can't go," I protested. She asked why not. "Because I have absolutely nothing to wear!" Aunt Lidia laughed. "But this can be remedied," she said. She bought me twelve new dresses, and off we went to Kislovodsk, a fashionable spa, with my governess in tow.

Aunt Lidia had many friends there. We stayed in the main hotel and went to the park where everybody went to take the famous waters. Each morning, we would go for a walk and meet someone Aunt Lidia knew; everybody was out to surprise everybody else with their beautiful outfits. In the afternoon, we would go sit at the café and gaze at all the passersby.

The park was huge, with a wonderful playground. I loved especially one swing—in Russia, we call it "the chime steps." It's a big pole, from which hang four or six loops—you put the loop around your body, run very fast, and then swing around the pole. It demands some skill. Many times I bumped my head on the big pole, knocked my knees till they were bruised and scraped, but nothing would stop me—I tried again and again, went back day after day.

One afternoon, I arrived at the playground and saw a lot of ponies and donkeys, all saddled, some loaded with picnic baskets. A big group of children and their matrons had assembled, all ready to depart. Without a moment's hesitation, I mixed in with the group and mounted one of the donkeys. The expedition went up into the mountains—beautiful scenery—and I had a delightful day. When in the evening we got back to our point of departure, I saw that it was already dark. And every one of the children had parents or a governess who had come to pick them up—every one of them but me. I began to feel a little bit lost—how could I get home? I stayed there quite a long time, until all the children had dispersed. And then, suddenly, one of the matrons noticed me. "Where is your governess?" she asked. I told her that I didn't know, but that I was staying in such-and-such a hotel. So she said all right, she would take me there.

As soon as I appeared at the hotel, there was a big to-do. The doorman stopped my companion and asked her, very sternly, "Where did you find this girl?" And then I understood that my aunt, thinking that I had been kidnapped, had called the police.

When I got back to the room, my aunt and my fräulein were crying. But they were not alone: there was also a general, one of my aunt's admirers, who took one look at me and decided that what I needed after making everyone so worried was a good spanking. "Can you imagine!" he said. "I call out all Kislovodsk to look for her and she's off picnicking in the mountains! You must punish her immediately." But my aunt was so happy to see me that she forgave me and embraced me instead.

One day, we went with the same general to dinner at a well-known restaurant outside of Kislovodsk, about one hour's journey from the town. I was happy to be included, because we went in an open carriage, drawn by a troika of beautiful horses. Along the way we saw many groups of people on horseback, each party accompanied by a guide. These guides were generally very handsome, always colorfully dressed. The road took us over several bridges, and often we passed other carriages going to the same restaurant.

During our dinner, we were served the local red wine, for which the Caucasus is famous, and the waiter even poured me a little bit, mixing it with water. I tasted that and decided it was all right. The general, who was very much taken with my aunt, was intent on their conversation; so at the first opportunity, I switched the glasses and drank his wine. And soon I began to feel very gay and started to giggle and hop around the table, which very much surprised my aunt and her general. Well, immediately he discovered that I preferred his wine to mine, and said, "What a number your little Chourochka is! And this time, I hope you will spank her, but good!" All the way home, I sang and giggled. And it was with great difficulty that they finally put me to bed.

The next day, my aunt summoned me. "Dear Chourochka," she said, "how would you like to have the general for your uncle?"

"Never!" I said. "All he wants is to spank me! He is not nice." And I asked her not to marry him.

She thought about it then and said, "All right. It will be the way you want it. Let us forget about him." And that was the end of *that* general.

At Christmastime, Aunt Lidia and I went to Moscow to visit *her* aunt—my "Moscow aunt," as I called her. I loved her and Moscow very much. On the first day of Christmas, we went to Dvoryanskoe Sobranie, the noblemen's club, to see the Christmas tree—it was enormous, almost to the ceiling in a room two stories high, and beautifully decorated.

Christmas fast became my favorite holiday. On Christmas Eve, there were parties—several families together in the drawing room of someone's house. The grown-ups came in their evening clothes, and we children in our best outfits. The servants would pass a big tray of cookies, with a gingerbread house in the center, and lemonade and tea to drink, as the boys gathered on one side of the room, the girls on the other. There were brought to us on a velvet cushion all kinds of little decorations—stars, hearts, trinkets—and each of us would choose one and pin it to her dress. And then the search began, for the boy wearing the same decoration would be your partner for the first dance. Next, the boys would each be given a fishing pole. They would stand behind a screen and dangle their fishing lines over the top. We girls, stationed on the other side of the screen, would put our little decorations on their hooks—the boys would reel in their catches and ask, "Well, who is this?"—and in that way we found our partners for the second dance, and so on. There were always little entertainments. We would make London Bridge or dance, sing carols, have our fortunes told, but not exchange gifts—it wasn't done.

Every morning during our holiday visit to Moscow, I ate for breakfast *juliki*—special little breads—with my tea. And every day at noon, my Moscow aunt would take me by the hand and we would walk to the skating rinks, where there was always music playing; the whole town was there. My Moscow aunt spoiled me terribly.

When finally Aunt Lidia and I returned to St. Petersburg, I found it very dull after Moscow. My aunt, it seemed, was going out every night, and I was entirely in the hands of my governess, whom I had grown to despise.

Then the spring came, and with it came my Moscow aunt for a visit. She arrived laden with cartons of nuts, dried fruits, little cookies, special candies, and gingerbreads—all for me.

Before long, I noticed that something special was going on in the house. There was some kind of excitement in the air. So I asked my Moscow aunt. "Ah, dear Chouritchka, we are getting ready for a wedding," she said. "And for you, we will make a beautiful frock." Well! I had never been to a wedding before. How interesting! But who was getting married? "Your Aunt Lidia will marry a very nice general," my Moscow aunt said. "You will live in a big house, and you will love your life again."

That same afternoon, the general came to take tea with us. My fräulein dressed me and brought me to the drawing room to meet him: I curtsied to my future uncle and gave him a good, long look. I liked him, I decided. And he conquered me completely when he reached into his pocket and gave me some money. Later, I learned that it was five rubles; but since I had never held any money in my hand before, I had no idea of its value. "So, what will you do with it?" he asked me. I thought about it, then said, "I will buy my aunt a house, so that we can live again the way we used to live." He laughed and said, no, that this money was strictly for me, not for my aunt, and if my aunt needed a house, it was he who would buy it for her. I must think what I want for myself. Finally, after consultation with my aunt, I decided on a house for my dolls. I had two of them: one, named Lidia, after my aunt, and the other, a little baby—this one I liked very much because I had to change the diapers.

ikhail Ivanovitch Batianov, my new uncle, was one of the highest-ranking generals in Russia, decorated with all the most prestigious medals. Born in Bessarabia, which is part of Romania, he was not pure Russian. He was sent to military school and at sixteen became an officer, defending Sevastopol during the Crimean War. He was in his late seventies; Aunt Lydia must have been in her thirties. A handsome man, dark, lively, mild-mannered, charming, not very tall, the general commanded everybody's respect. He was a great lover of women. He came to his marriage to Aunt Lidia, his third wife, with eight children by his two previous wives, both of whom had died. (Later, when my aunt Lidia had died and he was eighty or so, I heard that he wanted to marry again. By our law in the Russian church, three times is the limit. For a fourth marriage, he had to ask for a special dispensation from the empress, and she refused to give it to him.)

I loved my new family. Most of all, I liked Machuta, the general's daughter by his second marriage. She had big blue eyes, fair skin, chestnut hair, and a quiet disposition—when she spoke, which was rarely, her voice was soft and musical. This new apartment was very big—eleven rooms that took up the entire floor of the building. Machuta, like my aunt, had two rooms all to herself. Every day, I would go and visit her.

In spite of my young years, I soon came to realize that our presence—Aunt Lidia's and mine—was resented in the big Batianov family.

Not that anyone ever said so, in so many words, but one could sense a certain tension. For example, Machuta's brother Vladimir, a handsome cadet, a second lieutenant in Her Majesty's regiment, was stationed in Peterhof. He would come to visit us but never hid his delight at returning to his regiment.

My aunt did not allow anyone to smoke at the dinner table. Once, coming into the drawing room, I overheard Vladimir hatching a plan with our butler, Vassily. "You will call me to the telephone," Vladimir said, "so I can have my smoke." And sure enough, at dinner that day, Vassily called him away from the table after the second course, saying that Vladimir's regiment was telephoning on some urgent matter of business. Vladimir excused himself, got up and left the table, and in a few minutes returned. And this same scenario was repeated every day until Vladimir went back to his regiment.

From the general's first marriage had come three daughters, each with children of her own. One of these grandchildren, Lenochka, told me that she and her mother had decided to move out of our big apartment. Somehow, in the midst of this big family, Aunt Lidia and I remained outsiders. Though initially we were made to feel welcome, we never were made to feel as if we belonged.

My refuge was my imagination. I would pretend that gypsies had kidnapped me and then, feeling sorry for myself, sit and cry. In the summer, we would all go to my uncle's big estate at Sarny, in the Ukraine, and then I would pretend that I was an explorer, embarking on the unknown.

The house at Sarny was big and simple, by no means luxurious but comfortable, with a huge dining room that seated all of us—and that first summer, I think we must have been more than twenty—at one big table. We brought along our seven servants and three dogs. The furniture was all rattan, upholstered in chintz, and upstairs every bedroom had a white handwoven spread. We slept with the windows open, and at night you could smell the lilacs and hear the nightingales sing.

All around the house were beetroot fields. (The general's fortune came from sugar.) In front of the house was a circular driveway planted with rosebushes. Every morning before breakfast, I would go out and pick a rose for Machuta to wear.

Everyone was left to his own devices at Sarny, to do whatever he pleased, and this arrangement suited me. I had my own life there. I would wander all over the grounds, "discovering" the servants in the kitchen, the strawberries in the garden—we called them "pineapple" strawberries because of their color, greenish yellow with a tinge of pink on one side. Every day at twelve, I went to the priest, who taught me to read; and then, after the lesson, I would go and watch the peasants work and the cows being milked. There were courts for tennis and a lawn for croquet, horses, a little river where one could go bathing, a vegetable garden, a smokehouse, a stork's nest—I had to visit everything.

Once, on one of my expeditions, I discovered the house where all the farmhands ate lunch. I sat down with them at the long wooden table and ate, too. In the center of the table was a big bowl filled with *vareniki*—ravioli filled with white cream cheese—the national dish of the Ukraine. With our fingers—no silverware—we dipped the *vareniki* in a dish of sour cream. It was delicious.

The last and favorite stop on my daily rounds was the chicken house, to see the old woman feed the ducks and chickens at six. I was a little busybody. By the time I had called on everyone and everything, it was already evening. As the day wore on, the plot of my little private drama thickened, and I imagined myself lost in the world. Then, just in time for supper, I would discover the way home.

The one law of the house, laid down by my aunt, was that we be on time for meals. Dinner was served at two, supper at eight, and a gong sounded fifteen minutes before. Latecomers who appeared just in time for dessert got only dessert, nothing else.

My "cousin" Somaripa, Aunt Lidia's nephew, came and spent the summer with us at Sarny. He used to pay Machuta special attentions. On the morning of her birthday, she came downstairs for breakfast and found that he had completely covered her chair with flowers. Well, Machuta was a very spartan woman, and she was a bit taken aback at this display. She didn't like it when anybody made a fuss over her. Now I understand that he was in love with her. But she never replied to him. Often, in fact, she tried to avoid him, because she was in love with another man, who wasn't in love with her. I knew him—he used to visit our house all the time. He liked glamour pusses, it seemed to me, and Machuta was too plain for him. No one told me so, but that was my *résumé*.

General Batianov's eldest son, who never came to visit us in St. Petersburg, was named Pyotr, and it was he who looked after Sarny, this big estate. Pyotr and Pavel—Peter and Paul—Day was his name day and also a big religious holiday in Russia. At Sarny, the morning began with a special pastry, called *krendel,* baked in Pyotr's honor. Then we all went to church in the local village. The peasants wore their national costumes and wreaths of fresh flowers on their heads; there was singing and dancing on the village's main street. And on this particular day, the village looked like a picture that had come to life: the sun seemed brighter, the colors more vivid. In front of each house, with its bleached walls, whitewashed every Saturday, and its straw roof, was a small garden where hollyhocks and a cherry tree grew. Inside the house was a sideboard full of crockery and, always in the corner to the left of the door, an icon draped at the base with a long towel embroidered in red and black cross-stitch. The bed, set to one side of the room, was huge, covered with a patchwork quilt, stacked with pillows almost to the ceiling; the pillowcases were trimmed with handmade lace. The floor of the house was dirt. All this made a deep impression on me.

For Pyotr and Pavel Day, our own house was hung with small lanterns strung on a wire through the trees. After supper there were fireworks. In the village, the peasants danced, accompanied by harmonicas, jumping over bonfires built in the main street. This day, I thought, was magic.

In my first year of grammar school, when I was seven years old, I was chosen to be a butterfly in the Christmas pageant staged by our ballroom-dance teacher, Mr. Nicholas Govlikovsky, a soloist with the Imperial Ballet of St. Petersburg. There was in this little scene a girl walking in a garden, singing. And my part was to fly around her in some sort of dance. I loved it! Apparently, I did it very well, too, because I received many compliments; people told me how light and graceful I was. Before that, I hadn't really understood what it meant to perform—I was just having a wonderful time doing my dance. But all those compliments turned my head a little bit, and I started spending hours opposite the mirror, trying all kinds of movements.

Somehow, one day—by accident—I went up on my toes. Fascinating! I called to my cousin Boris, "Come see the trick I can do!" I thought that this was my invention. Boris was very impressed with what he saw and told me that I must demonstrate this trick to my aunt. I was a little bit afraid of what she would say, but she also was impressed. "My goodness, Boris!" she said. "She will be another Pavlova. She will be a ballerina!" Boris agreed. "Do you want to be a ballerina?" my aunt asked.

I had never seen a ballerina; I wasn't even sure exactly what a ballerina was. But I said "Yes," and then and there, my future course was decided: I would become a ballerina.

Aunt Lidia and General Batianov read in the newspaper that the Maryinsky School in St. Petersburg had received two hundred fifty applications. I overheard that my uncle had to call somebody very important for my application to be considered, because I was then eight and a half years old, and ordinarily the school accepted new students only from the ages of nine to twelve.

Once the application was accepted, I had to go to the school one day in May for two examinations—one physical, the other artistic. There were two hundred thirteen girls, and we were competing for seventeen places. Even so, I was not at all nervous.

First came the medical examination, in private, with a doctor and a nurse. They looked to see that I wasn't bow-legged or near-sighted. (At that time, before contact lenses, a ballerina with bad vision could miss the ramp for her exit or run to the wrong partner.) The doctor also checked to make sure that I had nothing wrong with my heart. I passed this physical test and was sent on to a big studio for my audition.

At one end of the room was a table. All the faculty, along with the Maryinsky company's prima ballerinas, some premiers danseurs, and even some actors and painters, sat behind it. So, many branches of the arts were represented, not just dance. Later, when I was a student, I learned names to go with some of the faces on that panel—Olga Preobrajenskaya, Mathilda Kchessinskaya, Tamara Karsavina, Agrippina Vaganova. They lined us up and looked at us from all sides, every angle, trying to guess how we would look when we grew up. Would we be too thin—or perhaps too fat? Too tall—or too short? They asked us to skip around the room, to run, to turn. Then they let us go home.

Three days later I was notified that I had been accepted. My family was pleased and very proud of me.

Early on the morning of August 20, 1911, I arrived at the school's main entrance, at number 2, Theatre Street, in St. Petersburg's downtown business district, near Nevsky Prospekt. Theatre Street was a cul-de-sac; at the end was the Alexandrinsky Theatre. The Theatre School, like so many of the buildings of the city, was made of stone painted pale yellow and white, with high arched windows overlooking the street and the gardens of the Dowager Empress Maria's palace. There were two entrances—one at the side, facing Nevsky Prospekt, leading to the offices of the director of the Maryinsky Theatre, and the main entrance, to the school. Next to our door was an arch, and through it, a square, with entrances to the rehearsal studios used by the members of the Maryinsky Ballet.

The doorman asked my name, escorted me inside, and introduced me to three ladies—one very beautiful, wearing a black dress with a high collar; the other two dressed in blue uniforms. I curtsied, as little girls do in Russia. The lady in black, the directress, told the others to take me to a classroom.

This room was full of little girls—new ones, like me. We stared at one another, asked one another's names. Before long, a loud bell rang and—a surprise—the boys came in. So, we would study together—the boys on one side of the room, the girls on the other.

Our lessons lasted until five o'clock. Between classes, there were intervals ten minutes long, when we emptied the room and a maid came to open the window and let in some fresh air. At the end of the day, we were sent back to the big hall. Already I had made a friend—Galina Sobinova, the daughter of Leonide Sobinov, a very famous Russian tenor. The doorman was calling her: "Miss Sobinova, please, they've come to fetch you." Galina told me goodbye and disappeared.

I was completely alone. "Where are my people?" I asked the matron. "You, Danilova," she said, "you stay in the school—until Saturday. You are interned." A boarding student! Why hadn't my aunt told me? How would I ever sleep in this strange place? I started to cry.

Before going to the dining room, we were paired off and lined up—little girls in the front, big girls at the end. Since I was the smallest in the school, I was pushed to the head of the line. In the dining room were four big tables, already set, with wooden benches along either side. "Danilova, you sit at my table!" one of the matrons ordered. A maid served each table at one end; we passed the plates down the line. Good soup, I thought, but only a few spoonfuls later, my neighbor passed me back her now-empty bowl. "Come on," she said. "Hurry up!" Two more spoonfuls, then another empty bowl. A few moments later, the maid came, picked up the empty bowls, and took mine, still half full. I was slow and clumsy. For weeks, I would hear, "Danilova! Eat faster and get the plates ready," at every meal. But when I would try to explain that I didn't have time to pass all the plates and eat, too, the matron would interrupt: "Nobody wants your opinion!"

After dinner, a big sideboard at the far end of the room was opened and the matron took out all kinds of packages. "You can bring your own sweets and fruits, and we keep them right here for you," she explained. A little girl came to the matron to show her the sweets she was taking. "My goodness," the matron said. "So very many, my dear! Put half of them back—you can't eat all those." "Oh, but I will give half to Danilova," replied the girl. How kind of her, I thought.

The girl and I left the dining room together. But as soon as we were a safe distance away, she suddenly snatched back all of what she had given me. I was shocked. "Thanks for the lift," she said. "Here— you can have this," and she gave me one piece of candy.

After dinner, we were all taken to a big square room; at the center was a large basin with several faucets, where the girls washed their faces and brushed their teeth. Along the walls were lockers. I was shown to the area where the little girls undressed and was assigned a number— 21. In my locker, I found a package containing underclothes and shoes, all labeled with my number. And in my drawer, I found my toothbrush and all my things that had been sent from home.

Then the matron showed me where I slept—my cot was the first in one of three long rows of beds, separated by passages that the matron constantly patrolled. She herself slept in this same room, behind a screen.

The youngest of us slept closest to her, the older girls at the back. Through an arch at the far end of the room was a smaller, more private chamber, with twelve beds, where the oldest girls in the school slept. We girls in our first year would cry because there was no one to tuck us in, so the eldest girls would come and kiss us good night.

Two

IN THE MORNING, I was awakened by one of the maids walking through the dormitory, vigorously shaking a loud bell. At the wash basin, another maid came to me and asked, "Are you Miss Danilova?" This was my maid, Xenia; and by way of introduction, she gave me an ice-cold shower—there was no hot water. Then she brushed my hair, braided it into one big plait, and wound it into a chignon. "But I don't wear my hair this way," I protested. Never mind, she told me, that was the way all the girls were required to wear their hair for dancing. She showed me how to put on my long pink cotton stockings, how to roll them with elastic at the hip to keep them up, and how to tie the ribbons on my ballet shoes. Then she helped me into my dancing outfit, which consisted of a light-grey starched cotton dress, with little puff sleeves, and a starched petticoat that gave the effect of a tutu. I was given a shawl, number 21. All this attention from our maids was only for the first day—from then on, we had to dress ourselves.

At the second bell, we had to be ready to assemble in the hall. There we lined up, two by two, from smallest (that was me) to tallest, and the matron on duty conducted her inspection. Like all the other girls, I curtsied, saying "Good morning," and, having met with her approval, entered the dining room. First, still standing, we said our morning prayers, led by one of the eldest girls. Then we sat down to our breakfast—a mug of tea, a little bread with butter, and one egg. Exactly fifteen minutes later, we all reported for our first class.

For academic subjects our classes were combined, though the boys were seated on one side of the room and the girls always on the other. But our dancing lessons were separate. We small children took dance class from ten to eleven; older students' lessons lasted an hour and a half. Then, after class, we all reported back to the washroom, where we changed out of our dancing frocks and into our uniforms—long, cornflower-blue wool challis dresses with long sleeves, white fichus, and black aprons over the skirts. Regardless of the fashions that came and went, this was the style for the girls of the school; boarding students who remained at the school on weekends wore these dresses with white aprons on Sundays. The boys wore black woolen pants and high-collar jackets, with a lyre—the emblem of Art—embroidered on each side of the collar.

Lunch would be *choucroûte*—cabbage with little sausages—or hash or occasionally fish, and again, tea; the little ones were forced to drink milk, which I hated. After we had eaten, we put on long coats distributed to us by the wardrobe mistress, and funny hats that were absolutely flat, like a plate, and went for recess in the inner courtyard. The older girls would use the time to read or prepare for the afternoon's lessons, while we, the little ones, would always play and run like mad. By one o'clock, we had to be back inside, and all the afternoon, until five, was taken up with our academic subjects.

While I attended the Theatre School, there were forty-eight girls and twenty-eight boys. Of these, only a few were day students; the rest were interns, or boarding students, like me. Most big schools in Russia at that time were boarding schools—probably because of the weather, and also, I suppose, because of the prevailing notion that somebody else could raise your children better than you could.

In the eyes of the school, we were all simply students; but in one another's eyes, some of us were much more important than others. We younger girls were taught to address the older girls formally, as "you," even though they called us "thou." To enter their washroom, which was separate from ours, we had to ask their permission. "What for?" they would reply. There had to be a reason—a present we had bought for one of them, a question we needed to ask. And then, as soon as we were finished, they would tell us to scram. They were very pompous, and we, in turn, were all humility.

We little fries had to wear our hair in one braid; it was only when we had reached the age of fifteen that we were entitled to two. When we put on our dancing outfits in the morning, we weren't permitted to wear our shawls folded in a triangle—that, too, was a sign of status reserved for the last class, the oldest girls. We called them "the goddesses."

In the center of the circular library, which was known as "the round room," was a table where our goddesses gathered to read, embroider, or knit, or sometimes just to sit and chat. When we had to cross this room on our way to a class, we were obliged to tiptoe, and we weren't allowed to talk, because it was their room. Frankly, we took a detour whenever we could.

While all of us wore grey frocks for our dancing lessons, the girls in the eldest division, if they were accomplished, received pink dresses to set them apart. Better yet were the girls in white dresses: in the whole school, there were only two—Olga Spessivtseva and Felia Doubrovska, members of the last two classes. I used to watch them closely. Both looked important and snooty—they paid no attention to anyone. Well, I thought to myself, so they should be, because they are so superior to us.

Friday was an important day—bath day. After dinner, from eight o'clock on, we were sent in groups to the steam bath, to be scrubbed down by our maids. Then we would return to the school, put on our bed jackets over our gowns, and let our hair down to dry.

My first Friday at the school, after my bath was over, one of my new friends approached me and asked, in a hushed voice, "Danilova, would you like to see a play?" Well, yes, of course, I told her. Then come to the Rich, she said—"the Rich," which we pronounced "Reech," was our name for a room that was off to itself, apart from our classrooms and dancing halls. It was said that a monk named Rich had hanged himself in that room. This was silly, of course. No one in Russia is named Rich, and the Theatre School had never been a monastery. But we chose to forget all that and believe the legend. We were a little bit afraid of the place, as if it were haunted.

At the door to the Rich another girl was stationed. "Are you alone?" she asked me. Yes. "All right," she said. "Give me three chocolate candies." I explained that I had none, that I was new and no one had told me to bring sweets along. The girl thought this over, then waived my admission, as long as I promised to bring double the usual portion on the following Friday night. As in many small theatrical productions, the actors in this one split the till—that is, they divided whatever candy they collected at the door among themselves.

Inside the Rich, the audience—all little girls—was impatient, and the "artists," the actors, were assembled behind the big chalkboard until the play began. On this evening's program was a play called *Vanka Kluchnik*, adapted from a song popular with the peasants, about a handsome janitor named Vanka, in love with a princess, who is young and beautiful but married to a man much older than she. One day, Vanka declares his love for her, but the prince, her husband, finds out and orders that Vanka be hanged. On his way to the executioner, Vanka looks up at the princess's window and sees that she is looking at him, crying for him. And he is comforted that she loves him. So on this night in the Rich, we had the little girls' dramatization of this song: the audience was absolutely spellbound, and some of us were even moved to tears when it came time for Vanka to go to his death. I felt very sorry for him, and thought what an awful man the husband was to hang poor Vanka. Eventually I, too, took part in Friday-night productions in the Rich, in a play called *Toreadors and the Bull*, in which we toreadors used the aprons to our uniforms as capes.

Our favorite day of the week was Saturday, when we went home. When our last lesson was over, we would tear up the stairs like hurricanes and change into our private clothes. After spending all the week in our uniforms, our own clothes—even our underwear—seemed so beautiful that we couldn't look at ourselves long enough in the mirror. Once we had changed, we hurried to the front hall, where we had to wait for someone from home to come and pick us up. And finally, just when I was beginning to believe that they had forgotten me, the doorman would call out: "Miss Danilova, it's for you." Then Masha, our maid, would take me back to our apartment in a carriage.

The first weekend, I was the guest of honor in my own home: for dinner, we had all my favorite dishes, and the conversation revolved around my week at the school. I told everybody about my job collecting the plates at the end of the meals, about opening my own bed to air it before I left the dormitory; and I explained that it was absolutely necessary for me to have candy, since it was the local currency. "Okay," my aunt said, "if everybody else has sweets, you will have them, too."

After dinner, my aunt and uncle went off to the theatre. I begged them to take me along, but they said no, operetta was not for children, and left me behind. So I spent the evening visiting Machuta in her room, watching her embroider.

The next morning, Masha woke me early and I hurried to my aunt's rooms, where I helped her choose which dress to wear and fastened her boots with the button hook. I never missed the opportunity to watch my aunt dress: I loved to see how Fenia, her personal maid, would do her hair, and to see which perfume she would put on, which jewelry she would choose.

After lunch on Sunday, we went to Vassilevsky Ostrov, a park on an island in the Neva, where people would go for a Sunday drive in their carriages. All St. Petersburg was there. And my aunt and uncle would nod first to one side of the carriage, then to the other. Suddenly, I saw someone *I* knew—my new friend Shura Barash, from my class at the school, coming toward us not by horse but in a car driven by a chauffeur. I nodded to her and waved, feeling very important for having seen a friend of my own there.

(Our name—Alexandra—was a popular one in Russia, the name of our empress; a lot of girls born at the time of her coronation were christened Alexandra, for which the diminutive is "Shura"—as it is usually spelled in English. Years later, after leaving Russia, I lived in France and so began to spell my name the French way. One charming man in Paris deciphered it *comme ça*: "*Mon petit chou et mon petit rat, ça fait* Choura." When eventually I moved to the United States, my friends urged me to change the spelling of my name to the English version, but I refused. "I'm very sorry," I said, "but it's too late.")

Sunday night was always sad, because the week stretched on ahead—such a long time to wait until I could come back home. I said goodbye to my aunt and uncle and, accompanied by Masha, returned to the school. We parted at the door, but not before I reminded her to come for me on Saturday—*please*, don't forget to pick me up. Then, very slowly, I went up the stairs, stones weighing down my heart.

But upstairs, there was a wonderful surprise waiting for me: three of my new friends from the week before—Sobinova, Barash, and Genia Svekish—had changed their status from day students to interns, like me. This meant that we could be together all the time.

Svekish was my "buddy": she and I made up the first, the smallest, pair at the front of the line for meals or baths or recess. We shared the first bench in the classroom; the arrangement was always the same. She was a very good student and very serious, beautiful but without great talent, and a bit fussy. When I did my homework, which wasn't always, I did it with her, and what I didn't understand she would explain to me. But when it came time to play, it was with the other two girls—Barash and Sobinova—that I would invent some new amusement. We were inseparable. Barash's name, which means "lamb" in Russian, was soon applied to us all: *"Barashki!"*—little lambs—the doorman would call to us on Saturdays "Your maid is come to fetch you."

A few weeks into the term, one of the matrons informed me that in addition to my classes during the day, I would be required to take extra dancing lessons in the evening with Maria Scherrer, one of the girls in the fifth, or last, class. Extra lessons! Goodbye to all the fun I used to have with my friends in the evenings. Immediately, Barash, Sobinova, and I had a little meeting to compare notes. Apparently, the eldest girls had each been given a handful of students from the first or second year, little ones, with whom they met every evening to review and repeat that morning's exercises. Each of us had been assigned to a different girl.

The idea of these extra lessons didn't appeal to our little trio at all, and we decided that we would hide someplace instead. But where? I suggested the big linen closet. So when the time came to change back into our dancing frocks for our evening class, we three went directly to the closet. We sat there a long time before we heard the matron's voice growing louder, coming toward us: "Where could those three girls be hiding?" And then the closet door opened. We were discovered, dragged from our hiding place, and, right there, sentenced to spend the weekend at the school—a very severe punishment. Of course, at the thought of not going home on Saturday we all began to cry and apologize. The matron scolded us but finally took pity on us because we were in our first year. Our sentence was reduced: we would go without sweets instead. So that was our first big enterprise—very unsuccessful. When Svekish heard about it, she shrugged and for a time ignored me completely—we'd been very stupid, she thought, to try and carry out such a plan.

By that time, we had all gotten to know one another quite well and had even gotten to know the boys a little bit. In our class were twin brothers—Mikhail and Nicholas Efimov, one older than the other by ten minutes. To tell them apart was impossible. So our teacher ordered Misha to wear a red tie. But the system was hardly foolproof. Whenever one of them was punished for some small offense—say, ordered to go stand under the clock for ten minutes while everybody else went out to play—they would share the punishment: one would stand five minutes while the other went outside, then the other would sneak in, put on the tie, and change places with him.

Once a week, we had a ballroom lesson with the boys, taught by Mr. Govlikovsky, the same man who had taught me ballroom dancing the year before, at my grammar school. This class we adored! All the girls would go to the big studio and wait on one side. "Now, gentlemen, please invite your ladies," Mr. Govlikovsky would say. And the boys would approach us, bow—we replied with a curtsy—and offer their hands, then lead us to our places on the floor. Sometimes, two boys would ask me to dance, both at once, and I wouldn't know what to do. "All right," Mr. Govlikovsky would say, coming to settle the question, "you will go with this one, who is more your size." So we paired off at the start of the lesson, but not always with the same partner.

It was only later, when we were older, that we girls found out that the boys decided on their partners ahead of time, in their quarters, before coming downstairs to class. Sometimes they would fight over certain girls. But at the time, we girls didn't give the boys a thought, except to hope that our partner would not be too clumsy.

One girl, named Nina, was always without a partner—nobody wanted to ask her to dance because she was not very attractive. And when I think back, I am really ashamed at myself, at how much we all made fun of that poor girl and how miserable we made her life. She took all our teasing and our insults quietly, however, and never complained.

Our routine at the school remained pretty much the same day after day, week after week, until Ash Wednesday. During Lent, we had no dancing lessons, no classes, and the Theatre School took on a completely different, rather mystical air. We were not allowed to run; we were instructed to read or paint or do needlework. And we ate a special diet: meat, butter, and milk were forbidden. Everything was prepared with vegetable oil instead of animal fat. This was the first time I had ever encountered this special regimen for Lent, and the greasy food didn't agree with me. But there was no substituting something else I might have liked better. So when no one was watching I would drop my food into my lap, squeeze out all the oil I could with my napkin, and then somehow maneuver the food back onto my fork. It was the only way that I could manage to swallow.

One day during Lent, Shura Barash came to me and whispered that she had chocolate. I said, "But you can't eat it, because there's milk in chocolate." "Ssh!" she told me. "First we'll eat it, then we'll confess it to the priest." I laughed and went along with her. And as soon as I ate the last piece, I felt very sorry.

Soon it was time for confession. Before going to church, we were all to go to one another and ask forgiveness for anything we might have done. So, of course, we all surrounded our Nina and asked her forgiveness.

Then we all went in small groups to the chapel, which was on the top floor of the school, to confess our sins to the priest. Finally, my turn came. I was very uneasy. I thought to myself that I mustn't say that it was Shura Barash who gave me the chocolate. . . . The priest listened to me very gravely, but finally he forgave me everything. And when he laid his hand on my head and prayed, I wanted to cry.

I can't honestly say that I worked very hard or was very attentive during my first year at the Theatre School. Looking back, I can see that many of the best pupils then turned out to be the worst ones years later, and vice versa. And in my case, though I was later considered one of the finest pupils in my division, I wasn't very serious at that time. I found the exercises rather dry and uninteresting.

Like any school, ours ended the year with examinations. The youngest students had no tests in academic subjects: we were simply promoted on the basis of how much progress we had made during the year and how well we had behaved in class. But the dance examination was for everybody, no exceptions. And there were no exceptions to the nervous state that came over us all the day before the examination, either. For it determined our future. Those who failed the test were dismissed from the school. Of the seventeen girls in my class that first year, only nine of us were allowed to remain.

And of those nine, our little triangle—Sobinova, Barash, and I— was left intact. In fact, because we had been so busy making mischief that we hadn't learned our lessons, the three of us had to stay behind and repeat the first-year curriculum. The rest of our classmates were promoted without us.

I was stunned. I think now that I was simply too young to understand the seriousness of being enrolled in the school and taking lessons. And so, when they put me on probation, I saw for the first time that I would have to work hard and concentrate; it was then that I began to grow from a little girl into a young woman.

Three

THAT FALL, when we returned to the Theatre School, I was still the smallest. "Goodness, how you have grown!" was the cry heard all around the room. "But you, Chourochka, you are still so little—you haven't grown a bit!" I was annoyed, but it was true. Even when the new flock of girls arrived, I was again at the front of the line.

One day, we were all collected in the big hall and arranged, as usual, by height. In came our inspectress, Varvara Ivanovna Lihosherstvova, and with her, Mr. Alexander Monahov, a member of the Imperial Ballet, a handsome man and an excellent dancer, who chose the children to appear in productions at the Maryinsky Theatre. With his hand, he divided our line into two groups. "These girls," he said, indicating my end of the line, "should go into the crowd."

We were to appear in the opera *Faust*. Of our little trio formed the year before—Barash, Sobinova, and I—I was the only one chosen. "But when will we ever rehearse?" I asked, excited at the prospect of being on the stage. The other girls laughed and told me, "You don't need any rehearsal—all you have to do is walk."

Well! Finally, the day arrived. After dinner, we five, the chosen, were bundled into a closed carriage and driven to the theatre with a matron as a chaperone.

It was a thirty- or forty-minute ride from the Theatre School to the Maryinsky Theatre, which was in another part of town, situated opposite the Conservatory of Music on a flagstone piazza; at the center stood a monument to Pushkin.

There were four entrances to the Maryinsky: the main one, the center door, for the public; the stage door, on the side, for artists and employees of the director's office; a private entrance, next to the stage door, leading directly to the imperial box for members of the imperial family; and on the opposite side, an entrance for the orchestra, stage-hands, and pupils of the Theatre School. This last entrance also led to the photographer's studio, where all the artists of the ballet and opera were photographed.

We entered, climbed six flights of stairs, and made our way through endless corridors to our dressing room. This route took us past the stage, where we glimpsed singers and ballerinas practicing alone, getting ready for the performance. We also passed the studios, above and behind the stage, where Bakst, Benois, Tchervachidze, and other painters executed the scenery. On the top floor was the wardrobe department, an enormous suite of workrooms with tutus of all colors hanging from the ceiling. There were ballet costumes one hundred years old, and bolts of new material—so many that during and after the revolution, the wardrobe department was able to go on for years making new costumes for new productions.

Our dressing room could accommodate thirty people—there were fifteen mirrors on either side. Next door were three small rooms for pupils who had just graduated and joined the corps de ballet.

Someone unfastened my hair and combed it down over my shoulders, then helped me get into a dress; the matron dipped a rabbit's foot in rouge and gave me rosy cheeks—that was all the makeup I got. Three loud bells announced the time until the curtain went up: one bell, half an hour before the start of the performance; two bells, fifteen minutes; three bells, everybody on the stage. Our matron made sure that we were all out of our dressing room after the third bell; we ran downstairs to the stage, and God help anyone who got in our way.

The leading members of the company had their dressing rooms downstairs—the men on one side of the stage, the women on the other.

We waited in the Green Room until it was time for our appearance; we loved it there because the stars' dressing rooms adjoined it. The doors were most of the time open, and we could peep at the ballerinas. (It was every dancer's envy to dress in one of these rooms off the Green Room; and years later, during my second season as a member of the ballet, I was assigned to one.) We shared the Green Room with the flowers to be presented to the ballerinas at the close of the performance; we sniffed them, admired them, and compared them to see who had been sent the best bouquet. Going onto the stage, we had to pass through an alcove, and this was the most exciting part of all, because it was there that the most distinguished guests, including members of the imperial family, would come to smoke and talk with the artists during the intermissions. Generally, there were at least two or three grand dukes; we would drop in deep curtsy as we ran past.

The house of the theatre was in the rococo style, all light-blue plush and gilt, with an enormous crystal chandelier hanging from the center of the ceiling and, above the proscenium, a clock supported by two golden cupids. There were four tiers of boxes arranged in a semi-circle around the orchestra seats. At the center of the first tier was a big box reserved for state guests; the second tier, which was the most fashionable place to sit, was called the "bel étage."

The Maryinsky stage was huge, larger than the New York State Theater's, as big as the Metropolitan Opera's. Standing in the wings, I couldn't understand what was happening or make out the words that were being sung. I stuck close by the other girls.

Suddenly, I was seized by both hands and taken for a walk among the crowd. There on the stage, I saw, was the devil, who was singing. "Who is that?" I asked. "Chaliapin, of course," I was told. Chaliapin! The most famous singer of them all! So many times I had heard his name in conversations at home, had heard his recordings on Boris's gramophone. And now, there I was, with him—on the same stage!

Soon, Chaliapin broke a barrel and all the crowd gathered round. Somebody whispered to me, "Now you drink the wine."

"Wine!" I said, in full voice, drawing a shush from the rest of the crowd.

"What's the matter with you?" those nearest to me scolded. "You don't talk onstage—if you want to say something, you must whisper."

Reprimanded, I took the rusty iron goblet someone handed me

and waited my turn at the barrel—but this wine was terrible! I no sooner took a taste than I had to spit it out. "Are you actually drinking this?" one of the girls asked me. "Are you crazy? This is water mixed with paint!" I was astonished, because I thought that everything on the stage had to be real. My friends in the crowd made fun of me, and, of course, the next day it was all over the school. But I didn't care. I was very excited, too excited to sleep that night. I lay awake, thinking about my first appearance on the stage.

The next morning, I told everybody that I had been on the same stage as Chaliapin, but no one seemed very impressed. "Well, it's not such a big thing," my classmates would say. "After all, you didn't *do* anything, you just walked. Real artists don't walk in the crowd." And when I went home for the weekend and told my aunt all about my debut, she said, "Well, show me what you danced in the opera."

"Dance?" I said. "Oh no, I just walked. But it was so interesting. . . ." And I told her how, if you want to talk onstage, you must whisper, or gesture; and I demonstrated how one could say something in mime, pointing at myself—that's "I"—and then at the far side of the room—"go there"—and so on. Already, I felt that I was on the road to becoming an artist.

At the next audition, another lineup in the hall, I was again chosen—this time for a role with real dancing, in a ballet. In the last act of *Paquita*, there is a mazurka danced by twelve children. Mr. Monahov would teach sixteen of us the parts, then choose the twelve best. And of these, I was the only new girl. Being the smallest, I was put in the lead couple with a Polish boy, Kohanovsky, who incidentally was my most frequent partner in our ballroom-dance class. We called him "Grandpa," because he had to repeat the first year, then the second, then the third. . . . But though he was a poor scholar, he was a brilliant dancer. All through our years in the school together, we had an unspoken respect for each other's talent. At our every performance in *Paquita*, the audience insisted on an encore, and we would repeat our little number from start to finish. For three years, Kohanovsky and I led the mazurka, keeping our place at the front of the line because neither of us grew.

After this, my debut, I was chosen again and again, for every ballet that required children. Rehearsals were usually in the afternoons, and we were called out of class to go to them. We were given extra assign-ments to make up for the lessons we missed, but none of us minded. The homework was a small price to pay for the glory of being on the stage.

In *The Sleeping Beauty*, I was a little page, carrying the queen's train. From where I stood by her side, I could see all of the dancing, and so I learned everybody's parts, which I still remember. In *La Fille Mal Gardée*, I danced the Pas des Sabotiers, a little duet for a girl and a boy—I played the boy. We wore wooden-soled shoes. My first night in the role, at our entrance in the music, I ran onto the stage, slipped, and fell flat—disaster before the dance had even begun! But I quickly recovered, got up, and went ahead with my part. The audience insisted on an encore. Later, Mr. Monahov commended me for not losing my head. "Good, Danilova! You came through like a trouper, like a real dancer!"

General Batianov and the rest of my family would often come to see me dance. But even on those nights when they were in the audi-ence, I wasn't nervous or afraid, just pleasantly excited—exhilarated, really. I discovered within myself a certain assurance, a confidence that my dancing would see me through whatever happened onstage.

Besides my appearances in ballets, I was also cast as an extra in more operas. Gluck's *Orpheus and Eurydice*, for one—there was dancing, choreographed by Mikhail Fokine, running all through the opera. We children were the cherubs in Paradise, wearing crowns of flowers and armed with little bows and arrows, which we shot directly at the audi-ence. Sometimes we would hit the men in the orchestra pit, making them furious. At the first full dress rehearsal for this opera, a man called to me from where he sat watching out front. "What is your name?" he asked. "Danilova." "Very good, Danilova. If you keep working, you will go far—you will be a ballerina." This was Mikhail Fokine, and his words of encouragement sustained me for months.

Two of us girls were chosen to be the little mermaids in the opera *Rusalka*, and we alternated in the role. Chaliapin was singing the part of the heroine's father. In one scene, he came to the spot on the sea where he used to fish and where Rusalka drowned, and he called for her in an aria. Then along came a little girl—me—and delivered a couple of lines, which I still remember: "I came from the water onto the beach, to where my grandfather was waiting, and he asked me to get from the bottom the money he threw in. But what is money? I don't know." Being a mermaid, I had no use for money. Instead, I brought my grandfather a handful of beautiful shells. He took me in his arms then and kissed me.

After the opening, Chaliapin gave me a present, a big box of chocolates, and lifting me high off the floor—he was such a big man, I thought that I would go through the ceiling—he kissed me on the forehead. When I arrived back at the school that night, I fought with the matron, refusing to wash my face because I wanted to keep Chaliapin's kiss.

The stage experience I acquired during my first years at the school was not limited to the Maryinsky Theatre. Once, for a play at the Little Theatre, adjacent to our school, I was called on to be a peasant girl. The occasion was a big holiday, marking three hundred years of the Romanov dynasty, and as part of the celebration there was a tableau of a famous Russian picture in which a child is reading and all the grown peasants sit listening to her. I played the child.

My aunt had always subscribed to the opera but refused to take me on the grounds that I was too young to appreciate it. Finally, toward the end of my second year at the school, Machutochka decided that it was about time I saw an opera from the audience and took me to *The Barber of Seville*, which I loved.

On big holidays, like the tsar's or the tsarina's birthday, there were no classes. We were given pastry in the morning and a box of candy, then taken to the theatre in the afternoon. We students were divided into three groups, each taken to one of the three imperial theatres: the Maryinsky, for the ballet; the Alexandrinsky, for drama; or the Mikhailovsky, for classical French theatre. Needless to say, all the school wanted to go see the ballet. But which of us would go where—this was the inspectress's decision. Because I was mixed up in every unfortunate situation—breaking a window once because I'd climbed up to see what was going on in the street, committing little sins with my friends—the inspectress had taken a disliking to me. So I never got to go to the ballet. While other students went off to *The Sleeping Beauty*, the inspectress's favorite, I was sent time after time to the French theatre. Once, as punishment for some misdemeanor or other, I was denied any theatre at all, left completely alone at the school while all the rest of the students went off.

Our life revolved around our classes and, outside of class, our little intrigues. The Theatre School was our nest. It gave us none of the freedom children have today: we were told what to study, where to go, when to eat. There was no one telling us, "Go do whatever you want now." How can little mites know what it is they want? Occasionally, we went against the rules, but never did we question the school's authority over us. We felt secure there and took that security for granted—which is the way it should be for children. Our education, our dance training, our lives would run their course, guided by the school. We proceeded from one day to the next, year after year, looking ahead sometimes but never worrying about the future. The routine carried us along on its own momentum.

When I was performing in ballets or operas on Sundays, I stayed at the school all weekend and so didn't get to visit my family for weeks at a time. But when I did, the world at home seemed larger than the world of the school. I heard the general tell stories of his exploits during the war, his memories of Japan: the gardens, the leaves individually cleaned with a damp cloth; the men taken prisoner, who gave their word of honor and were permitted to walk wherever they wanted. These stories impressed me, and I vowed that someday I would go to Japan and see all of this for myself.

Boris and Vladimir sometimes quizzed me about important dates in history, or state capitals, or how to say such-and-such in French, to find out what I didn't know. I hated their questions. Even when Boris talked about ballet, which was often, I understood that he saw a side of it that was beyond my view as a student. He would discuss his favorite ballerinas—names I had never even heard—and scornfully turn to me and ask, "How can you be enrolled in the Theatre School and have no idea who the best dancers are today?" My aunt would come to my rescue: "She is still so young—give her time!"

My aunt was proud of my dancing. On the afternoons when she received, she would ask me to come say hello to her guests. "What do you dance?" they would ask me. So I would hum for them eight bars of music from my most recent opera appearance and strike my pose. "What is it?" they would ask when I was through. "There must be more." "No, that's all," I would answer, not realizing that my part was only a little patch of the big stage picture, and that we children were used primarily to create false perspective. The stage was raked, and we stood all the way at the back, giving the illusion, as the people got smaller in the distance, of a crowd much deeper than the stage. So my part, all by itself, made very little sense.

One weekend, I returned home from the school to find no one there except my aunt. "Where is everybody?" I asked. And she explained that Volodya was sick and that everyone had gone to visit him in Peterhof. Somehow I sensed that this was only half the story, that something awful had happened that they didn't want to tell me. Months passed, and then one day my aunt told me that Vladimir was coming home. But he was changed, she warned me—he had had an accident, and he was no longer so handsome, because his face had been harmed. I must not be afraid, and I mustn't stare. My goodness—poor Vladimir! But what kind of accident? My aunt would say no more, only that we were not to talk about it, and I was not to ask.

What a horrible sight he was—not at all the handsome cadet that I had first set eyes on at my aunt's wedding. One side of his face was now completely disfigured. I kissed him hello on the other side. "You see, Choura," he greeted me, "I am alive! The bullet went in this side and came out here." And he explained that he had only one eye left— the other was glass, implanted during an operation in Berlin. "Tell me, Choura," he asked, "you're not afraid of me?"

"Oh, no, Vladimir, no. But you will excuse me, I have to go now," and I ran to my room. What bullet could he be talking about, since there wasn't any war? I had no idea what it all meant. That Vladimir seemed different, a little bit strange—this was as much as I knew. It was only later, when I was grown up, that I learned the truth about Volodya's accident: he had attempted suicide. It seems he had fallen deeply in love with one of his cousins; they had asked the church for a special dispensation to marry, and the answer was no. Vladimir, heartbroken, shot himself in the head but somehow failed to kill himself.

My aunt and the general went away, on a short trip to Kiev, for a special gala performance in the presence of the tsar and tsarina. For weeks after their return, my aunt related to the family and our various guests the horrible event: it was at that performance that Pyotr Stolypin, the premier, was assassinated and the Russian Revolution set in motion. In my presence these conversations, though they began in Russian, always ended in French. I understood that my uncle was not at all pleased with the political state of affairs, and see now that he wanted to shelter me. Later, when war was declared, the general followed its progress on an enormous map, with each army's position marked by flags on pins. Every morning, he would summon his secretary and dictate his column—a daily political analysis for the Petersburg *Gazette*. He was, I understood from other people's attitude toward him, greatly respected for his opinions. But despite his popularity, he was never a member of the court of Nicholas II, I think because he disliked Rasputin. In political debates at home, the line was always very clearly drawn, with the general on one side and on the other Vladimir, a member of Her Majesty's private regiment, advocating the position of the tsar and the tsarina.

It was in 1912, during my second year at the Theatre School, that my aunt came down with meningitis. One night, I was called home from the school and taken to her room, which smelled of medicine. She wanted to bless me before she died, according to Russian custom, but by the time I arrived she couldn't speak. She made only faint, pathetic sounds with her voice as I sat crying, trying hard to hear words in those sounds. She died later that week.

Everyone was shocked. The body, as Russian custom dictates, lay in state in the apartment. People came and went throughout the day and evening, attending the brief memorial services that went on continuously, joining in prayers led by a nun or a monk. My Moscow aunt arrived in tears. Aunt Lidia was buried in Alexander Nevsky Lavra, a cemetery that is to St. Petersburg what Père Lachaise is to Paris. General Batianov then bought himself a plot next to hers.

Suddenly, the apartment seemed very empty. "And what will she do, your little ward?" friends who came to call would ask the general. "She will be a ballet pony," he would declare with pride. So my place in the family was secure. There was then a custom in Russia that after dinner, on leaving the table, children would say "thank you" to their parents, as a guest would to his hosts. It was a good custom, I think, because it reminded us that someone else had earned our daily bread for us. I had always thanked my aunt. Now that she was gone, I got up, thanked the general, and kissed his hand.

Aunt Lidia's place was immediately taken by Machuta, who became the mistress of the house and my new "aunt," caring for me, tucking me in at night before I went to sleep. Our friends changed—more young people came to call on us, and some of the tension that had strained the atmosphere at home now lifted. I think my aunt must have named me as her sole heir, because from then on, I was often told, "You will be very rich, my dear, a nice fiancée."

The annual school performance, held in the Little Theatre, was the culmination of all our hard work during the year. Our teachers or sometimes members of the company would choreograph ballets especially for the pupils who were graduating. At the end of my second year, there was Olga Spessivtseva, a beautiful dancer who everyone predicted would be world-famous. The ballet done for her, called *Tsarina of the White Night*, was the story of a little girl lost in the forest: she goes to sleep, has a vision of a beautiful princess, and when she wakes up, the princess shows her the way home. The princess was, of course, Spessivtseva; the lost little girl was me. The pride and joy I felt at being cast in this role were enormous, and very soon I decided that the principal part in this ballet was really mine! After all, *I* was the one who got lost in the forest, and the princess appeared to *me*—she was there on my account.

The performance went well, and Spessivtseva was truly a vision. We all idolized her—she was so beautifully built, with a face like an Italian madonna. Technically, she could do anything, and with such grace! The now-standard double pirouette into a fishdive in the grand pas de deux in *The Sleeping Beauty* was devised for her in 1921; she brought it back to the Maryinsky from the Diaghilev company. Before that, the choreography called for a different step entirely. Spessivtseva had a smooth développé, rather high for that time, that was very striking, and I modeled my développé on hers.

Spessivtseva had one fault: she was not musical. When she performed, the répétiteur would station one of his aides at every corner of the stage, in the wings, to count the music so that she wouldn't miss her entrance. But in everything else we tried to copy her. And we took communal pride in her, as if, by being trained at the same school, we would all one day share in her success.

Each ballerina in the company had her following among us students; there were little rival factions. We were fanatical in our devotion. God forbid your favorite should make a mistake! Then the other girls would point to you and say, "Ah, *your* ballerina did that!"

There were Mathilda Kchessinskaya's fans. She was a marvelous dancer—very light, very fast on her toes. She was the first Russian ballerina to do thirty-two fouettés, the only one who could measure up to the Italians in virtuosity—a real *con brio* dancer. In *Le Talisman*, an allegorical ballet, there was a scene in which we children—eight girls—represented little flickering lights. Pierre Vladimiroff was Wind, flown in on a wire from the top of the stage; he danced with Kchessinskaya. We did more posing than dancing and spent most of our time onstage devouring her with our eyes. Often, for our own little Friday-night shows put on in "the Rich" after our baths, we would try to re-create her performance.

Her best role was in *Esmeralda*. In it, she was in love with a very handsome officer who was romancing her while he was betrothed to another woman—the usual story—and of course he wouldn't marry her. She was burned at the stake. Very tragic. I always cried at this last scene, no matter how many times I had seen it before. Often, Kchessinskaya would have to encore the coda of her dance five or six times. She had complete command of the stage and a certain diamantine brilliance which she "sold" to the audience in her performance. I have never seen another dancer as fast as she was on her toes, doing échappés or bourrées. In the *Don Quixote* pas de deux, the variation usually danced with the fan, most ballerinas have a hard time keeping up with the speed of the music. Kchessinskaya, however, had the conductor double the tempo.

Her retinue within the company included Vladimiroff, her frequent partner, who received the highest salary ever paid a first dancer and was granted many more privileges than Nijinsky had ever had at the Imperial Theatre. Vladimiroff was our Clark Gable, a strikingly handsome man, besieged by admirers wherever he went. Kchessinskaya had a special dressing room built for him.

Her entourage was the most conspicuous and the most powerful. In Russian society, dancers, like other theatre people, were considered citizens of the demimonde. At every performance, the first few rows of the theatre were filled with balletomanes, many of whom had mistresses in the company. And just above the box for the tsar was one for the grand dukes, who had easy access to the dancers: a special passage led directly from their box to the stage. I would say that maybe half of the dancers in the company had "protectors," but they were discreet about it—those things were kept secret then. Kchessinskaya was the exception. She flaunted her affairs with her grand dukes, because she thought it showed the world how attractive she was. They gave her precious jewelry, built her a magnificent palace. My aunt warned me that under no circumstances should I ever accept an invitation to Kchessinskaya's palace, because it was considered not nice. Girls went there to pick up a protector or to be in vogue with the men.

We loved to see Kchessinskaya and Olga Preobrajenskaya, both marvelous actresses, pitted against each other, fighting over the same man, in La Bayadère, which was one of our favorite ballets. In one scene was the hunt: there was a big waterfall onstage, and at the top of this waterfall appeared a lion, played by two extras—one for the front legs and one for the back. Someone shot the lion and he collapsed—a dramatic moment. A scene like that would be laughed at today, but at the time we were all taken in by the spectacle.

Preobrajenskaya had her admirers, but my friends and I were not among them. We did respect her. But she was not very well built—small, rather wide and square. And she never did two pirouettes, always one; well, you can imagine that that didn't impress us students very much. She left the Maryinsky Theatre while I was still in the school and gave a lot of performances all over St. Petersburg, for charity. Her repertoire included some modern dance, which later I would have been very interested to see, but at the time we wanted nothing but tutus and toe dancing. We liked Tamara Karsavina because she was pretty and well dressed, with thousands of admirers—very glamorous. Preobrajenskaya, with all her charity benefits, seemed rather dull by comparison.

But she must have been a good woman, and later, in Paris, a good teacher to have produced Irina Baronova, Tamara Toumanova, Vladimir Dokoudovsky, so many fine dancers.

My own favorite was Karsavina, who was not as good a technician as Kchessinskaya, lacking Kchessinskaya's dynamics, but a very beautiful woman and very feminine in her style of dancing. It was said that everyone who met her fell in love with her—Fokine, all Paris. I loved her in *Paquita*—she had such charm and warmth.

Pavlova had already left Russia, and so she had no following at the school. I saw her only once, at Narodny Dom, the huge people's theatre. She was astounding—so ethereal. But it was my memories of Karsavina's performances that stayed with me and nourished me. Her femininity and warmth and beauty were my inspiration.

Of other forms of dancing, besides ballet, we knew practically nothing. Several years later, I went with some of my classmates to see Isadora Duncan perform. She was fat, but it didn't matter—her dancing was so dynamic, so different from anything we had been taught. And her life, according to all the rumors, was so undisciplined—she was, I think, the first hippie. After the performance, my friends and I went backstage, but she had already gone. There was a bottle of champagne, almost empty, on her dressing table. And I thought to myself, rather smugly, "Well . . ." Twice, she established a school in St. Petersburg, but her method was too disorganized to produce even one remarkable pupil. She was like a comet that passed across our field of vision and then was gone. We went back to our ballet.

Not far from the Theatre School, on the other side of the Neva, was a chapel made from a hut that Peter the Great had built with his own hands; inside was the icon that protected the people of Peter's city. Before final examinations, this chapel was always packed with students who came there to pray and light candles. If one couldn't manage to visit this chapel, the alternative was to carry a small replica of the icon, tucked into one's décolletage. But not even the replica was all that small, and we little girls especially, during the days leading up to our exams, took on a most peculiar shape, and kept it until we were certain we had passed.

Unpopular as I may have been with the inspectress, I was well liked by my teachers. At the second year's end, they awarded me good marks in all my classes and a scholarship. For each of the first two years, my family had paid three hundred and fifty rubles—quite a lot of money— for my tuition and room and board. There were only a few scholarships, reserved for students who were extraordinarily gifted or promising, funded by the tsar's private capital.

The tsar was like a deity to us, and when he came to the school, it was not so much a visit as a visitation. His father, Alexander III, had been very fond of the ballet and on rare occasions would have supper with the students. There was a story passed down to us that once he was at the Theatre School, walking in the corridor on his way to one of the studios, when a little girl ran up behind him and kissed his hand. "What do you want?" he asked her. "Oh, Your Majesty," she said, "I want to be a boarding student." "All right," he said, "granted."

I thought dancing was everything, that it wasn't necessary for me to learn academic subjects. I was a complete moron. I loved history, thanks to one teacher, a charming man with great enthusiasm for his subject; but it was only as I grew older that I came to see the importance of knowing about something besides ballet.

Dancing came easily to me. We girls went on pointe at the end of our second year—just exercises in all positions at the barre, to build strength in our feet. And that seemed to me perfectly natural, since I had gone up on my toes instinctively when I was much younger. Adagio I found maybe a little more difficult than allegro, though it wasn't until later, when I began to dance for Balanchine, that I worked on my extension, because he wanted the legs higher. But at that time, during my years at the school, we didn't lift the legs high—it was considered not classical, rather daring, a little bit vulgar. "You are not in the circus," our teachers would scold if développés or grands battements got too big. Just a teeny bit above the waist was as high as we were allowed. The Victorian attitudes still prevailed.

Even more modest than our développés were our costumes for Fokine's ballet *Eunice*. The story was about a slave girl in love with her master, who of course couldn't marry her. In the last scene, the master and slave died together; roses fell from the ceiling as the curtain came down. It was a very sugary ballet. The choreography was à la Isadora Duncan: we strewed flowers and picked them up again, hippity-hopping around the stage in tunics and veils and "bare" feet, which were actually covered in flesh-colored tights made like gloves, with toes. (Feet that were really bare would have been censored as too risqué.)

As we were promoted from one year to the next, we were passed on to new teachers—from the first class, under a kindhearted man named Mr. Veransov, to the second, under Mme Ruslakova, a soloist in the Imperial Ballet. In the middle division, we were taught by Mme Kulichevskaya, a former soloist retired from the stage, who bestowed on me the coveted pink dress while all my classmates were still in grey. One year behind me was a girl named Lidia Ivanova, a promising dancer who was also singled out to wear pink.

So she and I were thrown together early on and often cast together in performances, both at the school and at the Maryinsky Theatre. We had many admirers, people in the audience who would point us out and follow our progress. Mostly, they were divided in their opinions—some were her fans, some were mine. But there was no rivalry between us. Our talents were different, and they complemented each other: she was a good actress, very expressive, coquettish, earthy, beautiful in adagio, with a big extension. And she used her extension in her jump, which was not very high but looked enormous because she could leap with her legs in a split. I was lighter, better in allegro, with good clear beats, a high jump, and a sharp attack. Like me, Lidia was small, but she was also a little bit plump. She had dark hair, a pug nose, and fiery almond eyes.

For our school performance the year before I was graduated, we danced the pas de trois from *Paquita*—Ivanova and I, with Georgi Balanchivadze—whose name would later be changed by Diaghilev to Balanchine. By featuring us so soon, before we were ready to graduate, the school cast a spotlight on the three of us and signaled that our future was full of promise.

Four

WE GIRLS HAD BEGUN to be aware of the boys in our class. The boys at the school were far more sophisticated than we girls were. They had more freedom, and when they returned from their weekends, they would tell us about the musicals they had seen, brag about the women they knew. We took it all in, in disbelief—our matron would have given us a good thrashing just for suggesting things the boys did as a matter of course. They tantalized us with descriptions of the world beyond our reach.

I became aware of one boy in particular—George Balanchine. He was not yet handsome, but he was interesting looking, with piercing eyes; he seemed somehow special. Every weekend, he stayed at the school, and often alone, as his family lived in the Caucasus, too far away for him to go home. His sister was enrolled at the school for a while but was dismissed—she wasn't very capable. And his brother, whom I had also met, was a student at the Conservatory; he later became a composer. George had a nice disposition, but while the rest of us were busy getting into mischief, he mostly kept to himself. He seemed very serious for his years.

Grigori Grigorevitch Grigoriev, an intellectual, one of the boys' schoolmasters, took George on as his protégé, inviting him to his apartment for lunch on Sundays, introducing him to music and books. George played the piano well, and it was Grigoriev who suggested that he attend the Conservatory. We were all in awe of this; professional music training was above and beyond the Theatre School's curriculum. We studied music, but most of us learned only as much as we needed to know to dance, for rhythm. Whenever there were parties at the school, George would sit down at the piano and play a little concert, making us very proud. Most of us took for granted that we would become dancers, but George then had another ambition: he wanted to become a conductor.

In Russia, a girl would not go all the time with one boy before she had finished school—it wasn't done, it would be considered compromising. Life for us was much more formal than it is today. St. Petersburg was a beautiful city, with wide streets and beautiful palaces and gardens. On a date, we would go for a walk, or to a barge on the river where they served beer and crayfish. In the winter, we would go skating on small ponds which were all over the city. Our pastimes were innocent.

Of course, that didn't stop us from having crushes. Mine was on Anatole Vilzak, a dashing young member of the company, and I shared my crush with my friend, Maria Komendantova. Together, we talked about how handsome he was, how beautifully he danced.

The Dramatic Studio then occupied the classrooms on the boys' floor, just above our own, and the boys in our class got acquainted with the drama students: the girls, according to our boys, were beautiful, sophisticated, and very "advanced" for their age. All this big talk was calculated to make us jealous. And it did. Often, we heard about Nellie O., who had dark hair and striking features; a good ten years older and married, too, she had taken up acting as a hobby. The boys promised us that they would arrange a meeting, so we could see this Nellie for ourselves. And, indeed, to our dismay, she was as gorgeous as they had said. Years later, after George and I had left Russia for a tour of Germany, I bought a new hat. When I modeled it for him, he said, "You look like Nellie." And I was so flattered. Her beauty was still, even then, the standard by which we measured other women.

In 1920, when he was sixteen, George asked and was granted permission to choreograph something for our annual school performance. So, to a piece of music by Anton Rubinstein, he made a pas de deux called *La Nuit*, which he danced with Olga Mungalova. It was what would today be called "a sexy number." The boy conquered the girl: he lifted her in arabesque and held her with a straight arm overhead, then carried her off into the wings—so, she was *his*! This was the first time we had ever seen a one-arm lift in arabesque, which is now almost commonplace. But the effect that pas de deux had on me was more than the surprise at seeing new steps. It awakened something in me as a woman. Until then, all my boyfriends at the school had been just friends—I had never felt the need for anything more. And then suddenly I thought, there is something else. . . .

One Saturday in 1917, Machuta and an officer, a friend of Volodya's, came to fetch me at the school. "Where is Masha?" I asked. "There has been some trouble in the streets," Machuta explained, "and we've come with the carriage to make sure you get home safely." Outside, I saw groups of people gathered here and there. And going back to school the next evening, I saw the groups of people again, still there. On Monday, we heard shooting in the streets.

Immediately, we ran to the windows, where we saw crowds of people running in all directions, soldiers and police shooting at each other. We were not allowed out; nor were we even allowed to go to the windows to see what was going on. But the sound of so much excitement right there below us, in the street, was too much for me—I simply had to have a look. When I was sure the matron wasn't watching, I climbed up into one of the windows, which were high and wide, with a deep casement. Just opposite the school, on the other side of the street, was a group of soldiers. One took up his rifle and aimed right for me. Before I knew what was happening, I heard the gunshot, the whistle of the bullet, and I fell to the floor.

"I am wounded, I am wounded!" I cried. The matron came running to investigate.

"Get up!" she said. "Don't be silly, you are not wounded. There is no blood—nothing. But this will teach you a lesson." I looked up at the window and there, near the top, was a small, clean bullet hole. That gunshot killed my curiosity.

Our maids brought us the news. Everything was confused: fights had broken out between the soldiers and the people; the Dowager Empress Maria's palace, close to our school, was occupied by the tsar's police. One evening, when we were ready to sit down to supper, the front bell rang—one long, loud, impatient, continuous ring. We froze in our places. Our matron on duty, white with fear, strode hurriedly to the entrance hall, which was quite a distance. The bell was still ringing when she got there. She opened the door, and there stood soldiers armed with bayonets. "Where are the police?" they asked.

"What police?"

"We are looking for them—the palace is in our hands!"

"There are not police here," the matron told them. "This is a school. There are only little girls."

"Very well," they said, "we will look just the same."

In no time, there were soldiers everywhere, poking around with their bayonets, searching every room, while we girls trailed along at a safe distance behind. When they got to the dormitory, the soldier in the lead crouched down to look under the first bed. "Go right ahead," the matron told him. "We have forty-one beds here." At that, we girls began to giggle, which seemed to embarrass the soldiers—they abandoned their search after two or three beds, satisfied that we weren't harboring any police. That evening, we were put to bed later than usual, after a long consultation in hushed tones between the matron and our directress.

Little by little, we began to lose our comforts. Food was rationed, but with every week there was less to buy, no matter how many coupons we were prepared to pay. There was no butter. The bread we were served was cut into smaller portions each day. And milk, when it was available, was tasteless and thin, diluted with water. There was no heat. We began to wear our shawls over our dresses all day long. When the weather turned colder, we put on our gloves. The boys and their schoolmaster would make regular trips to the attic, which had been our infirmary, to gather loose floorboards for firewood.

Meanwhile, the government, preoccupied with its revolution at home, had stopped fighting in the European war, and the Germans seized the opportunity to close in. Suddenly, without warning, Machuta, Volodya, and I, with our cook, our maid, and our kitchen maid, were forced to flee St. Petersburg, on foot. We were not alone—the road was thronged with people, running.

We made our way to Eisk, a town in Kubanskaya Oblast, the Cossack region, where we spent the winter and most of the spring. Rumors of the changes brought on by the Revolution reached us even there. Finally, when it was clear that St. Petersburg was safe from the Germans, we went home.

I had done exercises every day while we were away, but even so, with no classes and no supervision, I lost much of the progress I had made at the school. When we arrived back in St. Petersburg, we discovered that the school had been closed: the Communists were not yet sure that they wanted to sponsor ballet, suspecting that it was too bourgeois an art form to be granted a place in their new society. Besides, they told us, it was hard to find enough food to keep a school going.

Fortunately, General Batianov had died, at the age of eighty-two, three months before the Revolution, and so had been buried as a hero, with a state funeral—a military band, an honor guard that marched behind his coffin to the cemetery, and a wreath of yellow roses from the dowager empress. Had he lived long enough to see the Communists come to power, he would almost certainly have been executed.

Our twelve-room apartment was now much too big for us, so we left it for a smaller one—only eight rooms, downstairs in the same building. How crowded we are now! I thought. General Batianov's daughter Elena came with her daughter to live with us. It was a comfort for Machuta and me to share our new home with our family, someone we knew. For very shortly, our three servants' rooms close to the kitchen were taken away from us and turned over to total strangers.

All of our servants left, and many of them made off with whatever pieces of our furniture they fancied. What remained we took with us to our bedrooms. Mine was furnished with the lovely Empire bed and dresser that had formerly belonged to Aunt Lidia. No one living in our apartment at the time used the kitchen; it was every man for himself, in his own room. We cooked our meals in Machuta's room, on a wood stove with one burner. The problem was finding enough kindling to fuel the stove. People picked up anything on the street and took it home to burn: sidewalks made of wood disappeared, plank by plank. When there was no more wood to be found in the streets, we resorted to breaking up our extra chairs.

Nor were there any clothes to buy. I had only one pair of shoes. I took one of the general's military coats to a seamstress and had it rearranged to fit me. Many people had new clothes made from their tablecloths and curtains.

Machuta and I had no idea how to cook, or how to clean the apartment, or how to do the laundry. Masha had married one of the general's orderlies, and they had moved to an apartment in our building. Often, I would go downstairs to ask her advice about our housekeeping, and she would give me step-by-step instructions for some chore or other.

Soldiers came to the apartment one day and took Volodya prisoner. That he was obviously a sick man and no longer active in the military made no difference to them; he was arrested and jailed for having once been an officer. From time to time, we would hear reports of the Communists lining up former army officers and shooting every tenth or twelfth one, at random, but Volodya managed to survive. For two years, he was held in prison. Machuta took a job in the restaurant next door to our building, and whenever we could, we sent him extra bread.

It was nearly a year before a man named Anatoly Lunacharsky was appointed the new minister of fine arts; he championed ballet and theatre and persuaded the Communists to reopen the school. And so, once again, our routine resumed. Again, we saw the same, dear faces.

But there were changes: new courses—in English, the history of dance, the history of art, the study of costume. The directress, whose power had been absolute, was now forced to share the governing of the school with a committee of students.

But the changes that affected us most had nothing to do with the administrative policies. There was no heat, and we had practically nothing to eat. All of us were hungry and began to develop boils—at one time I had five, but that was nothing compared with George, who had thirty. There was no nourishment. With our coupons we would go to restaurants, where they would serve us some thin soup—dirty water with potato peels in it—or seal meat. We tried to mix flour with coffee grounds to make patties we could eat. Sometimes we were given horse feed. The horses, meanwhile, were dropping dead in the streets. During the night, people would come with knives and take whatever they could from the carcasses; in the morning, there would be only bones.

It was during these desperate times that we girls got to know the boys a little better. The eldest students, those of us in the last class, took turns cutting the bread for the entire school. Every third week, we got up half an hour early and reported to the kitchen, where the boys would insist on showing us how to slice the loaves into pieces that weighed exactly one-eighth of a pound, how to cut so as not to make so many crumbs, how to balance the scales. And, naturally, flirtations developed.

The boys continued to raid the school's attic for firewood, dismantling the floor and whatever furniture had been put there in storage. As time wore on, we marveled that the building was still standing.

Ivanova and I were forbidden to wear our pink dresses because, the Communists thought, such distinctions created jealousy among the students. So there we were, everyone in grey. Before long, the school's supply of pointe shoes was exhausted, and we had to wear soft shoes for class. As soon as the ballerinas at the Maryinsky Theatre threw their pointe shoes away, we students would snatch them up and try all kinds of tricks to make them last a little longer, so that we could wear them once or twice before they gave out completely.

That Christmas was the first that we had all spent at the school, and it was to be our last, in the traditional sense, for years to come. We were given a coupon for a Christmas tree, and the boys went out and brought us an enormous one, which we all decorated together. By the next year, all the trees had been chopped down for firewood. When the trees had disappeared, people began to burn everything: their furniture, their libraries. . . .

Ordinarily, the school was closed at Christmas, but that year it remained open. We would go home to visit our families, most of whom had no heat or hot water, and then hurry back to the school, which was at least slightly better off. There was a party for the students in the last class. George, I remember, came wearing a navy-blue suit instead of his uniform, looking very grown-up and debonair.

The school began to offer evening courses as a means of opening itself to more students. From these classes came Vera Volkova, Igor Schwezoff, Eugenia Delarova, Natasha Branitskaya (who later joined the Diaghilev company), and Tamara Geva, whom I had met a few years earlier at a birthday party for my classmate Nina Nikitina. Tamara was the daughter of Nina's godmother, and she had always been interested in what we did at the school. "Show me how you do développé," she would say. "Like this?" And she would lift her leg very high. "Well," we would say, "that's very good." The new policy at the school after the Revolution made it possible for Tamara to enroll.

The new government also offered ballet tickets for little or nothing to the labor unions, for the workmen and their families. Every Thursday was factory day, a closed performance, always sold out. The old royal boxes in the theatres were transformed: the tsar's box was for the directors, the grand dukes' box upstairs for artists from any of the three official theatres. Actors, opera singers, dancers could come and watch one another's performances whenever they pleased.

In our last year, we studied under Agrippina Vaganova, who was very strict, very stern—I was terrified of her. She would call me "trash" whenever my performance in class was not as good as she thought it should be, which was almost always.

It was through Vaganova that we got our news of Diaghilev's Ballets Russes. Karsavina wrote her letters and occasionally enclosed a program; we would pore over it before class began.

For our graduation, I danced a pas de deux with Kola Efimov, to music by Delibes, from *Sylvia*. It was Mme Preobrajenskaya's choreography—long, not interesting, an awful number. Then I was taken into the company. This came as no surprise—the students who were not suited for careers in ballet had been weeded out all along the way. Only five of us girls finished the school that year, in 1920, and we were all hired for the season that would begin in the fall.

We asked one another to sign our yearbooks. George wrote a few bars of music in mine. When I went to the piano and played the notes, I discovered it was Lensky's aria from *Eugene Onegin*: "I love you, I love you." I thought it was a joke, just a nice thing to write. I didn't take it seriously.

Five

ALL OUR YEARS at the school looked toward that day when we would be members of the company. But when that day finally arrived, the changes in our lives were really not very dramatic. I moved back home to my family's apartment, which was a two-mile walk from the theatre. Otherwise, my daily routine was as before—class in the morning, rehearsals in the afternoons, and performances in the evening.

It was amazing to see how some girls, having finished at the school, no longer practiced, content to spend their careers, as the saying went, "near the water." In the last act of many of the old story ballets, there was often a tableau with a big fountain situated all the way upstage. And around this fountain there was always a group that never danced, just posed—for decoration. These girls were "near the water," and my school friend Galina Sobinova soon took her place among them.

Mme Vaganova continued to teach us and coach us in our new roles. Karsavina still wrote to her from wherever Diaghilev's company was touring abroad, and she would bring the letters to class for us to read; they were our window on the world outside Russia. Paris sounded so glamorous, and sometimes ridiculous: Karsavina wrote that she had just bought herself dark glasses, because everyone there was wearing them. Apparently, they were all the rage. "Can you imagine!" Vaganova said. "How stupid," we agreed. "How difficult it must be to read!" We didn't understand that the people in Paris didn't wear their dark glasses all the time. Karsavina had neglected to tell us that the glasses were for the sun.

About Diaghilev we knew only that his ballet was the most advanced, the most amazing, but we had no details. Spessivtseva returned from dancing *The Sleeping Beauty* with his Ballets Russes in London and described to us the company, the repertoire, the dancers. Vladimiroff used to tell us about how fabulous a dancer Nijinsky had been, but we also knew of the scandal that had led to his dismissal from the Maryinsky, his refusal to wear bloomers over his tights (and there were no dance belts at that time). Later, when I joined Diaghilev myself, people were still talking about Nijinsky—about his dancing, his choreography. It was really very tiresome. I never heard anyone say that he choreographed a disaster, or that one night he gave a bad performance. Everybody agreed that there wasn't a thing he couldn't do, reliving their memories of this dancer I had never seen. To me, Nijinsky was the Kilroy of the ballet.

Besides Mme Vaganova, we were taught by Mme Johansson, the daughter of Karsavina's teacher and a famous teacher herself; she accepted only professional pupils. While I was still a student, she had approached me after one performance and said, "When you grow up, I will teach you to dance." And now, as a member of the company, I began to study with her. It was she who had taught the Maryinsky's ballerinas and watched over their technique. Once, I remember, Karsavina returned from a season with Diaghilev and her dancing was so untidy—knees bent, positions unclear—that the management refused to allow her on the stage until she had had three months in class with Mme Johansson, to straighten her out.

The theatre was a refuge for us, almost a paradise. Outside lay only the chaotic aftermath of the war and the Revolution. But regardless of how the government had changed, what went on inside the theatre was more or less the same. The repertoire was carefully maintained.

There were over two hundred dancers in the company, dancing all the time—if not in ballet, which was performed twice a week, then in the opera. It was a big family.

It was also a very class-conscious society, stacked according to our ranking in the company, with those of us in the corps at the very bottom. The soloists, who occupied more exalted positions, hardly ever spoke to us. This was simply the way of the company, standard practice, not at all surprising; even so, it was occasionally disappointing. Boris Chavrov, a handsome soloist whom I danced with and immediately fell a little bit in love with, refused to acknowledge me off the stage. "How do you do?" he would say when we danced together. But when we met in the corridor or on the street, he would turn and look the other way.

Higher even than the soloists were the ballerinas. Kchessinskaya, Karsavina, and Preobrajenskaya, the three we had worshiped during our years at the school, had all by this time fled Russia. Others had risen to take their places. There was Olga Spessivtseva, whom we adored. Lubov Egorova, who was, I would say, just an ordinary ballerina—her one distinguishing feature was her beautiful arms, so that her best ballet was *Swan Lake*. Xenia Maklizova, with a profile like a cameo, who came to us from Moscow. Elena Lukom, whose last name means "rest room" in Swedish; when she went to dance in Sweden and introduced herself, everyone would titter, until finally she was obliged to change her name to Lukova for her Scandinavian tours. Also, Elena Smirnova, whose roles we expected Lidia Ivanova to inherit because the two of them were the same type. And Elsa Vill, a beautiful dancer who was not quite a ballerina but more accurately a première danseuse, and strictly a soubrette. Her repertoire was limited to three ballets—*Coppélia, Harlequinade,* and *La Fille Mal Gardée*—but her technique was fantastic. One variation she *began* with sixteen entrechats six, enough to make another dancer collapse.

The repertoire during this time was a little bit of everything. There were the old Petipa ballets, in the classical style—*Paquita, Raymonda, Swan Lake, The Sleeping Beauty, Don Quixote, Esmeralda, La Bayadère.* We still performed *The Nutcracker*, although it was later changed by the Bolsheviks because of its Christmas setting; they didn't want any ties with tradition. And then there were the more modern ballets.

Fokine's *Eros* had a story line similar to *Le Spectre de la Rose*. A young girl is in love with a statue of Eros in her garden. One night, she falls asleep and the statue comes and kisses her. She awakens to a big storm;

the statue falls and is broken to pieces. The music for this was Tchai-kovsky's Serenade for Strings. Spessivtseva danced the part of the girl, Vladimiroff the statue, and I was one of four maidens, the cream of the corps de ballet.

We had *Les Préludes*, also by Fokine, to music by Liszt, with scenery by Bakst. The choreography, I recall, was abstract, without a story, danced on half-toe and full of droopy hands. I loved this ballet, which we considered very modern. It was not very popular—people liked the old things better. The Russian public came to the ballet to see toe-dancing and tutus.

Fokine wasn't the only forward-thinking choreographer, but he was perhaps the most popular. Pavel Petrov made a ballet called *Solveig*, to music from Grieg's *Peer Gynt*; but it wasn't very profound, and it didn't last.

More adventurous than either Fokine or Petrov was Feodor Lopu-khov, the company's artistic director. In 1922, he choreographed *The Creation of the World*, to Beethoven's Fourth Symphony. The first scene was an adagio for Lidia Ivanova and me, with a corps of boys. The ballet was too modern to meet with much success: half the audience ap-plauded while the other half whistled, which was considered terribly insulting. After one season, it was dropped from the repertoire.

But Lopukhov had become our mentor. He was blond, middle-aged, not handsome but *vivace*, with a long-nosed profile, like Gogol's. He was very fond of the young dancers and would scold us when we got morose: "What's the matter? You are young and talented! Go to the theatre, go to the museums, see everything! Study languages, study history. Go to concerts." He believed that I had talent and would some-day be a ballerina. So I followed his advice—took up French and the history of art and began to go to concerts. Without him, I don't know what I—or any of us—would have done. Despite all the gloom that pervaded our lives then, Lopukhov never let us lose sight of the goals he had set for us.

He pushed us, casting us in roles that were always just a little bit beyond our capabilities at the time in order to make us work harder. We would struggle to master the challenge each new part presented and finally feel the triumph that came with performing it. This policy gave us encouragement and developed our confidence. There were exceptions. I was given the Bluebird pas de deux in *The Sleeping Beauty*, but it turned out to be too much for me technically; I didn't have enough stamina. And Lopukhov invented something I couldn't cope with—very fast double chaîné turns on the diagonal (where dancers now do single and double piqué turns), and sissonne tombée en tournant, where before there had been coupé–rond de jambe en tournant. The original choreography looked too slow somehow, and he wanted to modernize it. But the steps he gave me were too fast. I was always behind the music. After one performance, the role was taken away. I was told that I wasn't ready yet and was sent back to class.

But technique was only one aspect of dancing, and not even the most important one. Lopukhov taught us that to be on the stage was to play a part. The art was in interpretation. One day you are the Swan Queen, the next you are the Firebird—both of them birds, but very different. Our goal was to find in each role some new side of ourselves to present to the audience, some aspect they had never seen before. To be the same in every role, to be yourself all the time, is boring for your audience. And five pirouettes is an impressive feat only if you can somehow make them serve your artistic purpose; otherwise, so many turns only distract your audience from the part you are playing.

The first role I danced after finishing school was in *Coppélia*—the Prayer variation. I think I was given it not only because of my dancing abilities but also because I had long, beautiful chestnut hair—Prayer dances with her hair down. The steps are simple, mostly bourrées all around the stage.

As a member of the corps, I was given a lot to dance. In the Kingdom of the Shades, the first scene in *La Bayadère*, I was the lead girl, which meant that I had thirty-one arabesques to do before the last girl in the line finally arrived. In *Swan Lake*, I was sometimes a big swan for the waltz in the second act, other times a little swan, one of the four cygnets.

My big opportunity during my first year came in Fokine's *Une Nuit d'Egypte*, a very dramatic ballet about the price one poor man pays for a night of love with Cleopatra. He is killed and his body is thrown out of her tent at dawn. Her procession moves on. A slave girl comes and finds him and kisses him. Lopukhov assigned the part of the slave girl, Ta-Hor, to two of us: Valentina Ivanova, who was older and established, already a soloist, and me. We were both to study the role and show it to him in a rehearsal; then he would decide which of us would finally dance it in performances. Well, for some reason—I don't know why—we were all at this time berserk about Egypt. Following Lopukhov's suggestion that we study a language, some of my friends had taken up hieroglyphics. I went one day to the museum, to the Egyptian section, to look at the sarcophagi. One of them was open, and when no one was looking, I got down on my knees and smelled the mummy inside.

Given my own case of Egyptomania, the role of Ta-Hor, which was all on half-toe, appealed to me very much. I practiced hard and won the competition easily. The only problem for me was the kiss, since I had never kissed a man before. How was I to do it? Just cross our heads and pretend or kiss the man—it was my heartthrob, Boris Chavrov—on the lips? Finally, I decided: anything for art. I kissed him for real. I must have danced convincingly as well, because from then on I was given one new role after another.

Next came the title role in Lopukhov's version of *The Firebird*, which suited me well because I was light but not ethereal, rather jumpy. Misha Mikhailov, one of my classmates, an intellectual who went on to become a critic, described me as "very graceful, petite, and with temperament." It was my success in *Firebird* that proved I was ready for principal roles.

At the end of my second year as a member of the company, I was told by the directors, "You have been so diligent and done so well, what would you like?" They would give me whatever I asked for, as a bonus. So I asked for firewood. And they gave me a huge supply, which unfortunately I had to unload myself—all day I hauled wood. But our apartment was warm again, all winter long.

Ivanova and I continued to be cast together. In *Coppélia*, I was Prayer and she was Dawn. In the underwater kingdom of *The Little Humpbacked Horse*, we were sea urchins. We danced Giselle's two friends and the two lead Wilis. In *Le Corsaire*, we did the pas de trois. In *The Sleeping Beauty*, we alternated in the Diamond variation: the consensus was that Lidia did the entrance better and that I was better in the variation.

Lidia took private lessons—something I should have done but never did—with Ekaterina Vazem, an old ballerina who helped many dancers in the company to improve their techniques. Her students all had better jumps and turns, but also, I must say, big thigh muscles from doing every day sixteen grands fondus développés at the barre and sixteen more in the center.

Having spent so much time together at the school, and now sharing a dressing room and going to the same parties, Lidia and I became friends. She was much more mature and sophisticated than I was—always smartly dressed, with a lot of admirers, especially among the officers of the Bolshevik elite, the "Blue Army," so called because their uniforms were khaki decorated with turquoise bands across their chests, and their hats had a blue star. During our years in the company, Lidia had a steady boyfriend, an engineer. Now I understand that she discovered sex before I did; in this regard, I was a little bit retarded. And Lidia never told me anything that might have disrupted my innocence.

It's not that I didn't have admirers. I was always invited to the theatre, to the opera, to all the new movies, to late-night restaurants with live music. One man I remember in particular, a Mr. Lorr: he looked like Richard Chamberlain, very handsome, and was close to thirty—I was not yet twenty. Mr. Lorr owned a chocolate shop and sent me boxes and boxes of candy. He would take me out for dinner and a ride in a troika, one of the many sleighs that made a special round in St. Petersburg, the way horse-drawn carriages do in New York City. The horses were fast and the seat very small, with a low back—young men loved to take their girls for a ride, because it provided them with an opportunity to hold them tight.

But most of my dates were foreigners living in Russia. We had a lot of Swedes: they would always bring us fabrics, like crêpe de chine, and beautiful gloves—things we couldn't buy. There was also a big German colony, and after performances we were often invited to the German or the Norwegian embassy for supper. But these boyfriends of mine were exactly that, just friends—escorts, really. There was never anything serious between us.

Soon after George Balanchine finished school, he married. His wife was a pretty girl I had met a few years before, Tamara

In *Waltzes from Vienna*, 1931.

Me at thirteen.

Machuta.

My Aunt Lidia.

My sister, Elena.

Taking class in the middle division of the Theatre School, in front of a portrait of the Tsar. I am second from right.

In an academic class in the first division, when I was about nine. I am standing, and dressed differently from the others because I was the only boarder. I think that the little boy on the far left is Mr. B.

With Nina Nikitina and Lidia Ivanova, in the early 1920s, with Mr. B. on the right.

In Monte Carlo, 1928. Left to right, Doubrovska, Lifar, me, Tanya Barash,
Mr. B., Mikerska, Lidia Pavlova, Nikitina.

In *Zéphyr et Flore*. Left to right, de Valois, Mikerska, Chamié, Tchernicheva, Sokolova, Soumarokova, Doubrovska, and me.

With Massine in *Pas d'Acier*.
Not a big success.

In *The Gods Go a-Begging*.

With Lifar in the first Lord Berners ballet, *The Triumph of Neptune*.

As the Fairy Queen in *The Triumph of Neptune.* You can't see it, but I am wearing a tiara.

In *Le Bal* my costume is by de Chirico; this was a ballet in which Mr. B. absolutely discarded classicism and made it very "Balanchiney."

In *Le Bal*, with Dolin.

Above and opposite: in *Apollo,* with Lifar. We
changed the costumes for this one so many times!

Again in *Apollo,* this time in the first costume Chanel designed for us.
Later she discarded this for just a little tunic.

Above: Chanel always had us in hats with little flowers. I think she was horrified by women's hair. Below: rehearsing *The Gods Go a-Begging*. Standing left to right, me, Sir Thomas Beecham, and Woizikowsky. Tchernicheva and Doubrovska are kneeling.

In the year before Diaghilev died. Luba Soumarokova is kneeling at the left, then Lifar is standing behind Balanchine, then me, then Tcherkas and Chamié, with the two Polish boys in front whose names I can never remember.

Geva. Tamara's father was a literary man, her mother a young, good-looking woman, and their home had become a salon for young artists.

The news of George's marriage came as a big surprise to all of us. Being friends from the school and very nosy, living in such close proximity, we generally knew everything about one another. In this case, however, we hadn't even known that George was courting Tamara. None of us were invited to the wedding. I found the news upsetting, although I wasn't sure why.

One day, not long after their wedding, I saw them on the street, both looking so young and so handsome. Tamara was beautifully dressed, and compared with her, I thought, I must look like God-knows-what, so I hung back—I didn't want them to see me. I felt suddenly very awkward.

Another day, after rehearsal, we happened to walk out together—George, his friend Slava Slaveninov (who later became an actor), and I. Tamara was outside, waiting for George. We were all headed in the same direction, so we strolled together down Theatre Street, and along the way, a gypsy stopped us. "Let me tell you your fortunes," she said.

Well, Slava thought it would be wonderful for the newlyweds to know the future, so he gave the gypsy a few pennies and said, "Go ahead, tell us what you see for them." She turned to Tamara and George. "You are just married," she told them.

Slava and I laughed. "Well, of course! Anybody could see it, the way you two walk around grinning all the time. . . ."

The gypsy looked at them more closely and said, "Give me some more money and I will tell you some more." So George added more money. "But this marriage will not last long," she said to him.

"Why?" we asked her. More money.

"Because you," she said to George, "will fall in love with a friend of your youth. And if you give me more, I can tell you her name."

By this time, we were all interested. Slava added a few more coins to her hand. Then she announced, "Her name is Alexandra." All eyes turned to me. I got red in the face.

"Then it must be you, Choura!" Tamara said. I chased the gypsy away and reminded them how silly this fortune-telling business really was, that these predictions didn't mean a thing. But I never forgot what the gypsy had said.

A s a dancer, George was popular and well re-
spected. He was given solo roles, most of them demi-caractère. In *The
Nutcracker*, he always brought down the house in the Candy Cane variation, with his sensational jumps through a hoop. His distinguishing
features, I would say, were speed, musicality, a big jump, and a sharp
attack. George was assured of a good career in the State Ballet, the
Maryinsky company.

But as a choreographer, he had no future there. His background
was so unusual, with the musical training he had acquired at the Conservatory, and his choreography was so innovative that he began to
seem threatening to our superiors. They were jealous. One premier
danseur who was also a high-ranking party official, Victor Alexandrov-
ich Semionov, argued that Balanchine was too modern, that he would
destroy the Petipa tradition.

So George had no choice but to do his choreography on the outside. He organized the Youth Ballet, an ensemble of young dancers—
all of us friends since school. We performed in the Gratskaya Duma, or
town hall, on Nevsky Prospekt. It was not a big theatre, not fancy, but
it served our purposes. George choreographed on us several experimen-
tal ballets—we danced with a choir, we danced to poetry.

George was influenced in his choreography by Kasian Goleizovsky, a choreographer who was at that time working in Moscow. Several
of us, friends from the Theatre School, had gone to see a performance
by Goleizovsky's troupe and found it very avant-garde. All I can remember of it is a ballet version of *Salomé*, which was magnificent, really
daring. Salomé wore a tulle leotard and under it a transparent brassiere,
so that she looked absolutely naked, but nothing was bouncing. The
dancers were all classically trained, but the movement was unusual,
sometimes bizarre. There were twelve boys who threw Salomé into the
air; they did all kinds of things. It's hard to imagine on the basis of the
story in the Bible what Salomé could have danced, that Herod would
give her the head of his prisoner. But this dance of Goleizovsky's was
so inventive and fascinating that it made sense of the story. It also made

a big impression on George. Goleizovsky's work inspired him, I think, and gave him the courage to stray far from convention, to try something completely different from what ballet had always been.

The Youth Ballet was just beginning to gather some momentum when, suddenly, we were summoned by the Maryinsky directors: if we continued to work with Balanchine, we would be expelled, they threatened. Balanchine they didn't even warn—he was expelled from the theatre, then and there, as punishment for his experiments. We were all shocked and discouraged. The Youth Ballet had had its roots in the school, in our expectations for George; we still felt proud of him, and loyal to him. And now the Maryinsky, which had been such a haven for us during these hard years after the Revolution, began to seem small and stifling.

George and Tamara continued to make appearances as a duo. And I occasionally did some concerts, what we called *haltura*—bread-and-butter engagements, strictly commercial, usually in restaurants—with my classmate Misha Dutko, a beautiful dancer who became quite an important soloist and later married Elizaveta Gerdt.

Even so, Russia began to seem a more and more hopeless place to launch a career. There was no heat, no food, no transportation. What was worse, there was no longer any personal freedom. To go anywhere, to do anything, one had to ask the government's permission. Everything we had ever heard about the West—my aunt's descriptions of Paris, Karsavina's accounts of Diaghilev's seasons, the little bit of information we had been able to gather from Viennese operettas that came to us by way of Budapest, plays by Ibsen and Shaw brought by German theatre companies, and American films—we had stored away, and now it all came back to mind as we began to wonder about the future we had once taken so much for granted. We were hungry, and there was no food. I wanted beautiful clothes, but there were none to be had. I thought that if I could not leave Russia, I would just rot there. I wanted to see the world. Russia was my home—I had no intention of leaving it forever. But I knew that I had to leave for a time, to see what lay beyond.

There was a singer named Vladimir Dmitriev, a member of the opera at the Mikhailovsky Theatre, which was our home for light opera, like the Opéra-Comique in Paris. Dmitriev liked pretty dancers and was always courting one or another of us. Often, he gave parties and invited young dancers. I was among them, and so we became friends. One day, he was dismissed from the theatre because he had begun to lose his voice: he was then in his forties. From the opera, he went to work in a private gambling club as a croupier. Before long he had made a lot of money, because it was the custom for everyone who won to give money to the croupier. Dmitriev agreed with me that we had to get out of Russia. Why didn't we form a little concert group, he suggested, and book ourselves a tour abroad for the summer, during our vacation from the theatre? He invited George and Tamara, Kola Efimov (who had been my frequent partner at the school), Lidia, and me. It was the cream of the young Maryinsky crop. Our conductor from the Maryinsky, Dranyshnikov, would accompany us as our pianist, along with a soprano from the Maryinsky Opera; I think she was his girlfriend. A Mr. Kessler, who represented a German piano manufacturer in Leningrad, arranged for us to appear in small theatres in Wiesbaden, Baden-Baden, and Frankfurt-am-Main and secured our visas, which were good for ninety days.

A month or so before we were to leave for Germany, Lidia came to the theatre with a sad face. "I am not going abroad," she announced.

"Why not?" I asked. "What happened?"

It seems that she had met at a party a woman who was clairvoyant. In the manner of the Count Cagliostro, who foretold Marie Antoinette's death by looking into a glass of champagne through her ring, this woman looked through Lidia's ring and dropped it into a glass of wine. And in this glass, she said, she saw a boat overturned and Lidia drowned. "Beware of water, I beg you," she said. Since we had to go from Leningrad to Stettin by steamer, Lidia had decided to cancel her trip.

About two weeks later, she called me with an invitation to go to Kronstadt for the day with some of her officer friends. From Leningrad to Kronstadt was half an hour by ferry. Kronstadt was our defense port, and there were always sailors and civilians making the trip back and forth. It was a pleasant outing on days when the weather was fine. I would have gladly accepted Lidia's invitation, but I wasn't at home when she called.

The following evening, she and I were both to dance at what had been the dowager empress's palace, now a public garden with an outdoor stage, where members of the company were sometimes engaged to give small concerts during the summer. But she never arrived. Not long before the performance was to begin, the adjutant to the commissar of the Maryinsky Theatre paid us a visit. The commissar's job was to see that all the artists of the theatre were doing what the party wanted. His adjutant informed us that Lidia had been killed the day before, in a boating accident on the river. We were stunned.

Somehow we went through with the performance. At the end, Lidia's boyfriend, who hadn't accompanied her on her outing the day before, arrived to pick her up and take her to dinner. We broke the news to him, and together the four of us—he, George, Tamara, and I—set out to find more information. We went to the pier where the boats for Kronstadt docked and there found the captain, who was distraught over what had happened.

He told us that a motorboat had been cutting across his path, scooting all the time under his nose; he tried to avoid it, hooting his horn, until finally he couldn't miss it, and the boats collided. Four people on the ferry were knocked overboard—Lidia and her three officer friends. The men were thrown life belts and ropes and rescued; Lidia was pulled by the current under the boat, presumably into the propeller, and never seen again.

Lidia had often been invited to the club of the GPU, the secret police. She was circulating on the highest levels of the party military. I went with her to this club once or twice, but instinct told me to be careful, not to trust those people one hundred percent, because the Revolution, though it was much less visible, was not yet over. It was not a quiet time. The power struggle between the Bolshevik and Menshevik parties continued. People were suspicious of one another. We warned Lidia not to spend so much time in those circles, but she waved aside our concern for her.

It was dangerous to be popular with the officers who were her friends. The circumstances of her death were suspicious: how does a motorboat manage to hit a ferry hard enough to knock people overboard? How is it that the three men were saved and not Lidia? People speculated that she somehow knew some secret information and that the accident had been carefully arranged.

The reaction to her death was no less mysterious. The following night, her three companions were reportedly seen out to dinner, laughing and drinking, toasting one another, having a high time. There was nothing in the papers save for a small item that gave a sketchy summary of the facts. The body never surfaced. A week later, Lidia's beau hired a diver, who saw the body at the bottom of the river; there was a hole in her head, he said. But the body was never brought up. There were no traces of the incident, of any kind. At the theatre, there was no announcement made, no memorial service. There was no funeral. We heard that Lidia's mother called for an investigation, but nothing ever came of it.

George told me that not long after Lidia was drowned, he saw her in a dream. "I am so lonely," she said, reaching out to me. "I want Choura." "No, no," he said, and he pulled me back, away from her.

We all loved Lidia and were terribly upset at losing her. But it was years before we understood what had gone on; the extent of the tragedy dawned on us only later. In a sense, she was a casualty of the Revolution.

Lidia's death made us all the more eager to leave Leningrad behind. The six of us set out, with Dmitriev acting as our manager. Our repertoire was limited but varied: Kola and I would dance the pas de deux from *Sylvia* that we had performed for our graduation from the school. Tamara and I would do an Oriental dance with tambourines, from *Khovanshchina*. I would dance two solos George had made for me, one to music by Scriabin and the other to a waltz George had written on the piano himself and dedicated to me. Tamara and George danced two numbers together, both George's choreography—very modern. As a closing number, George, Kola, and I danced a Russian sailor dance, based on a popular folk dance, which George also arranged.

The tour would last the summer. We intended to return in time for the start of rehearsals at the Maryinsky in the fall. I was looking forward to the next season. The directors had promised me the part of Kitri in *Don Quixote*. It was a big bravura role that would suit me well, and an important step in my career. So when I left Russia in June 1924, it was with the assurance that new success would be waiting for me when I came home, in just a few months.

Six

WE TOOK THE BOAT from Leningrad to Stettin, in Germany. Soon after we arrived on board, a maid came to my cabin and offered to help me unpack. "There's nothing to unpack," I said. My one small suitcase contained only a change of clothes, a nightgown but no dressing gown, one change of underwear, and two pictures, of my aunt Lidia and Machuta. I had wanted to bring my picture of General Batianov, too, but then changed my mind and decided that I didn't have room for it. I had also packed my icon (a year or so later it was stolen from the nightstand in my hotel room, somewhere on tour, along with my coral necklace, my only jewelry). I was wearing my best dress, which was tailored, very simple; like all my "good" clothes, it had been either copied by a seamstress from an old magazine from Paris or made from one of the patterns we obtained through some ambassador friends from Sweden and Germany. For a tour that was supposed to last ten weeks, this wasn't much to take along, but it was most of what I had at the time. That didn't matter—I was traveling light. I was conquering the world.

Germany seemed to us so clean, so comfortable, so punctual. I loved Berlin, especially—there were so many trees. The bleakness that had become a way of life for us in Russia was behind us. We felt optimistic and very prosperous. I bought a shiny purple-and-grey sweater on the street. It was awful looking, really, but it was cheap and I was thrilled with my purchase.

I also bought a big hat that caught my eye one day as I was walking past a milliner's window. The hats were displayed on stands, which were draped with chiffon veils. Well, I thought, that is the style here. So I bought a chiffon veil, which I draped over my face as I had seen the veils arranged in the window, one corner dangling down beneath my chin, and then put the hat on over it. Everybody turned and stared at me on the street. Well, I thought, I am so chic that they can't stop looking at me. It never occurred to me that the veils were simply part of the window display. There was nothing that I wouldn't do for fashion.

While we were in Berlin, the four of us went to see Max Reinhardt's production of *Die Fledermaus:* during the famous waltz, one dancing couple made a circle of the stage while the floor revolved—we were flabbergasted.

Best of all was the food. Coming from Russia, where we had been slowly starving, we could hardly believe all the food in Germany. The supply of bread seemed unlimited. We would wrap a few extra rolls in our napkins and smuggle them back to our rooms, just in case we got hungry. We had forgotten what it felt like to be full.

Our performances were well received. We were one act on a bill with many others, playing variety theatres in the spa towns along the Rhine. One of the other acts was a clown, who made eyes at me as part of his routine.

We didn't know anybody, and so we were thrown together and forced to depend on one another. The four of us—George, Tamara, Kola, and I—became a family: we lived in the same hotel, ate together, saw the sights together. Going down the Rhine by boat, we passed one old castle after another, all of them breathtaking. George, Tamara, and I would stand on deck and nudge each other and point and make a fuss over each castle as it came into view. Kola would say, "What are you getting so excited about? It's just an old house, full of holes," and he would go downstairs and nap.

From Germany we went to Vienna especially to hear Rachmani-

noff play his own works. After the concert, we went backstage to introduce ourselves. We were very admiring, paying tribute to him as if he
were a god. "I would like very much to choreograph a ballet to your
beautiful concerto," George told him.

"A ballet!" Rachmaninoff shouted. "To my music! Are you crazy?"
And he threw us out of his dressing room. This was probably one of
the biggest mistakes Rachmaninoff ever made. From then on, whenever
his name came up, George would slam the door on the conversation.
"Lousy music," he would say. He never did choreograph to it.

It was in July, while we were on tour in Germany, that an invitation arrived from the Empire Theatre in London. We were asked to
come for an engagement in November. The others agreed immediately
and signed the contract. But I at first refused to sign. We were expected
back at the Maryinsky on September 1, to begin rehearsals, so the decision to go to London was also a decision not to go back to Russia—
not just yet. But the West was for us an adventure, and we were not
ready for it to be over. In the end, I signed.

London in 1924 was a city of power, majestic and orderly. All I
could think about was Conan Doyle—I wanted to see Baker Street.

Our repertoire remained the same. Again, we were on a variety
bill. One night after the performance, Lidia Lopukhova, Feodor Lopukhov's sister, came to our dressing rooms to see us. She had left the
Maryinsky to dance with Diaghilev's Ballets Russes, then married an
Englishman—the great economist Maynard Keynes—and retired. We
gave her our by this time stale news of her brother and the Maryinsky
Theatre.

It seems that Diaghilev had heard of our tour and sent his cousin
Pavel Koribut-Kubitovitch, who acted as his advance man, to Germany, to bring us to Paris. When he got there, we had just left. Finally,
he caught up with us in London and delivered Diaghilev's note: Would
we please come to see him in Paris? Well, of course, we were very
flattered. As soon as our engagement at the Empire Theatre ended, we
left for Paris, where we were summoned to the home of Misia Sert. It
was a beautiful mansion, the kind of house we would call a palace in
Russia. We were met by a butler at the front door and shown up a
curving stairway to the drawing room, where we were presented to our
hostess—a pretty, rather motherly looking woman, dressed in deep red.

I recognized Diaghilev immediately, with his streak of white hair. He was very charming, with a high-society manner. With him was a handsome young man, Boris Kochno, his secretary and companion.

Tea was served, and we all set about making conversation. Misia turned to me. "Mademoiselle Danilova, how do you like Paris?"

"Well, I like it," I replied.

"You are not very enthusiastic."

I said, "Well, I like very much the Place de la Concorde. But, you know, Paris smells so."

She looked shocked. "Paris smells? But why?"

"I don't know," I told her.

"Where are you staying?"

"In a very small hotel," I said, "near Les Halles." At that she laughed. "Oh, now I understand!" I never again stayed near the markets, and from then on, whenever I would see Misia, we had a standing joke between us: she would ask me how Paris smelled. "Oh, beautiful," I would reply.

After tea, the furniture was moved to clear a space at the end of the room, where Tamara and George did their number in costume but in bare feet. It was George's choreography to some Arensky music from *Une Nuit d'Egypte*—very modern. When they had finished, Diaghilev turned to me and said, "And you, Miss Danilova, what will you dance for me?"

"Dance for you?" I said. "What do you mean?"

He said, "Well, they danced, and I thought maybe you would— it's like a little audition."

"Do you know that I come from the Maryinsky Theatre?" I asked him, indignantly.

"Yes, I do," he said.

"Well," I told him, "if I am good enough for the Maryinsky Theatre, I am good enough for you." Can you imagine how fresh I was!

Diaghilev laughed. "Yes, you are absolutely right."

Nevertheless, I did in the end dance something—a few movements from the *Firebird* Berceuse, Lopukhov's version. Afterwards, Diaghilev asked me how much I weighed. Nobody had ever asked me that. I got very insulted. "What are you buying," I asked, "a horse? Maybe you want to see my teeth?"

The four of us were given contracts. We would join Diaghilev's Ballets Russes in London just before Christmas.

But in the meantime, we needed money—we had nothing to buy food with. So we held a conference. We decided that we would have to sell our clothes. Tamara and I had nothing very exciting in our wardrobes. The only one with something to offer was George, who had a suit that was fairly new and well cut. So we decided that he must make the sacrifice and give up his suit to be sold. The boys took off, and when they returned a few hours later, they brought back a feast, and we celebrated. There was just enough food left over to last us a few days, to hold us until we went to London, where we could get an advance on our salaries.

Our welcome into the Ballets Russes was not very warm. Bronislava Nijinska, Diaghilev's ballet mistress and choreographer, didn't want another ballet master, especially one as young and promising as Balanchine, so she resigned. Diaghilev had had to dismiss a few of his less talented dancers in order to hire us. So already the company was growling. Then here we came, four Soviet refugees, not particularly elegant—scruffy looking, really—and rather arrogant. We went once to Nijinska's class, but we didn't approve because it was different from the Maryinsky's, so we never went back. Soon after we arrived in London, the company gave Nijinska a farewell party, and we weren't invited. Diaghilev asked us to dinner that evening, instead.

The dancers in the company were not very good, I thought. They seemed limited, without much technique. One of the first ballets I saw them dance was *Le Train Bleu*, with choreography by Nijinska. The Blue Train took high society from Paris to the south of France, where everyone went on vacation. The ballet was sporty and not very interesting. Anton Dolin had a gymnastic variation, with a trampoline. When Diaghilev asked me what I thought of the ballet, I said, "Where is the dancing?"

Leonide Massine's *Cimarosiana* was on the same program, and that I liked better. It was a divertissement from Cimarosa's opera *Le Astuzie Femminile*, without a plot. I saw Vera Nemtchinova dance in it, and she was good technically, though not a very attractive personality on the stage. Later, Diaghilev added to *Cimarosiana* a pas de trois for Serge

Lifar, Balanchine, and me, with choreography by Balanchine. After that season, my first, Nemtchinova left the company to join the Cochran Revue and never came back—she wanted to, but Diaghilev was furious with her for abandoning him. I took her place in many ballets.

His other ballerinas when I joined the company were Lubov Tchernicheva, Lidia Sokolova, and Felia Doubrovska; and now there was also Tamara Geva. Among the male dancers were Dolin, Leon Woizikowski, Taddeus Slavinsky, and Stas Idzikowski. Vera Savina, Massine's ex-wife, was a soloist. There were about sixteen girls in the corps. They were well trained, but the quality of dancers today is much better; the standard for the corps is certainly higher.

This particular season in London was at the Coliseum, a music hall. We danced twice daily, as part of Oswald Stoll's revue. Following us on the program, there were variety artists—a juggler, a dog trainer—and then a movie.

My first role came in Massine's *Contes Russes*, a colorful ballet of Russian folk tales to music by Liadov. It was never very popular, because nobody in the audience knew the stories. But we were a Russian company—these were the stories we had grown up with, and the dances were in our blood. My little number was a popular character dance called *komarik*—"the mosquito." It had belonged to Ludmila Schollar, but she left the company with Anatole Vilzak that season, and I was cast to replace her and dance with Leon Woizikowski. He was very indignant and at the first rehearsal refused to work with me. "Who she is?" he said. "I don't want to dance with some little nobody." I started to cry. Serge Grigoriev, our régisseur and the go-between in all our dealings with Diaghilev, left the studio. In a few minutes he returned: it was the wish of Diaghilev that I should dance with Woizikowski, he said, and under no circumstances was I to withdraw. But I was so upset that I couldn't even understand any of the steps being shown to me. Finally, Tchernicheva, Grigoriev's wife, took me in hand and showed me the number. "Stop crying," she said, "and show him how you can dance." My debut was a success, and after the performance, Diaghilev called the whole company together on the stage. Then, in front of everyone, he told me that I had danced the role better than anyone ever had before. In time, Woizikowski and I became friends.

From London, we moved to Monte Carlo for a three-week ballet season in January and then three months of dancing with the opera.

There were countless telegrams from the Maryinsky Theatre demanding that I return at once, threatening me with expulsion. These threats came from the management, never from Lopukhov himself. I wrote occasionally to my family, telling them that Diaghilev had engaged us, that we were going here and then there, describing the sights. They didn't reply. Only my sister, Elena, wrote to me. She had been adopted by a family in St. Petersburg. She lived more modestly than I did with General Batianov, but her mother was kind to her and often took her abroad, to Menton for vacation in the summer. During our childhood, we saw each other twice a year at the most—my aunt wasn't anxious for me to see anybody who would bring back memories of my family. Elena and I had turned out rather similar, with the same eyes, the same nose, but I was fairer and more delicate. In her letters, she told me that I should come back to Russia.

I missed Russia, and I wanted to return to the Maryinsky Theatre, but at the same time I saw that what Diaghilev was doing was different and exciting. And I didn't feel completely uprooted, anyway. Since my childhood, I had been connected with Balanchine. I had always believed in his genius, and now Diaghilev was giving him new ballets to make. More and more I came to understand that this was where I belonged. One day, Diaghilev brought us new passports—Nansen passports, with red covers. It was only then that I realized our decision to leave Russia was final.

By that time, our days had settled into a new pattern. From ten to eleven o'clock every morning we had company class, taught by Enrico Cecchetti, whom we didn't like because he never gave us enough exercises at the barre to get our muscles warmed up for the center. He would start as usual with pliés, then straight away—no tendus first— twelve grands battements, cold. Then sixteen battements tendus. Then sixteen quick tendus. Ronds de jambe par terre—eight en dehors, eight en dedans. No fondus. Only four développés on each side. Then ronds de jambe sur le coup de pied. Then we moved to the center and did a long adagio, during which I always got cramps in my legs because my muscles were not ready for it. Later Cecchetti revised his method of teaching, and today, of course, the Cecchetti technique is very different. But at that time, his center work was much better than his barre. Cecchetti had certain movements for each day of the week: on Monday, we did assemblés; Tuesday was jetés; Wednesday was ronds de jambe; and so on. The whole class was set. I didn't like that, because I think that in class you must also exercise the mind, so that your brain is trained for work with a choreographer and you can learn new combinations quickly. In Cecchetti's class, everything became routine, which is not interesting. But Diaghilev insisted that we take company class, and in Monte Carlo there was no one else teaching ballet. We were always relieved when the time came for our seasons in Paris and London, where we could take class with private teachers. Eventually, Cecchetti was replaced in Monte Carlo by Mme Tchernicheva.

The uniform of the Diaghilev company, for class and rehearsals, was black—a black crêpe-de-chine tunic and skin-colored silk tights. I hate wearing black, and in Paris and London, where I took lessons apart from the company, I dressed in every color of the rainbow, like someone who has been starving and is suddenly allowed to eat anything.

From eleven-thirty until one we had rehearsals, supervised by Grigoriev. Then lunch. Generally, during the ballet and opera season, we would snooze for an hour after lunch, then start preparing for that evening's performance. By the time we had washed our tights or sewn our shoes, it was time to go to the theatre, because the curtain was at seven-thirty. So we would have tea and arrive by six, warm up, do our makeup, try on our costumes, practice our difficult steps, feel out the stage. During rehearsal periods, when we had no performances in the evenings, we would prepare new repertory for Paris and London.

I felt very secure in the Diaghilev company. We were all busy dancing, and Diaghilev's authority was absolute. In many ways, my life as a dancer was the same as it had been back in Russia, at the Maryinsky. But there was one important difference: at the Maryinsky Theatre, everything was handed to me. I was told what to do and shown how to do it; Vaganova or Lopukhov would personally rehearse me in a new role. In the Diaghilev company, I was on my own. Our only classes were for warming up or for maintaining technique, not for improving technique or even building stamina. At the Maryinsky, we had gone through rehearsals marking the steps, saving our strength, not pushing ourselves; often we would have three months of rehearsing a role before having to perform it. But long rehearsal periods were a luxury the Diaghilev company could not afford. Soon after I joined, Grigoriev came to me and said, "You must dance full out when you rehearse, and then you will gain in technique—this is your training." And I saw that he was right, that this was the way Diaghilev's dancers became stronger.

If you had a difficult variation, you had to go into a corner and work it out for yourself. At first, I couldn't understand that—I was waiting for someone to work with me. During rehearsal, I would wait to go through my variation and then the time would be up; rehearsal was always over before they got around to me. "We don't have time for that," they would say. "Go somewhere and work on it by yourself." So I would get a studio and practice. If I needed coaching in a role, some kind of help with interpretation, I would ask George for advice, or sometimes Tchernicheva. Occasionally, after a rehearsal, she would come up to me and ask, "May I say something? The step wasn't like that. . . ." Or, "So much better if you do it this way. . . ."

In Monte Carlo, we were left pretty much to our own devices. In London, however, we could take class with Nicholas Legat, who was a wonderful teacher. In Paris, we had a choice: Egorova, Preobrajenskaya, Trefilova, and Kchessinskaya all had their own studios to which we could go for lessons and coaching. Kchessinskaya's classes were primarily a social event, filled with people who had come to see who she was. Everyone in the Diaghilev company went to either Egorova or Trefilova. I went to Mme Egorova, who paid close attention to technique, and her classes improved my dancing. But coaching was extra, and it cost more than I could afford.

The theatre at Monte Carlo was nothing like any opera house I had ever seen before: the stage was not especially wide, but it was very deep. The pit was large, with room enough to seat a full orchestra. The house was quite small by comparison, with only a few hundred seats— big, comfortable armchairs. The interior, in the Beaux Arts style, was decorated with gold leaf, mirrors, and cherubs. On the second floor, in the center, was the box of the Prince of Monaco. This jewel of an opera house was not a commercial theatre; it had not been built to earn money.

Our audiences were different from those in Russia; their tastes were not so old-fashioned. The Maryinsky Theatre, even after the Revolution, was an institution, with a classical standard by which the audience measured new ballets. But the only standard our audiences knew was the modern one Diaghilev himself had introduced. So when he mounted a full-length production of *The Sleeping Beauty* in London, it was well received but without the usual enthusiasm. People were much more interested in short ballets—three different ideas in one evening.

In spite of this very advanced attitude, there were still many people in the company who couldn't see what a promising choreographer Balanchine was. For them, Fokine was the ideal, and Balanchine was too modern. But Diaghilev must have been impressed by the choreography he saw during our little audition at Misia Sert's, because he immediately gave George an assignment. The opera season in Monte Carlo was three months in the spring, and George was asked to choreograph all the operas. He was also given *Le Chant du Rossignol*, a score by Stravinsky choreographed a few years earlier by Massine; Balanchine's new version was to have its premiere in Paris that June.

While we were still in London, Balanchine was summoned by Diaghilev to go with him and Boris Kochno to see a young dancer. It seemed that Astafieva, a former member of the Maryinsky now living in London, had telephoned Diaghilev and told him about a little girl who had suffered a great tragedy: her father had lost all his money in America and committed suicide, leaving his widow with four daughters. One of them, Astafieva explained, was a very talented dancer. So Diaghilev, Boris, and George went to see this girl, who was named Alice Marks, and they liked her very much. She was very small, very charming. Well, George decided, if we are doing Stravinsky's *Rossignol*, she will be the nightingale.

The ballet, set in China, was about an emperor who is always melancholy; the members of his court bring a nightingale to cheer him. Alicia Marks was renamed Alicia Markova and, in her debut as the nightingale, was a great success. It was in this ballet that Balanchine introduced chaîné turns with the arms open, then closed, then open again—no one had ever seen that before.

Our season at the Coliseum in London featured *Aurora's Wedding*, a little one-act salad Nijinska had arranged from *The Sleeping Beauty*. She substituted a pas de trois—two women and a man in the center—for Petipa's Four Precious Stones, using only the entrance music. At the Maryinsky, the grand adagio was followed by Aurora's variation, then the coda, when the full cast joins in. But in Diaghilev's version, Nijinska used the coda music for a folk dance called The Three Ivans, which was very popular with the audience because at that time everything Russian was in vogue. This was, of course, Diaghilev's doing;

before his Ballets Russes arrived, Europeans thought that all Russians ate children for breakfast.

There were to be five different casts for the Bluebird pas de deux; this was Diaghilev's gimmick to get people to buy more tickets. The ballerinas were Felia Doubrovska, Vera Savina, Alicia Nikitina, Alicia Markova, and me—I was to dance with Anton Dolin.

I had gained weight since leaving Russia—all that German food had made me plump. When I started to rehearse with Dolin, he complained about having to lift me. "What do you think I am, a piano mover?" he asked.

One night, I asked Balanchine to go out into the audience and watch me. He came backstage after the performance and said, "You want the truth?" "Yes, of course," I said. "Choura, you look terrible—you've gotten so fat. What's happened to you?" The next morning, I went straight to the pharmacy and bought a bottle of diet pills—one in the morning, one in the evening, the directions said. Well, I thought, I'll take five and I will melt immediately. The next thing I remember, George was shaking me—I had passed out. He picked up the bottle and asked me, "Is this what you took?" "Yes," I answered. He opened the window and threw the bottle out, then gave me a lecture about how I should lose the extra weight: no chocolate, no desserts, and I should wear a sweater with a high collar and wool leggings for class so that I would perspire more. I did as he told me. I tried everything. Finally, somebody suggested that I eat only fish, and that was when I began to lose weight—fifteen pounds altogether. It was the first time I had ever had to watch what I ate. Life in Russia had been a diet in itself.

It was then I began to see that I had to make some rules for myself—rules for dancing, rules for living. Where romance was concerned, I was still uninitiated, although a lot of men were after me. I made a rule that I wouldn't sleep with just anybody, whenever I fancied, but only with someone I loved seriously. I settled on a certain discipline and stuck to it. Many of the girls in the company were butterflies, but I didn't want that kind of life for myself. One day, Diaghilev caught me crying—there were men saying that they had had affairs with me, and I was upset that these rumors would ruin my reputation. "Stop crying," he said. "What a nuisance. You should cry when they don't talk about you—as long as they are talking about you, you are interesting."

During my first year in the Diaghilev company, I became more conscious of my image as a ballerina. Every woman has an image—mother, princess, ballerina—that she must uphold. I was privileged to be a ballerina and I therefore had a duty to my audience. They must never be disappointed in me. I had always worked at my dancing, but now I began to work on my image.

The first season with Diaghilev, I danced in *Swan Lake*. Diaghilev cut a lot of the mime speeches. I was all for that. Instead of pointing at yourself, then pointing at some place on the stage, then waving your hand, all just to say, "I go there," you cut the mime and just ran there. I thought that this made much more sense. I don't believe that anybody understands mime speeches, even in Russia, except the people who really study what the gestures mean. Mime is so primitive; to me, it's not real theatre. Real theatre is not waving your hands in such-and-such a way to tell the audience that you are unhappy. It is much better to incorporate that emotion into your dancing. In *Swan Lake*, for instance, Odette is supposed to say, "Yonder lies the lake of my mother's tears"—how are you going to communicate *that* idea? Well, it's a very complicated thought, but the feeling behind it is simple. Diaghilev had Balanchine make Odette new choreography, with droopy hands and sloping shoulders, to show that she is unhappy and in mourning, so that all her dancing is subordinated to this one idea—her sorrow.

We were all a little bit afraid of Diaghilev. He knew this and did nothing to make us feel at ease. One day, I ran into him on the street in Monte Carlo. "Where are you on your way to?" he asked.

"I am going to get a pedicure," I told him.

He was outraged. "No," he said, "they will cut the skin and you will not be able to dance." He forbade me to go. We parted, and I, of course, went on my way, by this time a little late for my appointment. Sure enough, the pedicurist cut my toe and it got infected. That evening, I reported to the theatre and told Grigoriev that I couldn't dance.

"Where is Choura?" Diaghilev asked George.

"She has something wrong with her foot," George told him.

Diaghilev knew immediately. "Did she have a pedicure today?" he asked. George said yes. Diaghilev said, "Then she will dance anyway." I could hardly get through the performance, I was in such pain, and my foot swelled so much afterward that I couldn't get my shoe on.

Because I was so young, I was probably even more afraid of Diaghilev than the rest of the company was. But once I spoke up to him.

The Ballets Russes *Swan Lake* was the second act alone, not the whole story, and when I saw it for the first time, I went to him and said, "Well, but where are the four cygnets?" He didn't know what I was talking about. His was a slightly different production from the one we had at the Maryinsky, and it may be that when it was first mounted, he didn't have four dancers in the corps who could dance the cygnets' choreography. I explained to him what we had in Russia—four little swans who come out and dance together, holding hands, with their arms crossed in front of them. I showed him the steps. He asked me to show it to the company, and we inserted the four cygnets in his production. It's funny—in life, I am very shy, but when it comes to art, I am not shy at all.

Most of the time, Diaghilev seemed unapproachable. When he went to lunch, there were never fewer than ten people around him—people like Picasso, Stravinsky, Cocteau, Derain, the Princesse de Polignac, Nicolas Nabokov, Vittorio Rieti, Christian Bérard, whom we called Bébé. And always Boris, Diaghilev's constant companion. Boris Kochno was from a very good Russian family, well educated, and somehow not frightened of Diaghilev. In this way, he seemed to me the only real friend Diaghilev had, because he was not afraid to speak up and say "Seriozha, this is impossible," or "No, Sergei, I don't think so."

Some people think that Diaghilev didn't know about dancing. But I was amazed at how much he knew. He was there at every performance and he saw everything—you couldn't skimp. In my first season with the company, in London, I was dancing twice a day and was very tired. It was new for me to dance so often. So one day I decided not to do the beats in my variation in *Aurora's Wedding*. The choreography was entrechat quatre, royale—four times. And I thought, I'll do changement de pieds instead, it will be much easier. As soon as the ballet was finished, I went to my dressing room and heard *knock, knock, knock.* "Yes?"

"Boris."

"Yes, Boris, what is it?"

"Mr. Diaghilev wants to know why you didn't beat today."

"What do you mean?"

"You know what I mean—you didn't do your entrechat quatre, royale." I was astounded. From then on, I always did everything I was supposed to do.

Although Diaghilev was quick to remark on dancing that was not up to his standards, he was just as quick to pay a dancer a compliment on a performance that he found particularly good. Once, he sent me roses after *Firebird*, and I was very flattered.

Nijinska's *Les Biches* was still in the repertoire, and I danced one of the two lesbians, with Tchernicheva. *Les Noces* was a better ballet, very beautiful, I thought. I also danced in it, in the corps. At that time, weddings in Russia among the peasants were mostly arranged by the parents. Very often, a young girl never even saw her fiancé until the wedding was already set, and it could turn out to be someone quite unattractive or an old man of thirty—she never knew until it was too late. And then it was goodbye to her freedom. Young girls might help their mother around the house, but mostly they would go to the woods to pick mushrooms or raspberries, or go on picnics. In the country, you would hear them singing while they did their chores—they lived care-free. And then, when they got married, they had to work in the house, on the farm, bear children and look after them—it was really an awful life for women in Russia. Russian women worked very hard. And all through this ballet, there was a sense of great sorrow, that this young girl's springtime was gone. The wedding celebration was very gloomy, there was nothing joyous about it. The ballet is really a tragedy. Stravinsky said Nijinska had understood his score, and it was true—the steps were perfect with the music. The musicians had a hard time counting it, and the dancers didn't even try. In *Les Noces*, besides piano and percussion, there was a choir. We sang along with them, and that was how we remembered when to do things, by singing and dancing at the same time.

I also danced several Fokine ballets. In *Schéhérazade* I played one of the three odalisques. In *Une Nuit d'Egypte* (which in the Diaghilev company was called *Cléopâtre*) I danced the slave girl, the role I had danced at the Maryinsky. *Carnaval* was about youth and old age: youth comes like a wave and washes time away. First I was Chiarina—I entered and a man caught me, declared his love, and kissed me; it was a very short, very passionate interlude. I danced that with George and with Slavinsky. Later Diaghilev gave me Columbine, the principal role. Both parts were delightful, very easy to dance—except for Columbine's entrance, twice around the stage, running on pointe, which required very strong toes. I loved *Les Sylphides*, and I'm sorry that so few companies dance it now. When I came to the Diaghilev company, I went straight into the corps de ballet, as one of the two girls with little solos, guiding the rest of the corps. Then I was given the first variation, a waltz. Later, I did the mazurka and the big waltz. There is only one male dancer in *Les Sylphides*, and he is Chopin; the sylphs are supposed to be his thoughts. The atmosphere is in the movement, in the port de bras. It's a very difficult ballet to dance for two reasons. First, you have to dance it perfectly. It must be like crystal, absolutely clear and faultless. The other reason it's so difficult is that it's sexless, spiritual instead of physical. You must be a creature of the air, not a woman—a weightless body with beautiful arms, untouchable. I used to imagine Chopin lying on his back on the top of a hill, staring up at the blue sky. A white cloud drifts into view and passes, then another comes. The music is very delicate, and so is the choreography. The corps de ballet makes little patterns—stage pictures.

Most of the ballets I danced during my first year with Diaghilev were roles that had first been choreographed on somebody else. But I did have a part in the new ballet that season. Leonide Massine had been brought in as a guest choreographer to maker *Zéphyr et Flore*, to music by Vladimir Dukelsky, who later became well known as the songwriter Vernon Duke.

I gave Mr. Massine a good looking-over and found him a very handsome man, with beautiful, heavy-lidded, suffering eyes that looked as if they had been painted by El Greco. I had already heard the rumors that Massine was bow-legged—when he danced the Bluebird he wore special tights, padded to make his legs look straight. For rehearsals, he wore specially made black alpaca pants, like those that flamenco dancers wear, to conceal the shape of his legs. This was very clever. The pants were high-waisted, with creases running down the sides instead of down the front and back. With these, he wore a white crêpe de chine blouse, also like those Spaniards wear, with full sleeves. The effect was very dramatic.

Well, he may have been carefully dressed, but he was not very amiable. One day during rehearsal, I asked him what time it was—I was just curious, there was no clock in the studio. He looked at me in great surprise and cut me short: "The time has not yet come for you to finish rehearsal!"

The choreography for *Zéphyr et Flore* was odd but not surprising or new. The principals were Serge Lifar, Anton Dolin, and Alicia Nikitina. There were nine muses—I was one, paired with Ninette de Valois, who called me "Dani." Lifar wore a short golden tunic with a big, wide belt; he was at that time beautifully built. Anton wore a silver tunic that was all leaves, layered one on top of the other. But the best costume was Nikitina's—she had a very small tutu, and her tights and bodice were painted with flowers. As muses, we were part of the landscape on Olympus; our job was to provide the background. Our costumes were awful—wool dresses with drop waists that made us look as if we were wearing burlap sacks.

Each of us had her own number or shared a number with one of the other muses. Doubrovska, I remember, was with Tchernicheva. Ninette and I had one of the best variations, mostly caractère in style. We came on from either side, crossed paths at the top of the stage, then, again crossing, came down and, facing each other, did some hideous movements. I did rond de jambe with one leg, rond de jambe with the other—nothing imaginative. The ballet didn't really work.

Balanchine, at twenty-one, was the ballet master and could do whatever he wanted. Diaghilev fed him ideas; sometimes he corrected Balanchine's own ideas or added something. But it was clear to everyone that Diaghilev trusted George, that he thought George was competent enough as a choreographer to guide the company artistically. Balanchine's ballets were always interesting in some way. I had a part in *Jack in the Box*, a short ballet, really more like a divertissement, for four dancers. Even when I wasn't dancing in his ballets, I loved to stand in the wings and watch.

That same season, in 1926, Balanchine made *La Pastorale* for Doubrovska. She played a movie star and Lifar a telegraph boy who fell in love with her. It was a perfect role for Doubrovska because she had such long, long legs and arms—though very beautiful, she looked different from everybody else, almost freakish. And Balanchine, in his choreography for her, used to exaggerate her uniqueness. (Later, in *The Prodigal Son*, he made her the Siren who devours the young man and had her wear a very high hat to make her appear even taller.) At the end of *La Pastorale*, the telegraph boy returned to his village sweetheart, which was Tamara Geva.

Little by little, we four refugees became part of the company. There were only thirty-five dancers altogether, so everybody performed nearly every night. In rehearsal periods, when we didn't have performances, we would sometimes go to the movies, or visit, or just sit in a café and watch the world go by. It was a different life in Europe.

I started to be friendly with Tchernicheva, and with Nikitina, who was a soloist. Balanchine and Tamara, Kola and I, we stuck together. When we first arrived, Doubrovska wasn't very friendly, but after a while she warmed up and spent time with us. And Roger Desormière, our conductor, was part of our circle, too—also, whenever Diaghilev wasn't around, Serge Lifar. We would organize ourselves and rent a house or private apartments together when we went on tour to the provinces. Hotels were too expensive, but in most small towns the stage door kept a list of places for rent, and we would stay at one of those.

Lifar always stayed with Diaghilev, at the same hotel, and sometimes he would invite us over to play cards. Diaghilev didn't mix with the dancers, only with Balanchine; if there was a new ballet to discuss, he would invite George to dinner, but never with Tamara.

Our life in the Diaghilev company was so much work, and the work threw us all together: we took class together, ate lunch together, rehearsed together, ate dinner together, spent our evenings together. I never thought about the future. I didn't have a steady boyfriend, but it didn't matter—there was always something to do and someone to do it with.

There were boys who admired my talent or my spirit, including one very handsome one who used to send me beautiful flowers, enormous baskets of them. I would scold him for spending so much money on them. He never listened—"Oh, I like you," he would say. But that was all there was to it. Each of us girls in the company had a few boys we were friendly with, who admired us as women or as ballerinas—a little *amitié amoureuse*. When we arrived in a new city, they would carry our bags from the station.

There were wonderful parties, especially in Paris. Count Etienne de Beaumont used to give an annual masked ball, and there was always a theme: he would ask his guests to dress in eighteenth-century costume, or all in black and white. Everyone as he arrived made an entrance. One year, someone came on an elephant, and that caused a big sensation. The Count would always arrange for another guest to escort me and, at the end of the evening, put me in a taxi. I would stand at the front entrance and hear the doorman calling out for the guests who were leaving as their cars pulled up: "Hispano-Suiza for Comte de So-and-So! . . . Rolls for Lord Rothermere! . . . Taxi for Mademoiselle Danilova!"

My wardrobe was still rather limited, but not as pathetic as when I left Russia. There was a very nice woman in Paris, Vera Franck, who copied the clothes at Chanel or Vionnet or Callot Soeurs, any house we wanted, and sold them to us quite cheap—for a few hundred francs. We would buy one dress and wear it for two years. We often traded clothes around, mistakes that we had bought and wouldn't ever wear. Sometimes a dress would pass through two or three hands before its time was over. Alicia Nikitina and I were the same size. When she was with Lord Rothermere, she ordered all her clothes at Chanel, and when she was tired of them, she would pass them on to me. I would parade around in my new clothes—her cast-offs—feeling very chic indeed.

After about a year in the Diaghilev company, I started to notice that Balanchine had changed—he seemed very somber, pensive, sort of alone. I asked him many times, "What's the matter?" And he would always say, "Nothing." One season, I had a bad foot, and the boys in the company would sometimes offer to massage it. We were in London, staying in little boardinghouses near the British Museum, and one evening George came to my room to massage my foot for me. When he was finished, he kissed it. I was a little taken aback, but then I thought, well, it's just an affectionate gesture, and I didn't think any more about it.

Then, a week or so later, Kola and I were talking, and I asked him if he knew why George was so sad. Kola said, "Ask him." I told him I had. He said, "Ask him again." So I asked him once again, and he said, "Well, don't you know? I love you."

"No, it can't be," I said. "How? What about Tamara?"

"Well," he said, "I don't love her."

I was absolutely shocked. I couldn't think what to say. So we left it at that for the time being.

But the more I thought about it, the more perturbed I felt. And then, one day not long after our conversation, I went to visit one of my girlfriends in the company, and Tamara was there. She said, "I hear that one of my best friends is taking away my husband." And I tried to explain. I told her, "It's not like that at all." But I felt that a stone was weighing on my heart, and I told George that Tamara knew about it, that he should talk to her. Little by little, people in the company were beginning to notice that George was paying special attention to me. I felt embarrassed and confused.

He was always very courtly. Sometimes he would visit me at night and bring me flowers. And we would talk. Finally, I said to him, "Listen, I will go back to Russia and you will forget me." I meant it. We have a proverb: "Out of the eyes, out of the heart." But he said no, that he really loved me, but that he couldn't marry me because he couldn't get a divorce—all his and Tamara's marriage papers were left behind, in Russia. "But then how can I be with you?" I asked him. In the sort of society I had been brought up in, people didn't live together. He said, "Well, if you won't be with me, I will go to America. I have an offer." And so I had to decide.

I wanted to be sure that he really was in love with me. One declaration wasn't enough. I thought it might be something passing, the kind of thing that happens with the boys: "Oh, I love you," they say, and then, a week later, "Oh pooh, it's you again." And then, he was still married. So I told him that I would go out with other boys, that I thought it best that he and I didn't spend so much time together. "Well," he said, "do what you want."

When he told Tamara how he felt, I could see that she was very hurt. She was never an easy woman; she had to have her own way, and I knew that things hadn't been going well between her and George. So I thought that if I more or less withdrew, he would be fond of her again. But Tamara said that she didn't want to stay with him anymore if he didn't love her, and she moved out. We were in London at the time. She left for Paris, to dance with the Ballet Chauve-Souris, and soon after that she went to America. George pinned me down: I had two weeks to make my decision.

I thought hard. It seemed that there had always been something between us, without our knowing it—the way you sometimes hear people say, "I didn't know I was in love with him until such-and-such happened." We had known each other since we were nine years old, we had watched each other grow up, we had danced together. In *Tannhäuser* at the Maryinsky, in the Venusburg scene, we had been paired together for the Bacchanale; the choreography called for us to embrace, and then, I remember, for the first time, my heart quickened.

George had been a hero at the school—not only a dancer but a choreographer and a pianist. When he was younger, he had been interesting looking, but now he was really handsome, very elegant in his own way. Diaghilev would take him to order his suits on Savile Row, from the same tailor he and Lifar used. (Balanchine could afford to dress well because Diaghilev paid him as both a dancer and a choreographer, two salaries.) George was also gallant—the girls liked him. Withdrawing from him, I missed him. I was afraid that he would go off to America.

George stayed by himself for a little while, waiting for my answer. I decided that I loved him, that I wanted to be with him. The summer started, and I moved in with him, happy to be with him but crying because I had always dreamed of being a bride and walking down the aisle in a long white dress.

The company was in Paris Plage, about forty miles outside Paris, for two weeks, for an extra engagement with the opera there, under René Blum's direction. Everyone was talking about George and me. Diaghilev summoned George to his hotel. I hadn't lost my fear of Diaghilev, and I knew somehow that he was against the idea of my being with George. But George went to talk to him and stayed two hours. What was said, I don't know—several times I asked, but George wouldn't tell me about their conversation. The people in the company thought that the whole affair was scandalous, and Diaghilev evidently wasn't pleased, but eventually everybody got used to us as a couple. From then on, I was presented as George's wife—nobody ever asked for documents in Paris, so that part was easy.

We had a good time together. Our life was very full. In Monte Carlo, we would get up, have our café au lait at home, then go to class and rehearsal. Then we would have lunch in one of a few little restaurants, none of them chic. At about three or four o'clock there would be another rehearsal, then we would go to dinner at a restaurant or sometimes at home—George loved to cook. After dinner, we would pay fifty centimes for a cup of coffee at the Café de Paris and sit all evening long, joined by our friends who congregated there. George was very sociable, very amusing, with a good sense of humor—he would tell little stories and act out all the parts, or do impersonations, which made us laugh hysterically. He was a wonderful mimic.

Ours was not the kind of relationship in which we would bare our souls—there was no need to, because we had known each other since childhood. George was easy to get along with—we never once quarreled. In a way, we were each other's best friends. I had also girlfriends with whom I could gossip and go shopping and do silly things. But George didn't really have anyone else, there was no one he could confide in, because there was no one of his caliber. He was very much ahead of the others, so it was more interesting for them to be with him than it was for him to be with them. George was a loner, and apart from the evenings we spent at the café, he kept mostly to himself.

That first summer George and I were together, Diaghilev asked him to come to Venice to discuss plans for the coming season. Diaghilev always spent his summers in Venice, and the composer, the choreographer, and the painter chosen to design the costumes and sets would all go there to meet with him about their next project. I stayed in Paris. After three or four weeks, George came back. He was very happy to see me.

If George was choreographing a new ballet and he liked certain girls in the company and wanted to give them parts, he always discussed it with me. There was no opportunity for me to be jealous, because he never went out with anyone without me, except for Diaghilev, who would ask George to lunch or dinner alone. I think in the beginning, Diaghilev was a little bit interested in George, until he saw that Balanchine was all for girls.

In Monte Carlo, we always stayed at the Hôtel de la Réserve, right on the beach. Massine and his longtime girlfriend Eleanora Marra stayed there, too. We would always laugh at them, because there we would sit on the terrace, talking and joking about things, and there they would sit, never saying one word to each other.

Massine was well known for his tremendous appetite, and this put a strain on his relations with the hotel management, since our breakfast was included in the price of our room. Once, coming out of the lobby, I was stopped by one of the proprietors, who said to me, in a state of great agitation, *"Mademoiselle, ce n'est pas possible—il mange tout—il gorge tout le menu."* Finally, he insisted that Massine pay him extra.

Vladimir Horowitz stayed at the same hotel, sometimes in the room next door. Every morning at eight, George and I were awakened by the sound of Volodya playing Liszt's "Valse Oubliée," which we heard through the wall. We never wanted to leave to go to class. Some mornings, we would all take our trays out on the balcony overlooking the sea and have breakfast together.

I was young and impatient; I was always wanting to go to night-clubs and dance the tango. "Why do you want to go sit in a noisy room full of smoke?" Balanchine would complain. If George was busy rehearsing, Volodya Horowitz would sometimes take me out Once he took me to the Schéhérazade, and while we were dancing, he told me one of his homemade jokes. A man asks a girl to waltz. She notices that when they turn to the right, he gets taller. When they turn to the left, he gets shorter. Finally, she asks him why. Because, he tells her, he has a wooden leg and he got it from a piano stool. Volodya would keep me laughing all the time we danced together.

Once Volodya told me that Debussy's "Serenade for a Doll" reminded him of me, and that from then on, whenever he played it, it would be dedicated to me—not publicly, in the program, but privately, in his mind. Years later, I would see advertisements for his concerts, and occasionally included on the program was "Serenade for a Doll." Is that still for me? I wondered.

Some days I would come home from my errands and tell George, "Oh, I saw such a beautiful dress. . . ." And he would buy me three dresses. I especially loved hats, and would go try them on and think, Will George like this one? I would buy the one I thought he would like best, then get home and try it on for him. "How do you like my new hat?" "Oh, that's awful," he would say. "Go and change it." This happened again and again. I proposed that he go with me so that we could choose the hat together, but one day he would be busy and the next day something else would come up. Finally, I thought, to hell with him. I will buy the hat I like. I took it home and tried it on for him. "Oh, how nice," he said. "It suits you."

George was generous with everyone. Woizikowski would lose at cards and come to ask for a hundred francs, and George would always give it to him. "Why?" I would ask. "He will never pay you back." Being so free with his money, George never seemed to have any for himself. I thought people took advantage of him, because he was so soft. Living with him, I began to worry about money.

When the time came to leave Monte Carlo, we didn't have enough to pay our hotel bill. George said, "Let's go to the casino." His number came up, and he won six hundred francs. Our bill was close to four hundred. George wanted to play more. I gave him one hundred francs and got out before he could lose the rest. I left him at the casino and went straight back to the hotel, where I paid the bill myself.

Moving from one hotel to another, from city to city, we lived like turtles, with our houses on our backs. After we were together a year or so, Balanchine and I decided to get an apartment in Paris. George still felt responsible for Mr. Dmitriev, and we still lived by our old agreement, that everything we earned would be put together and divided evenly. Mr. Dmitriev wanted to open a photography studio, to do portraits of society people. He moved with us into the little apartment we found in the Passage d'Oisy, off the Avenue Wagram. Our sleeping quarters were on a balcony overlooking the salon; Mr. Dmitriev had a tiny room opposite. Downstairs were a dining area and a kitchen. After paying our first month's rent, we had no money to furnish our four rooms. I told George to ask Woizikowski and the other boys who owed him money to pay back their loans. He did, but they refused to pay up. "What?" they said. "You're so rich that you can get an apartment, and now you want money from me?"

But little by little, we got what furniture we needed. Our first pieces were a divan, a bedroom suite, and a piano. George played often, mostly Bach. "Not Bach again!" Mr. Dmitriev would complain. I was tired of hearing Bach, too. "Why don't you play something nice?" I would ask George. "Why don't you play Scriabin?" "Bach was a genius,"

George would tell us. "He wrote pure music." The apartment became our headquarters. George and I entertained our friends, especially on Easter, when he would make a traditional Russian supper. For the first time since leaving the Theatre School, we had a home.

Seven

THE BALLET that George had planned with Diaghilev in Venice that first summer we were together was *The Triumph of Neptune*, to music by Lord Berners. It was the first ballet he made for me in the Diaghilev company. The story was about a journalist, a foreign correspondent who decides to go to Fairyland and write an article about it. His guide is a sailor, danced by Serge Lifar. When the journalist gets to the Frozen Wood, a snow scene, he meets me—the Fairy Queen. In the end, the sailor decides to marry Neptune's daughter—also me. Balanchine himself danced a very small part in this ballet, as a drunk, in blackface.

The music was a string of little numbers—one was Scottish, one was a polka, one a waltz. Lifar and I had a pas de deux, in which we repeated the lift Balanchine had used in his first choreography—Lifar lifted me in arabesque up over his head, on a straight arm. I had two variations—one in the first act, after the pas de deux, and another in the last act. As soon as my second variation was finished, I ran quickly into the wings and put trousers on under my opera-, or knee-length, tutu, ran back out onstage, and danced the hornpipe—this was always an enormous success.

It was a subtle little ballet, rather Victorian in style—sort of nine-teenth-century with some twentieth-century spice. For that reason, it seemed very up-to-the-minute, not really old-fashioned. The positions were classical, as in Petipa, but the steps were speeded up, faster than they would have been if Petipa had choreographed them. A port de bras that in Petipa would take two measures, Balanchine did in one measure. In Petipa's ballets, you might have a balance on two legs. Balanchine had me stand for one moment on both legs, then lift one leg and balance on the other. So it was a little more interesting than traditional classical choreography. It was also a more conscientious interpretation of the score than Petipa's choreography. Balanchine's steps had a more detailed relationship to the music.

George trained me—he trained all of us—to pay attention to the music. We had to count—it was all very precise. In ballets by other choreographers, we could get away with being a little off the music, and it wouldn't ruin the effect; but in Balanchine's choreography, close was not good enough. He made me understand how exciting it could be to see someone dance right on top of the music, and after that, I started to appreciate what a musical dancer Leon Woizikowski was. I used to love to watch him. His dancing was musically always very ex-act, on the nose.

Soon after he made *The Triumph of Neptune,* George hurt his knee in rehearsal. All this time with Diaghilev he had continued to dance: as the Prince with Vera Nemtchinova in *The Sleeping Beauty;* in the pas de trois with Lifar and me in *Cimarosiana;* in small solo parts in his own ballets. In Paris, in 1927, he underwent an operation on his meniscus, at the hands of a famous Russian surgeon, Dr. Alexinsky. This operation had worked for some dancers, but for George it was not successful: afterward, his range of motion was limited, and his knee stiff, not elastic enough to rely on in jumps. As a choreographer, George was becoming quite successful, and as a result, he had less time to practice dancing, so gradually he gave it up. For most dancers, the prospect of not per-forming any longer is terrible to contemplate, but to George I think it came as a relief, because it meant that he could concentrate on making new ballets.

When he was working on a ballet, it was on his mind all the time. In Paris, where we had a piano, he would play through the score at home. Sometimes he would talk to me about his choreography. It seemed that there was never enough time for rehearsals.

For *La Chatte*, he had only two weeks. He was making it on Spessivtseva, and he used to talk to me about how difficult it would be for her because she was so classical-minded and he was trying to give her something a little different. The music, by Sauguet, was gay and lively, but because Spessivtseva wasn't musical, she couldn't learn to count it. Balanchine had to count it for her all the time in rehearsals, and he worried that she would miss her entrance. I was very curious. I asked him, "May I come and watch?" But he said, "No, it will upset her. Don't come yet." Only Boris Kochno, whose opinion he respected, was invited to come and look at his ballets in the studio, before they were finished. I never saw what George was doing until the general rehearsal.

When he was working on *The Prodigal Son*, he was very worried. We were staying at the hotel on the beach in Monte Carlo, with a terrace overlooking the ocean. I remember sitting out on that terrace one evening, and George saying to me, "I don't know what to do when the son comes home, crawling on his knees—there are six pages of music. . . ." I thought to myself, Well, that will be terribly boring— what can you do on the knees? George was more or less thinking out loud. "I thought maybe he could have a staff, the way shepherds have, and he can hang onto that," he said. I didn't see how that idea would fill up so much music, but George seemed relieved, as if he'd solved the problem. Mostly, I didn't understand what he was talking to me about. He was a genius, twenty-five years ahead of the rest of us. I always knew that he could do everything, even when he wasn't sure himself. I never had any doubts about him.

Some of my favorite roles were ones I inherited. Diaghilev put me into *Petrouchka*. I loved playing the doll that falls in love with the Moor because he is gilded, dressed in flashy clothes. She doesn't see that next to her, in tatters, is a beautiful soul who has fallen in love with her—he isn't attractive enough for her to notice. My part was cute; the movements were very mechanical, because the doll is dumb, not much of an intellectual. Well, let's be honest—she is a gold-digger and goes where the money is. The Moor is pompous and handsome, strong, gaudy— this was Lifar or Dolin. And here, meanwhile, is Petrouchka, someone who is ugly, who has no money, and he gets stepped on. But in the end, he is the one who survives, because he is a moral being.

Diaghilev told me a wonderful story about *Petrouchka*. The ballet was supposed to finish with Petrouchka murdered by the Moor and dragged off by his legs by the magician. But during the final rehearsals, Diaghilev suggested that Petrouchka appear again above the little theatre and stick out his tongue, mocking the magician, proving that he is alive forever. Fokine, Stravinsky, and Benois were all against the idea. "No, Sergei," Benois said, "that is the end." But Diaghilev insisted and threatened to throw away the whole ballet unless the end was changed. There is in Russia this tradition of Ivanushka Durak—Ivan the Fool. Everybody takes him for an idiot, but in the end he outsmarts them all. In old Russia, there were these men who were elevated—not saints, not monks but holy men who would wander the countryside on foot and then one day suddenly turn up at the gate of some big estate. They were simple people, not at all sophisticated or educated. But they were always welcome, because it was said that they could guide people, that they were prophets. They would be taken in and given food and a place to sleep until they were ready to move on. Diaghilev understood that an ending that confirmed this tradition would make the ballet stronger. The new ending was brilliant; the ballet survived because of it.

When Nemtchinova left to go to London to join the Cochran Revue, I was put into *Les Matelots* in her place. This was a ballet by Massine to music by Auric, about three sailors—Woizikowski, who was Spanish; Slavinsky, who was American; and Lifar, who was French. My character was flirtatious, as usual. I was the girl who belonged to Woizikowski. And Tania Chamié was the other girl—she would go with Slavinsky, then with Lifar. The curtain opened and Leon and I danced together; then the other sailors came in. Then, in the second scene, Tania was standing and watching, waiting for the sailors to come. Well, it wasn't much of a story, just girls and sailors, and in the finale we all danced happily together.

Everything was on the toes. I always used two pairs of shoes in *Les Matelots*—one pair, already broken in, for the first scene, and a new pair for the second scene, in which I had a lot of bourrées and hops on one point, doing beats sur le coup de pied with the other foot, and pirouettes—it was difficult dancing. The pas de deux was more a dance alongside Leon than a traditional adagio. My costume was very pretty, a pink satin dress with three-quarter sleeves, with a little white apron, a blue scarf, and a blue flower in my hair. For the second scene, I had a red dress, and my apron was black with big white polka dots, which is very Spanish. I also wore a black cross around my neck, like a good Catholic girl.

It seems to me that *Les Matelots* must have been the inspiration for *Fancy Free*, the ballet Jerome Robbins choreographed much later, in 1944. In *Fancy Free*, there are also three sailors and two girls. The steps are jazzier, the style is freer, but the situation among the characters is exactly the same.

I also danced in Massine's *Soleil de Nuit*, the ballet to music from Rimsky-Korsakov's *Snow Maiden*. It was about a peasant gathering in primitive Russia, and I was the maiden who danced and worshipped the sun. My variation was not on pointe but in *lapty*, the handwoven leather boots that Russian peasants wear, and the choreography was strictly character dancing. I was good at it—I could do Russian dances very well—and this particular role remained all mine.

One season we put together a command performance in Monte Carlo for the Duke of Connaught, who had a villa in Villefranche. "What would you like to see?" Diaghilev asked him, and his reply was *Le Spectre de la Rose*, with Anton Dolin and me. For this performance, Anton brought me a real rose, the largest I have ever seen, very fragrant. "It's dangerous," I said. "You can slip on the petals and fall." But he insisted. He thought that a real rose would inspire our performance and lend it something special for the occasion.

There are some ballets you can express your soul in, some roles you like to dance better than others because they seem as if they were made for you personally. I think these roles change with age. My "soul" ballet while I was still at the Maryinsky was one I never got to dance: *Don Quixote*. I thought Kitri would have been a girl like me, very close to my heart. But if I had danced the role, it would all have been the dreams of a teenager. At that time, I was not yet a woman, on or off the stage.

While I was dancing in the Diaghilev company, my soul ballets seemed to change from one year to the next. I was changing, too. But my Russian roles—in *Contes Russes* and *Soleil de Nuit*—were always among them. I never felt homesick for Russia, but away from Russia, I felt in some ways more Russian than I ever felt when I lived there.

Nijinska returned for one season as a guest to choreograph *Romeo and Juliet*, and I was given a small part at the end. It was not Shakespeare's version; the scene was a dance studio, where Romeo and Juliet—Lifar and Karsavina—meet. Toward the end of the ballet, three girls—Doubrovska, Geva, and I—came in, looked at ourselves in the mirror, and started to do some movements. We finished with turns—fouetté, fouetté, double. Nijinska was very pleased and asked Diaghilev to come and see. At the end of our fouettés, he said, "Cut that variation."

Nijinska said, "But Mr. Diaghilev, it's so beautiful—they're so wonderful. Why?"

And he said, "That's why—because they will kill Lifar and Karsavina." It was too brilliant, he thought; we would upstage them.

In 1927, Massine put me in his new ballets: *Le Pas d'Acier*, which was very Soviet in style, to music of Prokofiev, and *Ode*, which was very modern, with a score by Nicholas Nabokov. In *Ode*, Doubrovska danced a variation, and then Lifar did a variation in front of a curtain, with a disc—an emblem of the sun—crossing the stage. The ballet was about the earth and the rest of the solar system, from the beginning of time. Massine and I danced a pas de deux. In it, I had to hold a bamboo pole over my shoulder. Hanging from the pole were curtains—I was in front of them, between them, behind them. Massine needed gimmicks like that to make his movement more interesting, unlike Balanchine, who put enough fantasy in the movement; George could think of enough ways to use the whole body, including the hands and the head, so that he didn't need a prop to work with.

During the pas de deux, Massine lifted me while I was balancing the pole—it was very awkward. We worked on it a long time in rehearsals. There I was, holding this pole and sitting on his shoulder, practically in a full split. It was very hard to balance. And then he asked me to slide down his arm in a split and land sitting in his hand. I was flabbergasted. Well, Massine didn't stop at anything. That was his character. So you had to be the one to call a halt. Very calmly, I told him that I just couldn't slide down his arm in that position.

For another scene in *Ode*, he made up his mind that he wanted the stage to look like water, so he covered us with a net and made us crawl

on our elbows, turning around and around under this net. It was humil-
iating. We said no, we wouldn't do it. Finally, Diaghilev heard that
there was some dispute and came into rehearsal. "What is all this non-
sense I hear?" he asked. We told him that we couldn't crawl because it
would hurt our female organs. In the end, Massine had to change the
choreography.

It was an odd ballet. It opened with a movie—nobody dancing,
just a movie of a flower. There was a rope draped across the back of the
stage—I think that was meant to be the Milky Way, with all the stars.
One end of the rope was loose, and Lifar danced a variation holding on
to it, never letting go. For the set, Tchelitchev continued the perspective to its vanishing point: there was a line of corps girls moving up the
stage, and then a row of dolls that got smaller and smaller, so it looked
as if the stage were very deep and full of people, much like it had at the
Maryinsky, when we children were positioned at the back of the stage
to look like adults seen from afar. Tchelitchev's costumes were white
leotards and tights—it was the first time we didn't wear anything on top
of our leotards. Doubrovska and I had white caps that covered all our
hair.

We understood that these costumes were appropriate to the choreography—many of the lifts, for instance, would have looked vulgar
in a tutu, with the partner's hand visible between the ballerina's legs,
whereas in a leotard and tights, the ballerina becomes a naked sculpture. But we were unaccustomed to wearing costumes that were so
revealing, and we felt uncomfortable at having our every contour
exposed.

Massine liked me, and he proposed that I come with him to dance
in America; at this time, he was a guest artist with Diaghilev, not a
member of the company. He and Eleanora Marra had just separated,
and he had an engagement in New York, at the Roxy movie house,
where they had not only films but live entertainment, divertissements.
The pay was very good. So I asked George. I said, "Well, he is offering
me big money." And George said no. So that was that.

Massine and I had nothing in common. I think he saw me as being
in a different camp, because between Balanchine and Massine there was
always a little rivalry, though only on Massine's part. He was unmerci-
fully jealous. Diaghilev used to laugh, because Massine would pretend

that Balanchine was stealing his ideas. Once Diaghilev spoke to Balanchine about some new project, and in a little while Massine went to Diaghilev and presented it as his own idea. "But Leonide," Diaghilev said, "Balanchine already told me his idea, and it's just the same." Massine said, "Oh, he did? So he stole my ideas from my head?" But Diaghilev paid no attention. "Don't be silly," he said. "How can he steal your thoughts?" George had a very amiable disposition, so the rivalry didn't bother him, but it bothered Massine all the time.

Diaghilev was exposing us to culture, to life. I am always astounded when I see how few dancers today are following in our steps. When we were in Spain, he would take us to supper in a cabaret, so we could see real flamenco dancing. He encouraged us to listen to music. He ordered us to visit the Prado, to look at art.

The years we spent with Diaghilev were Balanchine's apprenticeship. There was never any question that George had talent, but Diaghilev put him on the right path. He sent George to museums, because in many paintings there are marvelous groupings, and in sculpture there are imaginative positions; these things could become inspirations for a choreographer. Diaghilev had taught Massine in the same way.

There were always a lot of interesting people around Diaghilev, and we often spent time with them. One night he brought to my dressing room George Bernard Shaw, and on another night, Lord Alfred Douglas, who was by that time old and very distinguished looking, with white hair—in Russia, we had read all about his affair with Oscar Wilde. Picasso was at that time married to Olga Khoklova, a dancer in the company, and he would always come to dress rehearsals and sometimes help with the lighting. He had the look of a real macho man, not tall but broad in the shoulders, and handsome. He seemed to us quiet, not at all self-important or arrogant—like an ordinary person.

Coco Chanel used to invite people for lunch—never for dinner, always lunch. I found her not particularly warm, but cute, with a retroussé nose and short black hair, and very elegantly dressed, always in her own designs, usually a black sweater and short black skirt with rows of pearls and bracelets on each arm. She had a villa in the south of France, behind Monte Carlo on the way to Menton, in La Pausa, a very small village that clings to the rock. There were no flowers, I remember, just heather covering the ground everywhere, like a hazy blue carpet.

Sometimes Chanel would go out on the town with us. One night, we all went to the casino in Cannes, and the doorman wouldn't let her in because she wasn't dressed properly—she was wearing a black skirt, a black sweater, and a lot of diamonds, but ladies were required to wear evening gowns. "But I am Mademoiselle Chanel," she told the doorman. "I don't care who you are," he said, "you are not properly dressed." Diaghilev had a good laugh at that.

Chanel and Misia, Diaghilev's two girlfriends, were in on everything. When we had a general rehearsal, we had to put on our costumes and parade around the stage. The three of them would sit out front and discuss whether the tutu was long enough, whether the color was right, whether something should be added or taken off. "Turn and jump and we'll see," Diaghilev would call to us. We were really very well protected by their standards and taste. Nothing went on the stage without their approval.

With Balanchine, I began to learn more about music. We went to concerts. I didn't know enough to venture my opinion, so I listened to what George had to say. We saw a lot of Desormière and Beecham, and Igor Stravinsky, whom we got to know quite well.

Stravinsky would come to rehearsals, and he always seemed to admire what I did, though he never made comments directly to the dancers. If he had something to say, he would tell Diaghilev or Balanchine. Stravinsky and Balanchine were like father and son; George's father had also been a composer. And Stravinsky's own family was musical. His father had been an opera singer, a basso, and his mother quite a good pianist. As a child, he was very devoted to his nurse, Berthe, who hardly spoke any Russian—his nursery language was German, like mine. He told me that he wasn't close to anyone in his family, except maybe his brother, Yuri. There had been three boys in the family—the other one had died in his youth—but Stravinsky didn't like to talk about his childhood. When he did, he spoke of his room as a prison. He wasn't allowed to play any sports because he was so fragile. He had not been a very good student.

Petipa had been a friend of his father's, and in childhood Igor was taken to see his first ballet, *The Sleeping Beauty*. Later, he learned about the ballet's steps and positions from Cecchetti, who was his great friend. Then, as Stravinsky grew older, he grew more disappointed in ballet, and it was only with Diaghilev's company that he started to be interested in dance again. His favorite ballerina, he told me, had been Anna Pavlova—he met her once, when Diaghilev took him to visit her at her house. Stravinsky wanted her to dance his *Firebird*, but Pavlova didn't like his music—she found it decadent and much too modern. Later, Stravinsky said, he found her dancing, despite her artistry, very remote from Diaghilev's art.

Stravinsky's great-grandfather was related to Diaghilev's family, which made them distant cousins. When we first arrived in Monte Carlo, Stravinsky was living in Nice with his wife and children and was very much involved with the Russian church. But as time went by, he saw less of his wife and began freelancing, and then we saw more of him. He was always very gay, he always had amusing stories to tell—he enjoyed life. He loved ladies, but his taste always ran to very voluptuous, big women.

Stravinsky at this time had already begun his liaison with Vera Soudeikina, a very beautiful—big and voluptuous—woman. He met her in Paris, where she had an atelier that produced theatrical costumes. Since Diaghilev always ordered our costumes from her, she was around all the time for our rehearsals. We had been seeing a lot of Stravinsky. Suddenly, we were seeing a lot of Vera, too. Some years later, of course, they were married.

Stravinsky didn't entirely like Fokine's choreography for *Firebird*, or for *Petrouchka*, which he thought was not clear enough. Later, when Ida Rubinstein wanted Fokine to choreograph *Le Baiser de la Fée* for her company, Stravinsky was very unhappy about it, and he was relieved when finally Mme Nijinska was commissioned. He admired her very much, and always praised her interpretations of his music in *Renard* and *Les Noces*. He also spoke well of Massine as a choreographer—Stravinsky liked his *Pulcinella*. But once he had worked with Balanchine, Stravinsky said George was the only choreographer who completely understood his music.

Apollon Musagète, which George choreographed in 1928 to a score by Stravinsky, is now regarded as a landmark in dance history, a ballet that gave birth to a new era. *Apollo* seemed to us different and a little more difficult than George's other ballets, and revolutionary for the simple reason that at times we had to dance on flat feet—that was astonishing.

Balanchine's idea for *Apollo* was that the three muses would be in love with this god. They have, as the French say, *un béguin*. It was an attraction between them, but cool, god-to-god; it was admiration, not passion—passion is human. In order to show that they are divine—superior, not ordinary—there could be no passion between them.

Apollo was Lifar, who by this time was a marvelous personality on the stage—it was a personality Balanchine had given him. The muses were Tchernicheva as Calliope, the muse of epic poetry; Doubrovska as Polyhymnia, the muse of mime; and Alicia Nikitina and I alternating in the role of Terpsichore, the muse of dance.

Lifar was a beautiful youth who couldn't dance in a purely classical style. But when Diaghilev requested a premiere for him, George had no choice but to use him. Faced with a premier danseur who wasn't classical, Balanchine created what we now call the neoclassical style.

After the opening, Apollo's birth, came a pas d'action between Apollo and the three girls. In much of the ballet, the three muses dance and stand with their feet together, parallel, instead of in fifth position, and this gives *Apollo* a different, more natural kind of beauty. Apollo gives each of the muses a gift. When he gave me the lyre, I was to appear to be very flattered because it meant that I was the epitome of dance. I always made sure that my first step as I walked away carrying the lyre was very light. Each of us danced a solo variation. Mine was last, and right afterward I danced the pas de deux with Apollo. Then came the coda, when we all walked upstage in some kind of ritual and went to Zeus, who is the god of the gods.

Some people tried to read something special into my role as Terpsichore, but at the time I didn't think anything of it: one of us had to be the goddess of dance, and it can't have been a very difficult choice for Balanchine, because the other two were definitely not Terpsichores. And if Balanchine was in love with a dancer, she became Terpsichore for him, his inspiration.

In rehearsals, I had to separate myself from him, to behave as one of the dancers, not as the choreographer's girlfriend. But in a way this was easy. In the studio, our relationship was different. I had so much respect for George that I just turned myself over to him as material to work with. Whatever he ordered, I tried to give him.

George would come to rehearsal with a definite plan in mind, but the details, the actual steps, he would mold on the dancers. He could choreograph them right there, straight away, because he knew the capacity of each dancer so well. He would show me what he wanted me to do. If it didn't work, he would say, "All right, then I will simplify it or make it different." The movements in *Apollo* were unusual and intricate, but the style and the sense we could pick up from Balanchine, because he always demonstrated.

Balanchine in rehearsal was not like any other choreographer I have ever worked with. The steps just poured from him. But with *Apollo*, he had trouble, and he couldn't put his finger on it. He worked and worked on Terpsichore's variation. It didn't click, and I could feel that it wasn't right somehow. When we got to Paris, Diaghilev still wasn't satisfied with it and decided to cut it. Stravinsky came and said, "Where is Terpsichore's variation?" And Diaghilev said, "Choura doesn't feel very well and she isn't doing the variation tonight." It still wasn't what it should be, but Stravinsky was upset that it had been cut, and I think Balanchine was, too. By the time the next performance was scheduled, Balanchine had made some changes in my variation that improved it: he added some soft, light, quick sissonnes, with the arms open. But for that performance, I *was* sick and couldn't dance. Diaghilev was very upset. "I brought this on Choura," he said. "She got sick because I said she was." But I danced the next performance, including the variation, and the new choreography worked fine.

There was a big to-do about our costumes. They were changed again and again, until finally Chanel gave us Grecian tunics made of tricot, a knitted material that took nicely to the body. They were very classic, very beautiful.

I was Terpsichore, but my only premiere was in London. One day during rehearsals, Diaghilev came to me and said, very openly, "Choura, you will have to give your part to Nikitina to dance in Paris." Lord Rothermere, her benefactor, had given Diaghilev a big check to help pay for the season, and one of the terms of his gift was that Alicia have a new ballet to dance. The premiere was to be in Paris. Well, I wasn't very happy about it, but there was nothing I could do. Besides, I reasoned, London was as important a city for ballet as Paris. I could tell Balanchine was upset, though he never said anything to me.

Apollo was a very hard ballet for me, because I had to stay on the stage all the way through, from my entrance until the end. We stood in a line, waiting our turn to dance our variations. I was last. When Tchernicheva finished her variation, Doubrovska and I jumped forward. When Doubrovska finished her variation, I jumped forward and began mine. The other two muses went offstage; they could run to the wings and collapse and breathe, the way all three of them do today. But I stayed on the stage all the time until my variation, and then I immediately started the adagio. Doubrovska and Tchernicheva didn't come back until the coda.

Apollo was difficult for Lifar, too, because it was such a new approach, different from anything he had ever danced before. In the pas d'action, he had to partner all three of us together.

Today, it's a different ballet. For one thing, the steps for Terpsichore's variation are different. What I danced was lighter, smaller, and quicker. I did fifth, arabesque, fifth, arabesque—nobody does that anymore. And then I did sissonnes—my version was jumpier than the one they dance today. Balanchine changed it when Suzanne Farrell learned the part, because she couldn't jump so well—she's taller than I am, and she couldn't move as fast. For example, in the first part, she goes down in plié and turns on a bent knee in arabesque where I did sissonne en tournant, jumping and turning at the same time. It's the same movement, really, but with a different accent—my accent was up, hers is down.

The adagio I did was the same as every Terpsichore's, but lately I notice that dancers tend to emphasize the angular aspects and accelerate everything in between, which I didn't do. I tried to do one movement like the next, always light, in harmony, so that the angular positions didn't jump out at the audience. Balanchine was doing something new, but he was not simply trying to shock.

Also, when we all went on the toes and then off the toes onto our heels, I was as light on my heels as I was on my toes. Now dancers go very light on the toes but then stamp their feet when they go on their heels. We didn't do that, and I don't think Balanchine wanted it to be done that way. The idea was to make all these things part of a whole, not to show the contrast between them. Going up on the toes was what everybody expected to see in a ballet; going down on the heels wasn't, but we didn't call attention to it, by making one movement graceful and the other movement awkward—we gave each movement equal weight.

Our job was to make it look as if we went on our heels all the time, as if it were not a big event, no more unusual than opening and closing the arms in pirouette.

We were the first ones to interpret Balanchine's movement, to find that path. The steps were very difficult to perform. It was for the second generation to take what we had done and build on it. After seeing somebody else perform a role, you can think, "Oh, I know how I can do it better. . . ." The dancers who came after us in *Apollo* could look to our performances and copy what we did or dismiss it. That was their privilege, but not ours—we had a hard enough time grasping that new style and finding a way to express it.

On opening night, we all felt the excitement of being in on something new, regardless of whether we had a success or not. We had molded this ballet ourselves. When we did *Apollo* at the Opéra in Paria, some people were applauding, some were booing, but it didn't matter—we knew that we had done something great.

The way the three muses are cast today, there is usually not much difference in height. But sometimes there is a big difference in age, ten years or more. In our first cast, I was the smallest. Between me and Tchernicheva, there were two or three inches, and Doubrovska was even taller. In spite of that, I think the ballet works better when the muses are more uniform in height, and also in age. *Apollo* doesn't just demand good dancers; it demands goddesses.

Suzanne Farrell is a goddess, but to me the ballet doesn't work totally with her as Terpsichore. I think the best Terpsichore I have seen is Heather Watts, because she is smaller and more fragile, the way the goddess of the dance should be.

Mikhail Baryshnikov is a wonderful dancer, handsome, but he is not Apollo. First of all, he's small, with a square build—he doesn't look the part. And then, he is too passionate, too human on the stage. Apollo to my way of thinking should be tall and blond and handsome—Peter Martins is Apollo, and he has something cold about him that strikes the right note: he is not human, he is a god. His love is completely platonic. Lifar was not passionate, either. He was good looking, with a fantastic body—a twenty-four-inch waist, thirty-one-inch hips. If not Apollo, he could have been Narcissus. He had an air of assurance.

The next ballet Balanchine choreographed for me was *The Gods Go a-Begging*. It was Sir Thomas Beecham's idea—he wanted to do a ballet for me and he put together some music by Handel, one of his favorite composers. Beecham was a great friend of Lady Cunard, who was known in London as Lady Emerald for her beautiful jewels, and because they admired my dancing, they were eager to launch this ballet. Diaghilev was skeptical. Audiences expected something astonishing and innovative from him, and this ballet was a charming little caprice, not at all avant garde. In the end, he went along with it, but instead of ordering new costumes and sets, decided that we would make do with what the company already had. The costumes, except for mine, and the set were Bakst's for the second act of *The Sleeping Beauty*, the hunting party.

The scene was a little picture out of the eighteenth century: a maid comes with a Moor as her escort and sets up a picnic for two noblewomen. While they're eating, a shepherd comes along, so handsome that the two ladies are enchanted and give him all their attention. They dance a pas de trois. But he isn't interested; he's giving his attention to the maid. Somehow, he and the maid get together, he dances with her, and they reveal themselves to be gods. Everybody bows to them, and that's the end of the story. Doubrovska and Tchernicheva were the two ladies; Woizikowski and I were the god and goddess.

Diaghilev's only new expense was my costume, which he commissioned from Chanel. She gave me some advice I never forgot: "Always make your head small for the stage," she told me, because a large head looks unflattering, duncelike, and often almost comical.

In Paris, I felt old-fashioned and a little bit dowdy. "La garçonne" was all the rage, the androgynous ideal, in chic clothes and short hair. Chanel had set the example: she did away with the corset and cut her hair, and suddenly women were liberated—and all for the better. Soon, every woman in Paris cut her hair, including me, even though people had always admired my long hair. "Where is your hair?" George asked when I got home. He was very upset.

The Gods Go a-Begging was part of Balanchine's romantic period. All the steps and positions were very soft, very lyrical. It was an enormous success; in fact, it got to be so popular with our audiences that it became our bread and butter.

But *Apollo* had sent Balanchine off in a new direction. For *The Triumph of Neptune* and *The Gods Go a-Begging*, his choreography was romantic. In

Apollo, the lines changed and the steps were made faster. Balanchine took the style he invented in *Apollo* and explored it in his next two ballets, *Le Bal* and *The Prodigal Son.*

Le Bal was bizarre, very modern—it could be danced today and wouldn't look out-of-date. The music was by Rieti, the décor by Giorgio de Chirico. The positions were angular, with the elbows and knees bent. The steps were very syncopated. On each note, I had somehow to do a double movement. It was a difficult ballet for me to learn.

The setting was a masked ball. A girl entered on the arm of her fiancé; then they went off in different directions. But for a moment before they parted, they took off their masks and said goodbye to each other. An officer, danced by Anton Dolin, watched them, saw that the girl was beautiful, and followed her. They danced together—a very tender duet. And then he asked her to take off her mask. She didn't want to, but finally agreed, and he saw not the beautiful girl but the face of an old woman. Horrified, he jumped back and ran from her, but she pursued him. Then he was again in the entrance hall, hiding, and again he saw this girl, with her mask on, and wondered, Is that the beautiful girl, or is it that awful old woman? She met her fiancé, took off her mask—she was young and beautiful. The fiancé offered her his arm, and together they left the ball laughing. It was all a joke, merely for her amusement, and the officer understood that he was fooled.

While all of this was going on, there was of course dancing at the ball and entertainment for the guests. There was a Spanish pas de trois, with Doubrovska, Lifar, and Balanchine; a tarantella; and then a big dance for the ensemble. Dolin and I did our adagio, and then a lot of passages across the stage—mostly jetés in front of the ball. He was pursuing me or I was pursuing him. In the second scene, I had to wear two masks, one of them the face of the old woman.

Our costumes were very modern—painterly, and rather awkward. I wore a dress, not a tutu, and a white wig. When the doors to the ballroom opened and the guests began pouring onto the stage, you could see, beyond the doors, all the way at the back, a statue of an enormous horse, painted on the backdrop. (Later, Elizabeth Arden's Institut de Beauté adopted that horse as its symbol.)

My variation was very angular—jumps from fifth to second in the air to fifth again, opening the legs at the top, and a lot of pointe work that went directly from the pointe to the heel. The arms were not in the classical positions, opened out in second or up in third, but angular, with the elbows and wrists bent. A lot of the positions were in profile. It was difficult for me, but I liked dancing it.

And then there was a beautiful adagio. In it, I did a step Balanchine later put into *Firebird*, for Maria Tallchief. Holding on to my partner with one hand, I reeled around on pointe, off-balance—I did it in ara-besque, Tallchief did it à la seconde. It was a very unusual adagio, with a lot of strange lifts. For example, standing facing Anton, I would go on my toes, do a deep plié on pointe, and then from there jump onto his chest, arched back with my arms open—he would catch me with his hands around my waist. The timing was tricky, but Anton was a very good partner and knew just how to help me.

It was Balanchine who made adagio more important. Before he came along, it was just développé à la seconde, arabesque, pirouette, and lift. Real dancing together—it's Balanchine who invented that. Fo-kine more or less liberated the man from his role as a porter, gave the man a new status as a dancer. But Balanchine made the man more equal to the woman in adagio. In the old ballets, it was adagio, his variation, her variation, and coda. With her partner, the ballerina did the steps she couldn't do by herself, or did other steps better than she could do them by herself. But in a Balanchine ballet, the adagio would be more like a dance, conveying a mood. The man and woman create something together. The pas de deux isn't dancing as an exhibition of technique but dancing as love or hate or whatever—there is a situation or a story to it, as in *Le Bal*.

At the premiere of *Le Bal* in Monte Carlo, all the soloists were given flowers at the curtain except me. Diaghilev was very cross with Balanchine and asked him how he could have overlooked such a thing. The next evening, Balanchine sent me one hundred roses, delivered on the stage in an enormous bouquet. There were so many I couldn't carry them all home—I passed them out to other people in the company.

The Diaghilev company was a big Russian family. We had our squabbles, but they didn't last long. When George was busy making *The Prodigal Son* in Monte Carlo, Diaghilev asked me to dinner with his friends and Lifar. After dinner, Diaghilev said, "Come on, let's go and see what George is doing." So we went into the studio, in our evening clothes. George was setting Doubrovska's variation. While we sat and watched, Lifar was trying to tell me all kinds of naughty stories, and I didn't want to laugh but I couldn't help it. I put my chiffon handkerchief over my face so no one would see. But it didn't help—whenever I laughed, the handkerchief would move. Doubrovska suddenly stopped and said, "They are making fun of me. I don't want to rehearse in her presence," and pointed to me.

We said, "No, we are telling a funny story."

She said, "I will not rehearse in her presence."

Balanchine stopped the rehearsal and said, "Would you kindly leave?"

Diaghilev got furious. "What do you mean, leave? When we come in, you should be pleased that people are interested enough to come and see what you are doing. You have no right to chase my ballerina out of her temple. Everyone is welcome in the rehearsal studio." Doubrovska was in tears, I was in tears, and rehearsal was off.

That night when we got home, George said, "Women! Can't you behave yourselves? Tonight I lost a rehearsal, and I don't have very much time." I tried to explain, but he didn't pay much attention to what I was saying. The next evening was *Firebird*, and Doubrovska refused to dance—I had to dance in her place. But the following day, she came to me and apologized, and it was settled.

There was another incident about the same time, also in Monte Carlo. Sokolova had been sick and missed a couple of months. The theatre in Monte Carlo had only two dressing rooms for women—one large one for the corps, about sixteen, and another one for soloists, a small room with space for only four. In this room, there used to be Tchernicheva, Nemtchinova, Doubrovska, and Sokolova. Then Nemtchinova left and I took her place; Sokolova got sick and Alicia Nikitina came in. One afternoon, when I was called for rehearsal, I arrived in the dressing room and saw all my things on the floor; somebody else's things were on my chair. So I asked, "Who did this?" And someone told me, "Well, Sokolova is back." "How dare she?" I said, and swept all her things onto the floor and started to dress. Suddenly, Sokolova came in and saw me and started to scream, and I started to scream back at her. Again, Balanchine was rehearsing, and we had disrupted his work. And again, he gave me a talking-to.

Some of us had more than our fair share of temperament. One night, I was practicing on the stage before the curtain went up on *Cimarosiana*. A very attractive man in white tie and tails approached me and said, "Good evening. What tempo will you be dancing this evening?" "I'm sorry," I said, "I don't talk to strangers, and I don't believe we've been introduced," and I turned on my heel and walked away. To my surprise, when the curtain went up, there was this man in the orchestra pit, conducting. His name was Malcolm Sargent, and he was filling in for Sir Thomas Beecham, who was ill. Despite what he must have thought of me, the tempo Sargent set for me was perfect.

But mostly our life with Diaghilev was calm and our relations congenial. George and I "adopted" little Alicia Markova, and for her sixteenth birthday we took her out to dinner, ordered her her first glass of champagne, and gave her her first bottle of perfume.

As a company, our home was Monte Carlo. Our audience there was small and very devoted; some people would follow us all the way from Paris. In Monte Carlo, we prepared new ballets, looking forward to our seasons in London and Paris. We loved both cities. In London, more of the general public came to the ballet than in Paris, but in Paris our audience was more international—there were young painters, musicians, and writers, students who had come from all over the world, and they all came to see the ballet.

By the time I joined the company, Paris had a reputation for bad luck. Opening night there was always disastrous. Before we took *Zéphyr et Flore* to Paris, I made a mistake during one of our performances in Monte Carlo—I went into the wrong wing for my exit and collided with Lifar. He fell and tore a tendon in his ankle, so he couldn't appear in Paris; he was all plastered in a cast. Diaghilev hated me for that. It was all my fault—I was in disgrace.

When it was time to perform *La Chatte* in Paris, Spessivtseva went to Egorova's class and turned her ankle; she couldn't dance. My turn came three years later, when I got the mumps and couldn't open in Paris in *Ode*. Each of us had his own superstitions about going on the stage, but opening night in Paris seemed to be jinxed for the whole company.

Spessivtseva was always a little peculiar. One night in Paris, after our performance, we went for supper at the Ritz Hotel—a large group of us that included Diaghilev and one of Spessivtseva's great admirers, Sir Saxton Noble. Diaghilev said, "Well, Olga, of course you would like a nice cold glass of champagne." "No," she said, "I would like hot champagne." So a waiter came with a silver chafing dish on a trolley and warmed her champagne for her.

Every year in Paris, George and I would invite our friends for the Russian New Year. In 1929, he cooked a big supper for fifteen or twenty people. Boris Kochno came, and Ivan Mosjoukine, a Russian actor who was a big star at the UFA studios in Germany, several dancers from the company, and a friend of ours, a lawyer, whose hobby was reading palms. He looked at Lifar's and told him that he would have a complicated life. Well, we said, that could mean anything. He told one girl, a Polish dancer in the corps, that her life would soon change and that she would have a lot to do with horses. At this we laughed—we had all signed our contracts for the following season; we knew that we would be with Diaghilev. I asked the fortune teller what he saw in my hand. He refused to tell me.

Not long after, on the last night of our season in Vichy, before we all went our separate ways for the summer, Diaghilev called the company together on the stage. It was always very emotional, ending a season and saying goodbye. Tchernicheva was leaving the company, and it was hard to imagine how it would be without her. Diaghilev was going to Venice, as usual. We were all tired and looking forward to a rest.

In August, I was in Nice staying at the Hotel Negresco with my friend Agnes Petersen, a Danish girl, Ivan Mosjoukine's wife. George was in England, working on some new choreography. One afternoon, I went to the hairdresser. "Would you like to see a newspaper?" he asked me. Yes, I said. I looked over the headlines and Diaghilev's name caught my eye: Diaghilev was dead.

I remembered the last time I saw him, on the stage at the end of our season in Vichy. He made a brief speech about how well the season had gone. Then he said, "I can't kiss everyone, but you, Choura, I will kiss." And he came to me and kissed me twice—goodbye.

Eight

WITH DIAGHILEV'S DEATH, the ground collapsed beneath my feet. It seemed that I didn't belong anywhere. I felt suddenly very small and insignificant. Maybe I should go back to Soviet Russia, I thought.

Where could I ever work again with Balanchine? By this time, he was becoming a well-known choreographer, working with dancers who were out of my league. Soon after Diaghilev's death, Jacques Rouché, the director of the Paris Opéra, called George and asked him to make a new ballet for Spessivtseva, who was dancing there with Lifar as a guest artist. I wasn't then an established ballerina; I couldn't compete with Spessivtseva. And I realized that every big company in the world had its own prima ballerinas. I worried that George would go off and work for big companies everywhere and I would be left alone.

During rehearsals at the Opéra for his new ballet, *Les Créatures de Prométhée*, George came down with pneumonia. There were complications; the pneumonia turned into tuberculosis. He was ordered by his doctor to go to a sanatorium in the mountains, at Mont Blanc in Switzerland. But before he left, he explained his plans for the ballet to Lifar, so that Lifar could finish it for him. "Do you think I can do it?" Lifar asked. *Renard,* the one ballet he had made for Diaghilev, had been a failure, and Diaghilev had given up on him as a choreographer. But George was reassuring—half the ballet was already finished, and the rest he laid out according to the music. Everything was ready: he had the skeleton of the ballet and knew exactly what he wanted it to be. Lifar finally agreed, and George left for Switzerland. I accompanied him there, stayed with him a few days until he was settled, and then returned to Paris. After about two months at the sanatorium, George came back and we went to the Opéra to see *Prométhée,* which was a big success. At the end of the performance, we went to congratulate Lifar, but the concierge at the stage door told us that we were forbidden to enter. "Well, there must be some mistake," George said, and he sent Lifar a message. A few minutes later, the answer came back, exactly the same: Mr. Lifar does not wish to see Mr. Balanchine. We were turned away.

Nevertheless, Balanchine was in steady demand. Soon after he got back to Paris, he received an offer to do the Cochran Revue, in London. There would be a part for me, too. This was wonderful news. A few days later, I met Alicia Nikitina for lunch. "Well," she said, "what are you going to do? What are your plans?" I told her about the engagement with Cochran. "Tomorrow, I am going to sign the contract," I said. The next day, I went to Mr. Cochran's office. The secretary was apologetic. "Mr. Cochran had to leave town unexpectedly," she said. "We will summon you as soon as he gets back." I left and never heard a thing, until a week or so later when George told me that Nikitina had been engaged in my place. She had called Lord Rothermere, and, as usual, he gave Cochran so many thousand pounds to hire her instead. So George left for London and I was left behind.

There would be no more ballet seasons for the Diaghilev company, but somehow, for the next two years, Mr. Grigoriev managed to renew our contract to dance in the operas in Monte Carlo. Tchernicheva, Vilzak, Schollar, and I reported there in January, for a season that lasted three months. Balanchine's place as choreographer was taken by Pavel Petrov, whom I had known in Russia, where he had been a member of the Maryinsky Ballet. He had choreographed many comic operas for the Mikhailovsky Theatre and one ballet—unsuccessful—for the Maryinsky. The ballets he staged for the operas in Monte Carlo were charming, quite good. He choreographed for me "The Dance of the Seven Veils" in *Salome,* and I danced it barefoot. This was a big success.

The other members of the Diaghilev company took work wherever they could find it. Kola Efimov, our schoolmate who had been with us ever since we left Russia together, had joined the Paris Opéra ballet under Lifar's direction and eventually married Vera Nemtchinova's sister. George and I never saw him again. Diaghilev's death had changed everything. Circumstances were scattering our friends, separating George and me. When the opera season in Monte Carlo ended, I went back to Paris. I had no job; I was just studying with Mme Egorova and practicing.

I got to know some of the Paris Opéra dancers because they also went to Egorova's classes. So did Lifar, George Skibine, George Zoritch, and Zelda Fitzgerald, though at the time we had no idea who she was—we knew her only as Zelda the crazy American who took private lessons. We all liked her enormously. She was fair, with red hair and green eyes, not particularly flamboyant but very pretty—she had the kind of beauty that you have to look at closely to discover. She was not a bad dancer—technically competent, good enough for the corps de ballet, if she had been willing to work hard. One day she came to the studio with a champagne glass in her hand, still finishing her cocktail. "No, no," we told her, "that doesn't go in the studio." "Why not?" she said. We had to explain to her that dancing is a serious business, that she could either drink or dance, but she couldn't do both. She had more ambition than dedication, and I think she was a little bit surprised by our attitude.

Mme Egorova's lesson lasted two hours. Every day we did pointe work. Even though dancers then didn't raise their legs as high in extension, Mme Egorova always insisted that we stretch at the barre.

I lived in the apartment George and I shared with Mr. Dmitriev, who was still with us. He was a strong personality, and during the years when we danced with the Diaghilev company, he refused to let go. George and I brought our salaries home, put them into one pot, and divided them three ways; Mr. Dmitriev didn't work, but he had brought us out of Russia. When Diaghilev died, it seemed the time to break with Dmitriev, but George said, "No, not yet—we are obliged to him." Although he took up photography, he never really made a career of it.

While George was away, I fell under Mr. Dmitriev's influence. He convinced me that George could never give me security. "He is so extravagant," he said, and told me that George had gone to a tailor in London, ordered full riding gear, and now went riding every morning in Hyde Park as if he were a millionaire—his boots alone, Dmitriev said, cost fifty pounds. Now I understand that all the luxury George wanted so much then was to make up for everything he had been deprived of in his youth, during the Revolution. But at the time I thought, What about our life together? How will we ever pay for this apartment?

While George was in London, I had no income. Something came up, some expense for the apartment, and I wrote to him, to tell him that I needed money. "Sorry," he wrote back, "I can't help. You will have to find the money yourself." But from where? One night, Lord Rothermere took a group of us girls to a casino. "Here is a bonbon for you," he said, and distributed to each of us a two-thousand-franc note. I went and changed mine, played a hundred francs, and kept the rest to pay my debts. Tania Chamié did the same.

In London, George gave a big birthday party for a young dancer named Tatiana Riabouchinska. I read about it in a magazine. All this time I was waiting, thinking to myself, After these glorious engagements abroad, George will bring back so much money—I was counting on it to help us. But when finally he came back to Paris, it was with a car: he had taken the money he earned and bought a big American car, a green Willis Knight, in Denmark. We had to pay an enormous duty on it.

George brought me a present, earrings made of lapis lazuli, which in Russia we didn't consider precious—there it was a building material, like marble, used for columns in churches or for banisters in private homes. I was in my own way, I suppose, as eager for fine things as George. I had been expecting diamonds, so I threw the earrings in his face. "But they are so pretty," he said. He also brought me Atkinson's perfume, and I threw that at him, too. "Coming to Paris," I said, "the city of perfume, and bringing me lousy English perfume!" Mr. Dmitriev took me aside and said, "You see, he comes from these fancy jobs and doesn't bring back the money. He will never, never give you the security you are looking for." And I thought, He doesn't love me, there will be no money. . . .

So when in 1931 I got an offer from Hassard Short to do a musical called *Waltzes from Vienna* in London, I took it. At least I will have my own money, I thought. From London I wrote George a letter saying that I thought it was much better that we go our own ways, because life was separating us. It might have been different if we could have been together all the time, but he would be working six months in one place, I would be six months somewhere else. So I told him that it was better for both of us to be free.

We were young, and neither of us had any family, no one to guide us and say, "Well, now you do this" or "Don't hurry" or "You must try to do this," no one we could turn to for advice. There were little differences that we allowed to become too important. George wanted beautiful things; I did, too, but first I wanted security. I wanted to go to nightclubs and dance the Charleston, and he wanted to spend the evening at home. So we parted too soon, while we still loved each other, before we'd had a chance to learn how to put our love into practice.

For a long time there was no answer from him. And then finally a letter came, saying that if I wanted to leave him, I should do exactly as I pleased. That was all. There was not a word to say "Let's try again." I was hoping so much that he would ask me to reconsider, that he would suggest that we give each other one more chance, but there was nothing. Well, I thought, here is the proof that he doesn't want me—he doesn't even ask me to stay, to come back, to try again.

Now, looking back, I think that in a way I was right. Sooner or later, George would have left me. Balanchine was like a painter who, over the length of his career, has several models, and he falls in love with each of them; his models are his inspiration and his passion. For George, his ballets depended on the women in his life. But for me at the time, I think I did the wrong thing, because I loved him and missed him very much.

Our love was like a boat that set out onto the ocean, went through a storm, and then, broken into pieces, was washed back to the shore. George and I had a perfect understanding. We both had a deep respect for art—that was our strongest bond, and it remained. I continued to feel great admiration and tenderness for George, and I think he always felt something for me, though we never talked about it again. Once I had written my letter, the damage was done—there was no repairing it. I had to make a new life for myself.

Nine

THE CHOREOGRAPHER for *Waltzes from Vienna* was Albertina Rasch, who was typically West End in style. At the first rehearsal, she asked me, "Do you know any tricks?" "What do you mean?" I said; I didn't understand. "Well," she said, "everybody has their tricks. Do you do some special kind of kicks, or maybe thirty-two fouettés?" "Good God, no," I said. I couldn't grasp her method of choreography. She explained, "All my girls have tricks of their own—we sort of stop in the middle of a number and each girl comes to the center and takes her turn, does her trick. So, what is it you will do?" And I said, "Anything you will choreograph." Finally, she asked me, "Can't you remember some movements from your ballets?" And I said, "Yes," and showed her a few of my variations. What a strange choreographer she is, I thought. Somehow, we hodgepodged a waltz—I don't think it was anything very good. But Hassard Short, who was a great admirer of mine, was kind to me—he knew that Diaghilev had just died and that I needed someone to give me a hand. *Waltzes from Vienna* might have looked like a step down for me, but I regarded it as a step between. There would be another ballet company, somehow. In the meantime, I had a regular salary for a year.

The show was about Johann Strauss and his son, and the rivalry between them. Both were writing music, but young Strauss's was much more modern. The last scene was the big waltz, "Le Beau Danube," which I danced in character shoes, wearing a grey crinoline and a beautiful white ostrich feather in my hair. Young Strauss was played by a dashing English actor named Esmond Knight. We had a big flirtation. He was married, though I didn't know that in the beginning. In the end, we parted gracefully and agreed to meet in the next life.

Every week, there were new rumors about a ballet company being formed. Ida Rubinstein was getting some dancers together, it was said. There was talk that somebody from America wanted to invite some of Diaghilev's dancers. And there was the Opéra Russe à Paris, which was very popular, now run by "Zerbazon"—Prince Alexis Zereteli, Colonel W. de Basil, and Ignaty Zon. Nijinska was choreographing for them *Tsar Saltan*, an opera that required a lot of dancing. The Russian Opera came to London while I was there and brought this production. It was a success, and so was the ballet within the opera. Since some of the operas were short, the direction decided to add a divertissement at the end of the program, to give the public a full evening in the theatre— two hours of opera and half an hour of ballet. Lifar and Doubrovska danced the Bluebird pas de deux, and Nemtchinova danced another number. Finally, the directors thought, Why not drop the opera and just bring the ballet? That was the start of a new company, the de Basil Ballets Russes.

In its first year, Balanchine was hired as its choreographer, with Boris Kochno as artistic adviser. The news reached me in London that Balanchine didn't want any dancers from the Diaghilev company, that two young girls he had discovered—Tamara Toumanova and Tatiana Riabouchinska—would be his ballerinas. A young man named David Lichine was engaged as premier danseur. The repertoire was completely new.

When my engagement with *Waltzes from Vienna* was over, I was told by my doctor that I had to rest, because I'd been dancing twice a day for a year and was very run-down. So I went to Surrey, where I stayed as a paying guest on a farm owned by a navy officer and his wife. When my vacation was over, I returned to London, with no idea what to do next; I was taking class but I wasn't appearing anywhere. I studied with Nicholas Legat, who was adorable—a dear old man as well as a wonderful teacher. A few years earlier, Balanchine and Vladimiroff had persuaded Legat to go for surgery to a certain Professor Woronov, who had become famous for implanting monkey glands in humans as a means of rejuvenation. For a few months following the operation, Legat seemed to bloom again, and then—nothing. The effects didn't last. Even so, Legat would from time to time make monkey faces in class and scratch under his arms.

Legat created André Eglevsky, who took a year off from de Basil's Ballets Russes to study with him in a private lesson every day. Eglevsky left the company as a member of the corps and returned a soloist, with magnificent beats, a jump like a leopard's, and fabulous pirouettes, usually ten or more. Later, when I danced with him, as I took my preparation for a pirouette, he would whisper in my ear, "Pull in your left hip," and my turns would be straighter.

Legat's classes were good mostly for ballon and beats. His method was simple: he made us beat everything in the allegro—we never did a simple assemblé, always assemblé battu. Every day at the end of class, he gave us sixteen entrechats six. After a little while, we grew accustomed to it, so it wasn't so difficult. From then on, beats were never a problem for me.

I was a ballerina without a company, but I had many friends. There was one I'd met while I was with the Diaghilev company, an auto magnate, who lived in Paris and was interested in dancers. Every Sunday, he used to invite a number of us for lunch. I knew both of his girlfriends, who were dancers: one was a soloist, the other was in the corps de ballet. So, he told me, he always had two luncheons, usually at his house. (He was married, and his wife lived in his "official" residence; he also had another house of his own, with a swimming pool where, the rumor had it, people went in the water *en nature*.) The first luncheon, for the one girlfriend, began at noon; I went to the second lunch, for the other girlfriend, at two. It was always very gay, with twelve or so of us at the table—dancers from the Opéra and others, like me. We would stay until four or five o'clock. Our host was charming and very intelligent, and he and I kept in touch. While I was living in London, he would call me from Paris and ask, "Would you lunch with me?" We would make a date for the next day. I always thought he had some business that brought him to London, but I found out later that most of the time, he had come just to see me. He gave me a beautiful emerald. During this time, he asked if I would like to join the Paris Opéra ballet—if so, he said, he would arrange it. It seemed like a good idea. But when the management at the Opéra told me that I couldn't be a ballerina, that I would have to go back and start from the beginning as a demisoloist or a member of the corps de ballet, I thanked him very much and told the Opéra no.

He was desperately in love with me and offered to divorce his wife and marry me. But he was such a nice man, and I didn't love him the way he wanted me to—I didn't want to marry somebody just because he could give me the world. And then what? I would have sat in my golden cage with nothing to do.

Instead I married a man named Giuseppe Massera, a tall, dark Italian in his forties. He had a lot of charm, an engaging sense of humor, and a good figure. He was well groomed and well dressed, very attractive; he always fit in wherever we went. Having been raised in Russia, he spoke Russian fluently. We met through Tania Chamié, my friend from the Diaghilev days. When I was dancing in *Waltzes from Vienna*, he would often pick me up after the show and take me to supper. I missed George and I wanted to do something to get him out of my system. Here was the man, I thought, a nice man who had nothing to do with the theatre—Giuseppe was an engineer and the owner of a company that manufactured ventilation equipment for diamond mines in South Africa. I thought that he would give me a nice life and the security I never found with George. He told me that he had been married a few years before, to a Russian variety dancer in Italy, but that they were divorced. He said that we would have to wait a little while before we got married, but he didn't explain why.

Our wedding a few months later was a civil ceremony, in London. For our honeymoon, we went to the south of France; when we got back to London, we installed ourselves at Grosvenor House. It was a different life for me. We didn't see many people, and most of the people we saw were not dancers, because Mr. Massera didn't like my being in the theatre. He wasn't interested in art at all. On weekends, we would go to visit his aunt, who was Russian, at her house in the country, at Windsor.

I hadn't intended to get married so that I could quit dancing. Maybe

Mr. Massera thought that I would, but I just couldn't imagine life without performing. Dancing meant more to me than anything else. I always took class; I never rested for longer than a month. After all, I didn't have anything but my art. I had wanted a man from the other world, the world beyond the theatre; but, as it turned out, he couldn't understand my ambitions as an artist.

My private life was always a disappointment, and my life with Mr. Massera was no exception. One day not long after we were married, he came home very agitated. It seems that a rival company was trying to take over his business, and he needed money to fight them. He asked me for my savings—it was a loan, he said, and he would pay it back with interest. I gave him all the money I had, one thousand pounds I had saved from my salary while I was appearing in *Waltzes from Vienna*. Well, I thought, we are husband and wife: what I have is his, and vice versa.

Time went on, and he seemed worried. Then finally he announced to me that he had lost everything, he was bankrupt. He would give me papers, he said, stating how much he owed me so that when he got back on his feet, I would be paid. I asked if he had already been bankrupt when he married me. He thought for a minute and then said yes. Was that why he had postponed the wedding? Yes. He said he was sorry; what shall we do?

I knew what *I* would do: I would join Colonel de Basil's Ballets Russes.

During the company's season in London, Colonel de Basil had asked me to come and see him. I went to meet him at his hotel, the Strand Palace, a second-class hotel across the street from the Savoy, where Diaghilev always stayed. De Basil's room was only a bedroom, not a suite like Diaghilev always had; and when I arrived, the bed wasn't even made.

Colonel de Basil was a man of average height, with an elongated head shaped like a melon, and very thick glasses—not attractive, from my point of view, and certainly not the gentleman that Diaghilev had been. De Basil's manner was very ingratiating, but at the same time, because he was a Cossack, he was very sure of himself; he had to be master of the situation. At least he could cover the bed, I thought. From the beginning, we never really clicked.

De Basil and his new ballet master, Massine, had agreed to invite me to join the company. De Basil offered me a contract, without pay. Being a Russian, he said, I should be proud of this marvelous organization he had built. "Besides," he said, "You've been making such big money in *Waltzes from Vienna* that you don't need a salary." I thought again of Diaghilev, who even when he put any one of the rich ladies around the company on the stage always insisted on paying her. In *Ode*, in *Les Fâcheux*, there were mannequin roles for women who were supposed to be goddesses; they had nothing to do but to stand and look beautiful. They were happy just to be on the stage, but Diaghilev paid them a fee. He taught us that nobody works for free, and that if they do, there is no control: you have no authority over someone who is doing you a favor.

I didn't want to tell de Basil that I was penniless, but I said, "I'm very sorry, but I don't dance without pay. Besides, I wasn't making such big money in this show, and before that, I didn't have a *sou*." Finally, he agreed to pay me something—forty pounds a week, I think, which even then was very little, barely enough to live on. But at least I would have my own income once again.

Giuseppe asked me if I was leaving him. I told him yes, that if he wanted to join me, he would know where to find me—I would be with the company. But he never did. From time to time, he would telephone me, but that was all.

Two years after I had left, I asked Giuseppe for a divorce, but he refused to give it to me. He was still talking about recovering all the money he had lost, and when he did, he said, he would come and get me back. A year or so later, he went into the hospital for surgery, for bleeding ulcers. I was somewhere on tour when I received a telegram from his aunt, notifying me that he had died of complications from the operation. And so I became a widow. I was shocked and sorry for him. I wondered if he had been lonely. But I didn't grieve. After two years apart, the memory of the life we had had together had faded. It seemed a long time ago.

I joined de Basil in Monte Carlo. On my way from London, I stopped off in Paris, where I ran into Balanchine on the street. He asked me what I was doing.

"Well," I told him, "I am joining the company." I knew that he had been working as ballet master for de Basil, that he had choreographed something new for the famous "baby ballerinas."

"What company are you joining?" he asked.

"The de Basil company," I answered.

"Not that I know of," he said. "Who invited you?"

"Leonide Massine."

"What does Leonide Massine have to do with de Basil?"

"Well, I don't know; I thought he was supposed to be ballet master," I said. "But he did invite me. And you don't have any ballerinas, so you really need me."

"No," Balanchine said, "you are much too old to be my ballerina." I was at that time twenty-eight. I was stunned. Well, Balanchine, because he was Georgian, had a cruel streak—he wanted to hurt me, and he did.

In Monte Carlo it became clear that Massine was in and Balanchine was out, but de Basil hadn't even notified him. Balanchine had to call and ask to find out that he had been fired.

De Basil was trying to model himself after Diaghilev: he would tour with the company and sometimes come to rehearsals. His secretary, Gerry Sevastianov, tried very hard to give him the air of an impresario, but it wasn't very convincing. De Basil lacked the respect and the authority that Diaghilev had had, because he didn't have Diaghilev's knowledge or his savoir-faire. In the Diaghilev company, we had been surrounded by painters, composers, writers, all kinds of brilliant, talented people—we had lived and worked in an atmosphere of creativity, because Diaghilev himself was such a creative man. But de Basil wasn't at all creative, and neither was Sevastianov. Everything depended on the choreographer, on Balanchine or Massine. With Diaghilev, we had always felt that the success of each new production rested on the collaboration of everyone involved, but with de Basil, we had the sense that the weight of the entire company had fallen on one man's shoulders—our success depended on Massine.

There was no company class. If we were in Paris, we would all scatter to different studios to take lessons with our favorite teachers. On tour, I would give myself a warm-up, and often other girls in the company would ask if they could join me. Usually, we were a group of six or seven, doing our own class. I would announce each exercise at the barre, then we would do an adagio and a few combinations in the center before we had to start rehearsal.

The de Basil company was a good company—most of the dancers were younger and technically more accomplished than Diaghilev's dancers had been. The corps consisted mostly of young Russian dancers, born in Paris and trained well by Preobrajenskaya, Egorova, Trefilova, and Kchessinskaya. There were also a few French and English girls. Rehearsals were run in all three languages—Russian, French, and English. The girls were dedicated, young and strong. There were wonderful soloists with great personalities, like Lubov Rostova, who was beautiful, very fragile, and Nina Verchinina and Nina Tarakanova, who were very individual—they sometimes danced the leads in small ballets. Verchinina left the company to go to Germany to study modern dance. When she came back a year or two later, she was a completely different dancer, with a style of her own.

The premiers danseurs were Yurek Shabelevsky, Roman Jasinski, and, later, Yurek Lazowski—Polish boys who came from Warsaw, where they had received good training at a state school like the Russian Theatre School—and David Lichine, who had been trained by Mme Egorova. Lichine was a capable, handsome artist, rather temperamental, not especially well-built. His dancing wasn't classical, but it was dynamic: he became the role he was dancing. As a partner, however, he was unreliable. One was never sure: Would he help you, or wouldn't he? It all depended on his mood. Offstage, he was a Romeo. All the young girls in the company were a little bit in love with him. There were innumerable intrigues, little scenes, many tears on his account.

But the star attractions were the so-called baby ballerinas—Tamara Toumanova and Tatiana Riabouchinska, who were teenagers. When I first joined de Basil, Toumanova had left to work with Balanchine, who had formed a company of his own, Les Ballets 1933, with the help of Edward James and his wife, Tilly Losch. The repertoire was by Balanchine, with Toumanova as his ballerina. But he also gave a special part to Irina Baronova, a girl in the corps, because he found her charming. When Les Ballets 1933 folded after one season, Toumanova returned to de Basil. In the meantime, Massine had engaged Baronova, who was not yet sixteen.

It was important for de Basil to establish a reputation for his company that would make it somehow different from Diaghilev's. To do this, he needed new stars. I had been discovered by Diaghilev, so already I was a little bit passé. De Basil took credit for discovering the baby ballerinas; he built them up and cherished them. They were getting all the attention.

Toumanova was beautiful, and she knew it—she was a glamour puss. Baronova was a good dancer, very capable—technically, she could do anything, much more than I could do, and she was a good-looking girl. Riabouchinska was a bit older than the others, and she had personality in her dancing. Each had something different, so they made a good trio: one with beauty, one with technique, and one with personality.

The atmosphere in the company was in the beginning not very professional, because these young girls didn't know how to make up, they didn't know how to behave—they were girls taken straight from the studio and put on the stage. The company, as a result, was a rather amateurish *compôte*. The girls were, each in her way, quite sweet, but they fought among themselves like cats and dogs. That was one reason why de Basil took me, to set an example. The critics wrote that I was a real ballerina, and I was conscious of my role, even when I was off the stage—I was never late, I always dressed properly for rehearsals, I never misbehaved.

Once, in Bournemouth, during a performance of *Swan Lake* in which I was dancing the lead, something happened that called on all the composure I had. I was already on the stage, in the middle of my variation. Baronova was in the dressing room, doing her eyelashes. At that time we didn't have false eyelashes; we used solid mascara, melted in a spoon held over a candle flame. Lubov Rostova was checking herself in the opposite mirror, paying no attention to the candle on Irina's table. When Lubov bent over, the skirt of her costume caught fire, and when she saw what had happened, she panicked and ran straight across the stage to where Lichine, her husband at the time, was standing in the wings on the other side. I heard the audience gasp. The orchestra paused. The theatre was packed, and for a moment it looked as if everyone would stampede. I thought, The thing to do is to continue dancing. And I did. The conductor picked up, the audience sat down again, and out of the corner of my eye I saw firemen covering Lubov with blankets.

In *Les Sylphides*. Bakst designed my sleeves.

With Woizikowsky in *Les Matelots*.

In *Carnaval*.

In *Swan Lake*.

In *Aurora's Wedding*.
(My costume was a beautiful
blue and white.)

3

Above and opposite: with Massine, in *La Boutique Fantasque*.

In Nijinska's *Snow Maiden*. I can't remember who danced the two trees.

Clockwise from left: In the *Russian Dance* Nijinska did for the opera; in *The Great Waltz*; and in *Choreartium*.

Above, with the Denham Ballet Russe in *Coppélia*; below, in the de Basil *Boutique Fantasque*; opposite, with Jasinsky and Petroff in *Cimarosiana*.

Opposite and left, on tour with Massine;
below, in *Capriccio Espagnol* costume
with Argentinita.

In *Gaîté Parisienne* with Freddie Franklin.

In *Coppélia.*

In the Denham *Petrouchka*.
Opposite, with Paul Petroff in *Les Femmes de Bonne Humeur*.

In the de Basil *Firebird*.

We all finished the performance in a daze. It was only after the curtain fell that we realized how disastrous the situation might have become.

Most of the girls, because they were so young, traveled with their mothers, who were forever glorifying them, smothering them, and pitting them against one another. There were always intrigues. Each mother would run to de Basil and scream that her daughter was more talented, that she should get a bigger part. Then along would come another mother and scream the same thing, only louder. It was really very tiresome, especially for the choreographer.

My entrance into the company didn't improve this situation. The mothers resented me. One, who had a sixteen-year-old daughter, used to take me aside and tell me, "You are too old—you will have to go." Another always had some remark to make on my appearance. If I had a new hairdo, for example, she would ask, in a horrified tone of voice, "What have you done with your hair?"

"I have just come from the hairdresser," I would answer. "What is wrong with it?"

"Oh," she would say, "how unbecoming." Then she would tell me how marvelous her daughter was, the best dancer in the company. I became accustomed to these insults after a while. "Well," I would tell her, "it's a matter of opinion."

My life under de Basil was very difficult, and nobody knew what I was going through. I was very much alone. I had no close friends in the company, no confidantes, no one who would stand by me, nobody behind me. De Basil was obliged to have me, because people knew my name from the Diaghilev company, but the new roles went to the three young ballerinas. I was given mostly roles from the Diaghilev repertoire—the Doll in *Petrouchka*, my old parts in *Les Sylphides* and *Les Matelots*. De Basil promised me that this would change, that when we went on tour I would alternate with Toumanova and Baronova in their roles. But they held onto their ballets with their teeth; they refused to let go of a role.

I had a strong belief that if I danced a role better than anyone else, it would belong to me. And that's what happened. For a while, I felt deprived of *Swan Lake*, because Baronova was dancing most of the performances. But I think the audience wanted to see me in the part, so I was eventually given more and more performances, until finally when the theatres booked the company they stipulated that I appear. Little by little, we each staked out our territory—I got my repertoire, Toumanova got hers, Baronova got hers. I established myself in *Swan Lake* and *The Gods Go a-Begging*, and *La Boutique Fantasque* became my ballet.

Massine and I danced together in the Diaghilev company, but it was in *La Boutique Fantasque* and *Le Beau Danube* that we really became a partnership. *Boutique* was a ballet about a toy shop, in which Massine and I played a pair of dolls. Two different customers bought us and agreed to call for us the next day, but we didn't want to be separated. So, in rebellion, the toys all came to life and attacked the shopkeeper. Massine was dressed as a French dandy, a cross between Valentin LeDésossé, depicted in the paintings of Toulouse-Lautrec, and Charlie Chaplin. I wore a huge, full-circle skirt. Together we danced the ballet's big number, a can-can.

When I was given this role, which was made originally on Lidia Lopukhova, I went twice to the Bal Tabarin, in Paris, to see the way real can-can dancers played with their skirts. The can-can had been invented by washerwomen, *les blanchisseuses,* who danced a certain kind of polka. They exaggerated it—kicking their feet more, picking up their legs, and hitching up their skirts—and eventually it found its way into the nightclubs. I did all the same steps, though I like to think that I brought some extra refinement to them. But every can-can consists of more or less the same movements; it's a little bit limited. My skirt was all ruffles inside, from the waist to the hem, and very heavy because of all those layers of material—so heavy that when I did pirouettes, I turned first and then the skirt turned after me. The costume slowed me down; I needed much more than the usual force to get around. So each time I danced *Boutique,* I had to try my pirouettes in costume on the stage before the curtain went up to get accustomed to turning in the skirt all over again.

My skirt in *Boutique* was part of the choreography; it was part of my character. When I played with it, the ruffles looked frothy, like foam. Dancers today don't have as many opportunities to wear a costume and become somebody else, as we did. When I used to prepare to play a character, I would arrive at the theatre two hours ahead of time and get into makeup, then into my costume. I always hated it if someone disturbed me—I didn't want to see anybody until I was ready to go on the stage. By that time, I would have become my character, I would see everything through her eyes. The other dancers always noticed the transformation, especially when, years later, I danced a silly little ballet called *Mademoiselle Fifi* with the Slavenska-Franklin company. I would come on the stage before warming up, and everybody would greet me as usual: "Good evening, Madame, how are you?" Then I would warm up, go to my dressing room, and put on Mademoiselle Fifi's costume, with her blond wig and black feather boa. "Hallo, Feef, how've you been?" everybody would ask when I went back to the stage. I used to invent all kinds of stories for Fifi's answers. "Oh, I've just come from Paris," I would say, "where I stopped off at Maxim's and drank champagne"—silly things. But it wasn't me. The costume transformed me: I became the part and I behaved like that character until my performance was finished. I can't imagine sitting in my dressing room, smoking a cigarette and drinking Coca-Cola before going on the stage to dance *Swan Lake*, which is of course what so many dancers do today.

With Massine's ballets, there was always a little story. In *Le Beau Danube*, I played a street dancer in Vienna. In the park where I was performing, I saw my ex-beau, an officer. That was Massine—there he was, walking with his fiancée, and I got jealous. I pushed them apart and chased the girl away. Then I went with all my love to him, and he remembered the first time he saw me and the times we had together. We danced a very romantic waltz. Then his fiancée came back, crying, as if she were saying, "Here I am, waiting for you to get married, and you are with that dreadful woman," and the hussar turned his back on me and went off with her.

There were nice little details to the story. The first time the fiancée came to chase me away from her beau, I didn't budge; she went away crying, and then her little sister came and took him by the hand and guided him back to her. I found that touching. "All right," I said, "you chose her, so stay with her. Just go." And I lifted my skirt, did a pas de chat, and ran off into the wings to forget about him. Well, it was a different mood from what people were used to seeing. In Paris, people weren't so interested in marriage; it was always *les petits intrigues*.

When I was first given the role, I didn't want to dance it, because I thought it was vulgar. And then, somehow, when I started to think about it, I decided that it wasn't such a bad part. After all, she leaves him—there is no shame in that.

I created a character, which then became part of the ballet. Before I began rehearsals, Massine's wife, Genia Delarova, whom I knew from Russia, warned me that the costume was not good and that the wig was terrible. "You know," she said to me, "we must change both." But I told her to wait, to give me a chance to decide for myself. I went to the wardrobe and asked to see the wig and the costume. I put them on. The wig was hideous, made out of very thin straw, and I decided not to wear it; I would wear my own hair. But when I started to move in the costume, to try certain steps, I thought, How very beautiful. And I decided to play with the skirt, to manipulate it and make it work to my advantage. "How is the costume?" Genia asked me the next day. "Beautiful!" I said. She thought I was kidding. But after my performance, she understood what I meant. I arranged my hair in the same style as the wig, I worked with the skirt, and everybody said that they didn't recognize the ballet, it was so improved. Soon I was dancing *Beau Danube* all the time, despite the other girls' protestations. The Street Dancer became one of my "signature" roles, and Danube the most famous ballet Massine and I danced together.

My other signature role in the de Basil company was the Firebird. She is a strong bird and rather ferocious—not a bluebird or a nightingale, more like an eagle. The Swan Queen is half woman, but the Firebird is completely a bird—an exotic creature, a bird of paradise. Because she is such an unusual bird, she has unusual poses, rather Oriental—one arm draped over her head and the other wrapped around her waist. Her port de bras is mostly in the wrists—not like the Swan Queen's, whose port de bras is all in the arms. The Firebird's arms are always above or below the shoulders, never à la seconde.

I loved Stravinsky's music for *Firebird*. You can hear the beginning of the dancing in the orchestra: the Firebird dives and the music floats. I had danced Lopukhov's *Firebird* at the Maryinsky and Fokine's version in the Diaghilev company. Both were based on the same story, but Lopukhov's was modern, while Fokine's choreography was much more classical. In the de Basil company's production, there were a lot of blank spots in my role, because no one exactly remembered Fokine's choreography. So I used to mix the two versions, adding some Lopukhov steps here and there, and they blended very well. No one seemed to notice.

In both versions, the Firebird's entrance was very strenuous, requiring a lot of stamina. In Fokine's, I had to stay eleven minutes on the stage; in Lopukhov's, I had to stay for nine. The entrance was on the diagonal, then I exited and entered again, sort of flying—everything was jumping, leaping, grand jeté, then temps relevé. I ran on, got into my pose, then picked up a golden apple from the tree and started to play. The breathing was difficult, and I had to train myself for it. At the beginning of rehearsals, I would do only a third of the part, then every day add more until I had built up to the whole.

In Russia, my costume for Lopukhov's version was by Golovine, the famous painter who often designed for the stage. With it, I wore a blond wig, which was attached to the bodice of my costume by two threads, and on top of the wig a band of pearls, with short, flat ostrich plumes on one side in pink and green to match my costume. My costume in the de Basil company, by Gontcharova, was the same as the one I had worn in the Diaghilev company—a yellow tutu, normal length, with some ostrich plumes and spangles on it, and a gold-colored bodice. Karsavina, Fokine's original Firebird, had worn an enormous, hideous headpiece. I wasn't given one when I danced the role with de Basil so I invented something different for myself—a tourmaline-colored turban, yellow mixed with gold, that covered my hair and fastened with a rhinestone clasp. For feathers, I wore pheasant plumes, because they're unusually thin and very soft, and they move beautifully. This looked more exotic and graceful than the headdress Karsavina wore, and it became my trademark as the Firebird. I put a lot of thought and work into this part, and in the de Basil company the role was mine exclusively.

Fokine had been regarded in Russia as a god—the most original, the most modern choreographer. But for those of us who had worked with Balanchine, Fokine seemed rather old-fashioned. One day in Paris, I went to study with Mme Egorova, and before class I was chatting with one of the other dancers about the de Basil company. Fokine had just joined us to supervise rehearsals of his own ballets. "That old fool wanted me to do such-and-such," I said, and Mme Egorova overheard me.

"What did you say?"

"The old fool," I told her.

"How dare you call the great Mr. Fokine this name!" she said. "You have no respect." And she brought me a notebook and a pen. "Now sit down," she said, "and write as I tell you: 'I, Alexandra Danilova, will never call the great Mr. Fokine an old fool again.' " This is silly, I thought. She made me feel that I, a ballerina, was nobody. The notebook was filled with similar statements, written by other students who had been in some way disrespectful. Now, looking back on it, I think it's sweet, the way she defended the reputations of Fokine and others.

In the de Basil repertoire, we had several Fokine ballets, which were always very popular—*Schéhérazade, Carnaval, Prince Igor,* and, of course, *Petrouchka* and *Firebird. Les Sylphides,* which many people now find rather boring, was a favorite with the audience. But *Les Sylphides* today is a different ballet completely. The steps are the same, but dancers no longer understand the style; they don't know how to project the mood it requires, an air of lyrical detachment.

I danced Ta-Hor, the same role I had danced at the Maryinsky and with Diaghilev, in *Cléopâtre,* and the second lead in *Les Papillons,* a charming ballet that takes place at a costume ball. One girl, dressed as a butterfly, falls in love and burns her wings. Fokine wanted me to dance the lead in *Le Coq d'Or,* but de Basil manipulated the schedule in such a way that I always had another rehearsal at the same time as Fokine's.

Though I had few friends in the de Basil company, I was never lonely, always being busy working and traveling. In every city, there were interesting people who loved the ballet, and they sought us out, inviting us to supper after the performance or to their houses in the country on the weekends. And we became more interesting as a result, more cosmopolitan. I was exposed to a broad range of ideas and interests, to the world beyond the ballet. For most of my life I slept and ate and breathed dancing, but I didn't need to talk about it when the curtain came down.

In London there was a very well-known restaurant called Hungaria, on Regent Street, and I often went there with a party of friends after a performance. I would walk in the door and the orchestra would welcome me by playing the waltz from *Le Beau Danube.* One night when I arrived, sitting together at one table were three princes, the three sons of George V—Edward prince of Wales, the duke of York, and the duke of Kent. After supper, my friends and I were lingering over a bottle of champagne when the proprietor came to our table and announced that His Royal Highness the Prince of Wales wished to dance with me. I was terribly nervous. We danced something simple—a waltz, I think—and got through the first few bars all right, until suddenly I thought to myself, My goodness, I am in royal arms! And, of course, immediately I made a mistake. Somehow we made it to the end of the song, but I danced abominably, feeling very self-conscious and finding myself all the time on the wrong foot. We thanked each other for the dance and I apologized, saying that I was very nervous, that I was not usually so clumsy. But the prince was very gracious: he assured me that it was all his fault, because he was so nervous dancing with me.

It was during this time that I renewed my friendship with Stravinsky. He regretted very much that he and Diaghilev had not been on speaking terms when Diaghilev died: Stravinsky had written the music for *Le Baiser de la Fée* for Ida Rubinstein and her company, and Diaghilev never forgave him for it.

Stravinsky was always such a social man, very charming, very gay. No matter how late it was or how exhausted he felt, he couldn't let the fun go on without him. He never changed. On his eightieth birthday, in New York, there was a big celebration with a series of several small parties—cocktails at somebody's house, dinner at somebody else's. At the end of the evening, after all the parties were over, Stravinsky stood up and announced, "Well, that was marvelous. Thank you very much. I'm going home."

And we said, "Very well."

"Well," he said, "isn't anybody else going home?"

"No," we said, "we are going on—for some drinks or some dancing."

"What?" he said. "You think that I'm going home to bed when all the rest of you are going out on the town?"

I was very lucky—there was always somebody courting me. But I wasn't planning to marry again. I was freelancing. In London, there was a good-looking Irishman who lived in the boardinghouse where I stayed. I went out with him a couple of times. He fell in love with me and wanted to marry me—he said that he had a farm in New Zealand, that we would move there and look after his sheep. I said, "No thank you. I am a ballerina, dedicated to my career. I am not interested in sheep."

There were many Spaniards in Paris, people I had met when I was with the Diaghilev company during our seasons in Madrid and Barcelona. One of them, a very handsome gentleman, a widower and a marquis, would invite me to dinner whenever he came to Paris. One day he called to say that he hoped I wouldn't mind if he brought along a friend. No, I said, of course not. That evening, they came to pick me up and I met for the first time the marquis's friend, who happened to be the most handsome man I had ever seen in my life. His name was Antonio and he was much younger than the marquis, athletic-looking, very striking—tall and blond, with black eyes. We went to La Coupole for dinner and dancing. I was dancing with the marquis when suddenly, one of the corner of my eye, I saw that his friend was dancing with another girl. I was furious. "How dare you dance with somebody else!" I said.

"Why not?" he said. "I didn't want to sit alone."

"Well," I said, "it's very bad manners."

"But you were dancing with the marquis."

I bawled him out, but good. It was only later that I understood that I was jealous.

A few months later, the marquis and his friend returned. Just before they were supposed to pick me up, Antonio called and said, "The marquis has some business to take care of this evening. Would you mind if just the two of us, you and I, had dinner together?" And this time, I fell madly in love.

On their next trip, the three of us went again to dinner as usual. Suddenly, the marquis announced that he wasn't feeling well. It was still early—he was terribly sorry to cut the evening short, but he and Antonio would see me home. Before we left the restaurant, I went to the ladies' room and wrote on a little piece of paper "Call me" and my telephone number. When we arrived at my door, I said good night, shook hands with the marquis, then shook hands with Antonio and passed this little message from my palm to his. Then, very innocently, I went inside. Half an hour later, the telephone rang. Antonio said, "I'm coming to pick you up." So we continued the evening: a café, a night-club, and finally a hotel.

Our next encounter took place while I was dancing in the opera at Monte Carlo, living in a room with a little balcony overlooking the Boulevard des Moulins. One afternoon, what do I see there in the street but a carriage, and in it is Antonio: he had just come to Monte Carlo, arrived at the station, and didn't know where to find me. So he engaged a carriage and told the driver, "I am looking for Mlle Danilova—just drive." As they came down the boulevard, I stepped out onto my bal-cony—the timing was perfect. I had three days off and we went to Nice and spent them together.

For five years I saw him perhaps once a year, at most for a few days at a time, but I was madly in love with him. Whenever I danced in Barcelona, he would come and meet me after the performance. Cur-tain time in Spain is always late—ten o'clock or so—so we would go out for dinner at one in the morning. Walking back from the restaurant along the boulevard where the flower sellers were, we would stop along the way, buying orchids from one merchant, lilies from another, roses from another, so that by the time we got back to my hotel it would be four in the morning and my arms would be full of flowers.

Antonio and I exchanged love tokens. I gave him my gold Russian cross, and he gave me his first communion medal, which I still keep with me always. But our romance was complicated. Somewhere at the back of my mind, I understood that it wasn't forever. I knew that his family was very much opposed to the idea of our getting married. A dancer was not considered a suitable wife for a nobleman, and Antonio wasn't strong enough to go against his family. Years later, I learned that during this time Antonio's father had died. I imagine that on his death-bed he extracted from Antonio the promise that he wouldn't marry me. Instinctively, I knew that we would never be married. It was *Swan Lake*—a grand passion between two people from different worlds, impossible to carry out in everyday life. Finally, I told him, "If you want me, you must come and get me," and I named a date. He never came. But I never doubted that Antonio loved me.

Years later, after the war, I returned to Barcelona to dance there and a little girl, about twelve years old, came to my dressing room after the matinee. "May I have your autograph?" she asked. I looked at her face, and in it I saw Antonio's. "My goodness," I said, "I knew your father." And then Antonio appeared and introduced me to his wife. We all went out to supper, and Antonio asked me for the first dance. He danced the second dance with his wife. I saw that there was an understanding between them. "In all my life," he said, "I have loved two women—you and my wife, my wife and you. I've told this to her, and I'm telling this to you." He was the great romance of my youth.

Ten

IT WAS WITH the de Basil company that I first be-
came acquainted with America, in 1933. We came by boat; the crossing
took six or seven days, and by the time we arrived in New York we
were all terribly seasick. Sol Hurok had engaged us for a season at the
St. James's Theatre, on Broadway, and reserved rooms for us at the
Wellington Hotel. I remember trying to get settled into my room, looking everywhere for the bell to call the maid. When the maid finally
arrived, I asked her to do something for me—unpack my suitcase or
wash my stockings—which was routine in Europe but not the maid's
duty in America, and she refused. That night, as usual, we put our shoes
to be cleaned and shined in the hall outside our doors before we went
to sleep. The next morning, they were gone. Immediately, everyone
was on the telephone: "I can't go out, I can't come and see you, I can't
rehearse—I have no shoes." Our shoes had been thrown away. New
York seemed very foreign.

One night after the theatre, we wanted to eat yogurt, which had
then just been introduced in Europe. We didn't know what to call it in
English, or how to explain. "Yogurt," we said, but nobody knew what

we were talking about. Our waiter brought us cream. "No, no," we said, "sour." "All right," he said, "I'll bring you another cream if this one is sour." No, no, we told him, but still we couldn't make him understand. In the end, he was furious with us. We didn't know that in New York there was no such thing as yogurt; it was years before yogurt was introduced in America.

Paris, London, Budapest, Berlin—all these cities have a beauty of their own, a certain identity that has to do with the way the buildings look, the way the parks are arranged. But when we came to New York, it seemed to us all concrete, very grey and inhospitable. The first people I met were the press, who had a completely different attitude from the reporters in Europe. There, the press was interested only in our artistic life: "Who was your teacher?" "Which composer do you prefer?" American reporters wanted to put their noses into everything. They asked all kinds of questions about my personal life. "How old are you?" they always wanted to know. "I am as old as I look," I would answer. Their ideal ballerina was blond and sixteen years old. So when the reporters would come after me, I would tell them, "I am not blond and I am not sixteen, so you don't want to interview me," and I would walk away.

To me, American women looked overdressed. You could see that they were spending money on themselves—well, it was a much richer country. I thought they were working a little bit too hard—they had too many curls, they were too pale and too pink for my taste. The fashion in New York was a few steps behind the times, not quite up-to-date.

But all this was only a first impression. Very soon, I developed a great respect for American women. They were the source of culture in America. There were women's clubs, like salons, all over the country, and year after year they brought us back. The engagements, which were often for one or two nights only, made it possible for people living in small towns to see ballet. American men were busy earning their money, and the women were busy spending it—but often as not they spent it on the arts.

We gave the same program, night after night, for a month at the St. James's Theatre. Then we were to go on tour, to other cities in New York state. But we had such a big success that Hurok decided to divide the company in two and leave one half behind, to continue on Broadway. I was part of the other half, and we made a little tour of the state, with another program: *Les Sylphides*, Balanchine's *Concurrence*, which was Toumanova's, and *Le Beau Danube*. I danced twice every night, in *Les Sylphides*—one evening I would do the waltz, or pas de deux, the next night the mazurka—and in *Le Beau Danube*.

Most American audiences had never seen ballet and didn't know anything about it. We could sense their astonishment from the stage. I loved dancing for these audiences; I knew that I was introducing them to ballet. By the end of that first American tour, I was longing to get back to Paris. But after New York, Paris seemed small and insignificant. From then on, I was always happy to return to America.

We returned every year for the next four years, embarking on longer, more extended tours that took us all across the country. We got to know the American people, and they got to know us. Eventually, each of us could claim certain cities as our own. Mine were San Francisco, Chicago, Houston, St. Louis, and Denver. I was these cities' favorite ballerina, and I looked forward to them on our tours.

Some cities we loved for the theatres we played in, others for their hotels, but Chicago we loved for both its wonderful old Auditorium Theatre and its Auditorium Hotel. In 1935 we spent Christmas there, and Colonel de Basil gave a party for the entire company at the hotel. I sat with two of my friends—Paul Petroff, a handsome Danish boy who was not a very good dancer but a wonderful partner and a real ladies' man, and Nina de Basil, the colonel's wife, a beautiful woman with blond hair that really looked like gold. She was very much alone. De Basil was too busy running the company to spend much time with her, so he assigned a Czechoslovakian boy by the name of Vania Psota to accompany her on our tours. In no time, Vania fell in love with Nina, which amused the colonel but annoyed her—there was no escaping Vania. That evening, though, for some reason, he hadn't come to our party, and Nina was having a fine time, grateful for the opportunity to be with us.

As much as I hated to call it a night, I had rehearsals and a performance the next day, so at two in the morning I excused myself and went off to bed. A few hours later, I was awakened by a commotion in the hall. My room happened to be next to Mr. and Mrs. Hurok's, and I could tell that there was something extraordinary going on. I put on my dressing gown and opened my door. What traffic! Members of the company were dashing back and forth, and Mr. Hurok stood in the midst of them. "What happened?" I asked. "Murder!" he said. Murder! Little by little, we all pieced together the story: Paul Petroff had been stabbed, near the elevator, and Vania had found him and helped him to his—Vania's—room. By the time Vania called the police, the mattress was soaked with blood.

Of course, the police asked Paul who had stabbed him. He told them that he didn't know, and that was all. Nothing was written in the papers—rumor had it that it cost Hurok a small fortune to keep the story quiet. But this was the version that was passed around the company: After I had gone upstairs to bed, Paul took Nina out to a night-club, and when they got back to the hotel, after he saw her to her room, he was stabbed. The wound was half an inch from his heart, but he pulled through and left the tour to recuperate. It was awful to know that one of our members was a murderer. But Paul never let on who it was. Nina and Colonel de Basil eventually separated; he married Olga Morozova, a dancer in the company, and Nina married Vania and went with him back to Czechoslovakia.

The de Basil company was the most chaotic organization I have ever known. Wardrobe, for instance, plays a big part in the ballet, because the costumes and tutus must be refreshed and washed, and this can be a long, difficult job. Our wardrobe mistress, however, was a dreadful woman, *une petite goulue.* De Basil's bodyguard, Vasiliev, had picked her up on the street in Paris and presented her to the colonel as his wife. She was a rather good-looking girl, on the thin side. But about costumes and the theatre she knew nothing. At my first performance, when I arrived in my dressing room, there was no costume. Finally, with time getting short, I had to send my dresser upstairs to ask where it was. The dresser came back and said, "Oh, she says there is plenty of time—she generally brings the costume five minutes before you appear." But I said, "No! Please bring it immediately—I must see if everything is all right." "Well," she said, "you had better go upstairs and get it yourself." So I went to the wardrobe mistress, and we had a little scene. "Don't you know the law of the theatre," I said, "that the costume should be ready half an hour before the performance starts?" Well, she said, she didn't care. If any of us looked more or less decent onstage, it was only because we took care of our costumes ourselves.

One evening she was distributing some photographs of herself. She had tried on all the stars' costumes and taken pictures. "How do I look?" she wanted to know. Her reign was rather short; there were so many complaints that finally de Basil had to fire her.

He tried to be nice to me. After I had been with the company a few years, de Basil came to see me and said that he had a marvelous idea for a ballet for me—Mickey Mouse. "I have been thinking," he said. "You know, it would be very popular." Mickey Mouse! "Well, no thank you," I told him. "I don't think so."

In 1934, de Basil and his co-director, René Blum, separated, dividing the company in half. One group returned to America; the other to Paris, London, and Monte Carlo. I was part of a little group sent to Monte Carlo to work with Bronislava Nijinska, under Blum's direction. This was to be the beginning of Blum's own company, and I was his only ballerina at the time. Whenever I sneezed, everyone would come running: "Are you all right?"

But Mme Nijinska taught me a lot. There was no pressure; we had all the time in the world to rehearse. I danced her ballets—*Les Biches*, *Pictures at an Exhibition*, and *Bolero*, which I never liked. I danced on top of a big table, with a lot of men seated around me—the ballet takes place in a Spanish tavern. The choreography was rather limited, because I couldn't move very far and couldn't jump on this table. But it was the music that was most to blame—the score is monotonous, easy to get lost in. The melody is repeated over and over again, and the only landmarks I could find were the crescendos; whenever the music got louder, the movement changed.

But *Les Noces* I loved. It is to my mind Nijinska's best ballet, a masterpiece. It was full of references to Russia. At one moment, I remember, the girls made a pose in a triangular formation that looked like *paskha*, our cake for Easter.

It was always hard for me to remember Nijinska's choreography, and in the beginning I couldn't understand why. Finally, I analyzed it and realized that it was because her dance phrase didn't finish with the musical phrase, as usual: sometimes the dance phrase would start in the middle of one musical phrase and finish in the middle of the next.

Nijinska was eccentric, very demanding, and often difficult. Her studio was like a classroom—no one was allowed to talk. She insisted on our undivided attention. Even when she was working with another dancer, we had to sit and watch. We weren't allowed to sew our shoes during her rehearsals. Because she hated touching dancers' bodies and getting their sweat on her hands, she wore white gloves, which made us feel as if we all had leprosy. But she and I got along very well. Once she took off her gloves while she was working with me, and I thought, Well! This is a compliment.

Nijinska taught me how to act with my body—how to sit, how to walk. A great actress expresses what she is feeling with her body and her voice, not by making monkey faces, and Nijinska helped me to find that expression in dance—how to convey sorrow by turning my back to the audience, or to make the distinction between misery, by holding my elbows close to my body, and gaiety, by keeping my elbows out. This was one of the most valuable lessons of my career, and I applied it to all the dramatic roles I danced, not only my roles in her ballets.

I had many partners in the de Basil company, but as far as the public was concerned, I had only one—Massine. Everything we danced together was a terrific success. We were paired on the stage for life. As a partner, Massine was terrible. He wasn't interested in anybody else. He considered lifting a ballerina or supporting her in pirouettes not part of his job and acted as if he were doing her a favor. Like Nijinsky, like Eglevsky, he never really wanted to dance with a partner; he preferred to dance by himself. Apart from Fokine's ballets, Massine danced only his own choreography. There were duets in his ballets, but no important adagios, no pas de deux in the classical sense.

Massine always gave himself the best parts in his ballets. He was always beautifully dressed on stage. Well, I thought, why not? I didn't object. He was a first-class dancer, very passionate, expressive, with a style of his own, in some ways more a modern dancer than a classical dancer.

He was a little bit jealous of me in *Le Beau Danube*, of all the applause I used to receive after my entrance. I became famous as the Street Dancer, and my fame in the role annoyed him. Finally, we had a conversation: I told him, "Mr. Massine, we dance together, this is your choreography. So my success, it's your success—it's your ballet." He didn't see that. But after a time, he didn't bother about it anymore. If Massine was angry with me, he would pinch me on the stage, while I sat on his knee or while he supported me in arabesque. I wouldn't flinch or say a word.

Offstage, we had nothing in common. I think we didn't really want to know each other. He stopped trying to woo me, the way he had in the Diaghilev company, by making erotic choreography for me. But he knew that I was a good match for him as a performer—the other ballerinas in the company were children.

Artistically, we understood each other perfectly. So when, in 1937, Massine asked me to join him in the Ballet Russe de Monte Carlo, directed by Serge Denham, I went with pleasure.

Massine was, I think, a genius, but not as great a genius as Balanchine. Massine loved, he hated, he did everything in the extreme. By nature, he was a real artist, with volcanic emotions. He was like a monk in his dedication, ascetic and rather violent. Working with him, we were dancing for the Grand Inquisitor, who tortured people in the name of God. He had no understanding or forgiveness for dancers who couldn't do what he asked. Every dancer has his or her own best movement— one is better on the toes, another in allegro, another in adagio. Balanchine, if he wanted to make a fast variation, would cast a fast dancer. The choreography, the actual steps, depended on how you could interpret what he showed you. But Massine didn't care who you were or what you could do. If he thought you should dance adagio, you had to do it, regardless. If you turned best to the right, he would give you pirouettes to the left. When he made *Zéphyr et Flore*, he decided that Zéphyr had to jump. Zéphyr was Lifar, who didn't have a particularly good jump, but Massine made him jump anyway. In *Les Matelots*, I had to dance so much on the toes, more than we ever had danced on the toes in Russia. There was a lot of jumping on pointe. Massine was unmerciful, and he couldn't have cared less. If he had an idea, he would absolutely break the dancer before he would change the step.

The result was that in Balanchine's ballets, everybody was at his best, while Massine's ballets sometimes suffered because they were miscast. The Hungarian movement in *Choreartium*, for example, he gave to Toumanova, but she wasn't supple enough for the role. When Vera Zorina first joined the Ballets Russes, Massine was taken by her beauty, and he gave her all my ballets. But they didn't suit her very well. She wasn't the same kind of artist.

When he was making a ballet, Balanchine was inspired by the dancers, but not Massine—his inspiration was his own. He refused to explain to us what a ballet was about. "What am I?" I would ask, but he would ignore my question. Once, he said in an interview that he didn't tell his dancers the story of the ballet they were working on because if they didn't know, he could squeeze from them whatever he wanted. But if they knew the story, they would bring to it their own interpretations, and he didn't want that. I found his attitude insulting.

Massine was not particularly loyal to his dancers. When he was married to Tania Dokouchaiev, a cabaret dancer who was Denham's niece, he informed me that she would be dancing *Schéhérazade*. "How come?" I said. "She is not a member of our company."

"She is a beautiful woman, Choura," he said.

"So what? Mrs. Hurok is a beautiful woman, and so is Mrs. Libidins," the wife of our manager. "So they all will dance *Schéhérazade?* Impossible."

I told all the first dancers of our company about Massine's plan, and we decided to strike. If she was going to dance on this particular evening, none of us would dance. Massine was furious. He called me. "You think you are a ballerina?" he said. "You are a lousy dancer. You can't do thirty-two fouettés."

"Neither could Pavlova or Karsavina," I replied. "Sometimes, Mr. Massine, you can't do two pirouettes. But for me you are still a very great dancer." He walked away from me without a word.

The steps you danced in Massine's ballets, to his way of thinking, belonged to him. Years after we had both left the Ballet Russe, I appeared on "The Jack Paar Show," dancing a little piece of my variation from *Le Beau Danube*. The next morning, I received a telephone call from Massine. "You are dancing my *Danube*," he said, "so I expect a payment."

"For goodness sake," I told him, "it is such a small amount they paid me"—three hundred dollars, I think—"and I need the money."

"I don't care," he said. *"Danube* belongs to me."

I said, "All right, I will think about it."

A few days later, he telephoned a second time. "So, how about *Danube?"*

"I'm still thinking," I said. After that, he never bothered me again.

But he could also be generous. During my first season with the de Basil company, he promised me a new production of *Coppélia*, because he thought that I would be good in it, and in 1938, with the Ballet Russe de Monte Carlo, he kept his word, engaging Nicholas Sergeyev, an old-timer, a former régisseur of the Imperial Ballet in St. Petersburg, to stage the dancing, and Raoul Dufy to design the costumes and sets. The production was a huge success, and Swanilda became one of my favorite and most famous roles. My Franz was Michel Panaieff, a marvelous dancer who happened to be a distant cousin of Diaghilev.

Coppélia is a typical story of a boy in love with two girls, and there is nothing enigmatic about Swanilda. I imagine her as very *simpatica* but mischievous and quite enterprising. I understand Swanilda and all of her doings, and if I were in her situation, I would do the same things myself.

Balanchine always worked very fast in rehearsals—the choreography would just pour out of him. But for Massine it was like having a baby: very hard and slow. He would pace back and forth, trying to think what to do next. He never smiled or joked during rehearsals, and he didn't like his dancers having a rest. If he could have, he would have rehearsed us for three hours straight, or longer. Massine always carried in his arms a thick book, given to him by Diaghilev. In it were mysterious symbols and writing, notations for old choreography. Massine kept his eyes on this precious book. No one was allowed to come near it, and God forbid if you touched it.

There was no softness in him. When Massine saw a woman, he had to have her. His adagio was always a conquest—the man conquering the woman, or the woman conquering the man—not a song of love, like Balanchine's. With Massine, there was no romance, not even in his ballets.

There was something dry and pedantic about his attitude toward art. When he began choreographing symphonies, he took up studying composition, because he wasn't musically very well educated. Once, when we were in London, he asked me, "Don't you study with Cecchetti?"

"Good God, no," I said. "I study with Nicholas Legat, who is a marvelous teacher. Why don't you come?"

"Oh," he said, "I am Cecchetti's pupil." Then one day, a year or so later, he said, "Choura, I am coming to Legat."

"Why?" I asked.

"To get the vocabulary I need for my symphonies."

Massine studied with Legat for three years, whenever we were on tour in London, because Legat had such a variety of movements and accents, and that fed Massine's imagination.

To me, Massine's most beautiful ballet was *St. Francis*, which was, I think, inspired by Balanchine's *Prodigal Son*. The music was commissioned from Paul Hindemith by Diaghilev, but by the time Hindemith finished the score, Diaghilev had died, so Massine picked it up and produced it himself. I didn't dance in *St. Francis*—it was Massine in the title role, as the saint by himself in the forest, with Nini Theilade as Poverty. Together, they danced an adagio which was more like a slow allegro. There was not one lift. They danced a lot of the same movements together, facing each other. There was no love story at all; it was an allegory, typical of Massine's choreography.

Massine's strength as a choreographer lay in the way he used the ensemble. His ballets were filled with rituals and patterns. He was very fond of hand movements and poses—hands crossed above the head or across the chest—and a lot of port de bras in groups. One group would run on and move the arms, then another three or four dancers would run on and form another group, making a pattern. He was obsessed with arrangements, creating a design on the stage. For that reason, I liked his symphonic ballets—*The Seventh Symphony*, to Beethoven, and *Rouge et Noir*, a battle of colors, to Shostakovich. I asked him what the story was behind *Rouge et Noir*, and he told me that white was for Russia, black for fascists, and red for communists. The most powerful part of this ballet was a solo for Alicia Markova, a cry—she bourréed all around the stage, changing the positions of her arms, of her body. She was weeping without tears, with her soul.

After Massine studied music composition, I could see that he improved tremendously. He found more phrases in the music to choreograph in his way, for three or four people. Massine's choreography was musical, but not to perfection the way Balanchine's was. Balanchine heard everything; he didn't miss a note. Certainly, Massine heard the music correctly, but I don't think he heard all the parts. Balanchine's steps sometimes made a counterpoint to the music, but not Massine's. Dancing Balanchine's ballets, one has to count, to be right on the music. But in Massine's ballets one could go by ear. I wouldn't say that

Massine's choreography was less musical, but it was less musically detailed.

His steps were strange and sometimes awkward. What made Massine's choreography interesting was its fantastic rhythm. The rhythm was all in the feet, the way it is in Spanish dancing, which fascinated him. Where Balanchine would create a rhythm with beats and pointe work, all kinds of pas de bourrées, Massine would use heel work instead. His steps came from character dancing: the farruca, the tarantella—always ticky-ticky footwork, the talking feet.

Massine himself was not a truly classical dancer. His dancing was demi-caractère, and that was his style as a choreographer, too. But Balanchine's choreography was always classical: he borrowed steps from character dancing and applied them to classical ballet. Massine did just the reverse: he took classical ballet technique and applied it to character dancing. Today, Jerome Robbins does what Massine did. Even when Massine choreographed a complicated variation on the toes, like the one I danced in *Les Matelots*, it was still character dancing.

Massine's choreography depended a lot on style, and so today it looks a little bit *démodé*. His ballets are like a beautiful carpet that has faded; the years have washed away the colors. People today don't know how to dance Massine ballets, because they don't know how to dance demi-caractère. In the revivals I have seen, the dancers were not educated enough in character and folk dances to interpret their roles; they didn't grasp the style.

It is difficult now for people to understand how important Massine was. He widened the horizon. The 1930s belonged to him, and he helped prepare the way for what came after. Some choreographers are important in this sense, that they make possible a new direction for someone else. Eugene Loring, for instance—I don't think Agnes de Mille would ever have made *Rodeo* if she hadn't seen *Billy the Kid*. Loring showed her the nail, and she hit it on the head. Massine was like Loring. He choreographed his symphonies, which were all mood, and then afterward everybody made abstract ballets. He introduced complicated footwork, and now everybody does it.

While he was with Denham, Massine collaborated with Argentinita, who was a marvelous Spanish dancer, on *Capriccio Espagnol*, a Spanish fiesta to music by Rimsky-Korsakov. This was a good ballet, one of

Massine's most popular, well danced, with a nice mood. Later, Ballet Theatre revived it, but they lacked the style; nobody danced *Capriccio Espagnol* better than the Ballet Russe de Monte Carlo. Half, maybe three-quarters of the credit should go to Argentinita, a charming woman who was very capable and knowledgeable. Very few people realize what a wide range of dances the Spaniards have, more than just flamenco. Argentinita knew dozens of different styles, and she set my variation, the jota, which was a lot of beats, brisés and jetés. The steps were small and quick, very gay but quiet. For this, I wore character shoes and a beautiful costume—a white kerchief and white blouse with a red-and-black striped skirt and a black fichu. My partner was André Eglevsky and later Igor Youskevitch. Argentinita danced the premiere in Monte Carlo with Massine. Over the door of her dressing room, she hung a sign: "Argentinova." She wanted to be Russian, like the rest of us.

Like any other choreographer, Massine had his share of disasters, but even they were usually interesting. When he made *Bacchanale*, a ballet about Ludwig II of Bavaria with décor by Salvador Dali, I wasn't in it—I escaped. But I still can remember certain moments in it. The opening was erotic and quite beautiful—a Botticelli-like scene with Nini Theilade, as Venus, dressed in a pink leotard, with long white hair, poised like a pearl on a shell at the rear of the stage. The music was from *Tannhäuser*. The stories say that Ludwig died mysteriously, that one night when it was raining he went out for a walk and was later found floating with his umbrella in the lake. In Massine's ballet, when Ludwig died, the crowd onstage opened umbrellas. There were sadists and masochists, all the vices. Dali's costumes for the men featured black tights with a red lobster appliquéed at the top, just below the stomach. Supposedly, in Roman times a lobster was the emblem for sex—the sign of the lobster indicated a bordello. Well, when we saw these men dressed in their tights with lobsters on them, we were all shocked. The audience gasped.

I did dance in Massine's ballet *The New Yorker*, based on cartoons from *The New Yorker* magazine and choreographed especially for one of our seasons in New York. The music was by Gershwin. This was supposed to be a funny ballet—not the kind of humor that makes you laugh but the kind that makes you smile. There was a series of brief pictures, several in a row, with characters taken from the cartoons. This sounds as if it should have been delightful, but it wasn't. We did it for one season only, and then it went into the wastebasket.

Saratoga was another short-lived ballet, but it is memorable for me because the costumes and scenery were designed by a young man named Oliver Smith. I had met him one weekend when I was visiting my friend Robert Pitney in New Jersey. "Choura," Robert said, "I would like you to meet a very talented young painter." After lunch, I took Robert aside. "Now, tell me," I said, "is he really talented, or was that just a nice introduction?"

"He really is talented," he said.

So I told Oliver, "Next week, if you are in New York, please come and call on me." The following week, I received word from the stage door attendant: a young man named Oliver Smith to see me. Who on earth is that? I thought. And then I remembered. But I am so tired. . . . Oh, all right, I suppose I must. "Please show him in." I took him by the hand down the hall and knocked on the door of Massine's dressing room: "Leonide Feodorovitch, I want to introduce you to a young painter." And I went with him through the same protests I had just gone through with myself.

"No, Choura," he said, "I am so tired. . . ."

"You will be tired tomorrow and the next day," I told him. "Better right now."

The Ballet Russe was about to mount a new ballet, *Rodeo*, and Massine asked a few painters—one of them Oliver—to submit their designs for it. Oliver won. I was very pleased, and when I congratulated him, he said, "Oh, I must do something for you. What would you like?" A sketch, I told him, and ten years later I got it.

One of the biggest successes of my career came in Massine's *Gaîté Parisienne*, in a role he had made on Nina Tarakanova. After my debut in it, she didn't dance it anymore. The scene was Paris in springtime, and in the beginning, there were girls sweeping the stage, getting a sidewalk cafe ready to open. I was a glove seller, trying gloves on each man who asked me to dance. I never could make up my mind which one to go with. A rich lady entered, and an officer and a couple of gentlemen. And each of them was kissing her hand, to each one, she paid attention. There was this perpetual flirtation. A South American arrived—that was Massine. And then a lot of soldiers came in together, and some can-can girls. Each boy found a girl; everybody danced. Finally, I went with the baron, which was Freddie Franklin, and we danced a waltz, very pretty— not Viennese, which is strict, but a free waltz, with lifts and jetés. Then twilight came, and everybody got romantic and drifted away in pairs. That was Paris. As the curtain went down, Freddie and I were at the balustrade, kissing.

In 1940, Warner Bros. decided to make a film of the Ballet Russe in *Gaîté Parisienne* and *Capriccio Espagnol*, and we reported to their studios in Hollywood for our screen tests. Nobody said anything to me. I looked at the schedule and thought, Why am I not called for rehearsal? Finally, Jean Negulesco, the director, took me aside and told me that it was because I was not photogenic. I was the only one who danced *Gaîté*, and when it came to the film, my part went to Milada Mladova, who was very pretty but not a dynamic performer. I said to Massine, "That is my part. Don't you want to dance *Gaîté Parisienne* with me?" But he ignored me. For the movie of *Capriccio Espagnol* (which Warner Bros. renamed *Spanish Fiesta*), however, I did dance my part, which was small but quite nice. Apparently, I photographed well enough to do that.

Eleven

LIFE WITH DENHAM was much more glamorous than life with de Basil. Toumanova, Baronova, and Riabouchinska arrived. Alicia Markova and Anton Dolin also joined, and we had a grand reunion. Denham had a lawyer to negotiate our contracts; his company was run smoothly and professionally.

There were new ballets every season. One was by a young, distinguished-looking Englishman who was very pleasant, with a good sense of humor. His name was Frederick Ashton, and his ballet, premiered in New York, was called *Devil's Holiday*. During rehearsals, any time we were in a studio and had a few minutes free, Fred would turn to me and say, "Choura, dance for me some old variations." And I would dance for him variations that I remembered from the Maryinsky repertoire. He wanted to see Petipa's choreography.

The Ballet Russe de Monte Carlo was famous for its intrigues. One night in Boston, Markova was dancing *Giselle*. She and I always shared a dressing room, and when we went back to it at the end of the first act, we discovered that her second-act costume had been cut to pieces. The skirt was gone. Alicia was frantic. Luckily, we also had in the repertoire

Les Sylphides, so we substituted her *Sylphides* costume for her *Giselle* costume. Her skirt was later found stuffed in a corner of the backstage ladies' room, but we never found out who committed the crime. It could have been any one of the two or three other dancers who shared the role with Alicia; there was no one designated as her understudy.

We all had our superstitions on the stage. If a cat crossed my path from the dressing room to the stage, that was bad luck, so I used to skip to get there quickly.

My other superstition was that anything lilac-colored was bad luck. This applied to everything but amethyst, which is my birthstone and a beautiful jewel—I never minded if somebody gave me an amethyst. But if my costume had purple on it, I would ask to have it changed. Amazingly, I went for years without being given purple flowers on the stage. Later, after I had stopped dancing, I learned that if I had been sent an arrangement with purple flowers in it or with a purple ribbon, Alicia would switch the card on my bouquet with the card on hers, so that the purple would go to her. Other dancers had good-luck charms that they carried with them everywhere, but I thought that it was better not to depend so much on some trinket, because if you lose it, you're frantic and your concentration is gone. The only thing I had in my dressing room was a picture of Diaghilev, not for luck but for inspiration.

Every soprano wants to sing Tosca, every actress wants to play Juliet, and like every ballerina, I wanted to dance the role of Giselle. Certain things I did very well; other things, I think, not as well as I should have—I hammed it up in the mad scene, I'm afraid. But then I got Mme Nijinska to coach me in it, and my performance became more successful. Nevertheless, I soon enough lost interest in the role—I found it very dated, with so much mime, and not really suited to my nature. I think maybe I could never love that much, to lose my man and lose my mind. Or maybe it is just that I am not so delicate. If Albrecht had left me, I would have suffered, but I would have worked myself out of it. I am not the type to give up on life; I would have fought back. So I gave up the role.

Other dancers, I thought, were better in it. Yvette Chauviré, who came as a guest artist, was marvelous in the first act. She had the gift of charm; it was in her smile. We have a proverb in Russian: "She smiles as if she's giving you two rubles." That was true of Chauviré.

But in the Ballet Russe, the role of Giselle really belonged to Markova, and for a time I danced Myrtha to her Giselle. In Russia, *Giselle* was a ballet for two ballerinas—Myrtha's part was larger than it is today. At the Maryinsky Theatre when I was young, Elena Lukom was the great Giselle, and Elsa Will danced Myrtha opposite her. Ballet Theatre was the first to assign the role of Myrtha to a soloist rather than a ballerina, and her dancing was cut because most soloists couldn't get through the part full-length. I danced the longer, original version and found it more to my liking than the title role.

After one of our performances at Covent Garden, a rather plain-looking Englishwoman, about fifty years old, with a long face and thin features, walked unannounced and uninvited into my dressing room and introduced herself. She told me that her name was Elizabeth Twysden and that she had just returned from Russia. She brought me greetings and a little wooden doll as a present from Mme Vaganova. I was thrilled and touched that Mme Vaganova still cared about me, and I thanked Miss Twysden. But that was only the beginning: she started to pester me, asking me all the time for lunch or dinner or supper. I became an obsession with her. Her persistence made me dislike her. Finally, at the end of the season in London, I agreed to go to lunch at her service flat, in Knightsbridge. After lunch, she declared that she admired my dancing and that she admired me. "But you hardly know me!" I said. I was stuck with Miss Twysden for the next forty years, until she died, in 1978. From that season on, she was everywhere, wherever the Ballet Russe happened to perform, coming to my dressing room to say hello. Sometimes I refused to see her: "That woman again! What does she want from me?"

Traveling in the thirties from Paris to London, I used to take the Golden Arrow, a train that went as far as Calais, where we got a boat to Dover, and then boarded another train that took us on to London. That was the smart way to go. Many times one met friends or fans or other artists on the trip, especially on weekends, when the traffic was always heavy. One day, I was on my way to London, and on the boat was standing a young man in rather shabby English clothes. He approached me. "You are Mme Danilova?" I said yes. "My name is Colville Barclay," he said.

I didn't catch the name. "Yes?" I said.

"Oh," he said, "I admire you." We started to talk. Finally, he asked, "Would you do me the honor of having lunch with me? We could go downstairs, to the dining room."

I looked him over and thought, He is spending his last pennies on me. "No, thank you," I said. "I am not hungry."

"Please," he said.

Well, I thought, I could have a cup of tea. So we went downstairs and I had tea and a sandwich, being careful not to order anything expensive. He was telling me that he had just come from Greece. "The boats there are so dirty," he said, "that everyone travels third class," because third-class sleeping quarters were on the deck. "Oh, I know," I told him, and thought to myself, Well, of course he would travel third class—he couldn't afford anything better.

Across the Channel, when we boarded the train, I jumped in first class and my young man hopped in with me. The conductor came to collect our tickets, and, of course, my young man couldn't find his and had finally to pay something extra to settle his fare. When we arrived in London, he offered to take me to wherever I was going in a taxi. "No thank you," I said. "I am going too far out of your way." So we said goodbye.

Just before the Ballet Russe season in London began, I received a card from Colville Barclay, saying that he would be at my opening night and hoped that we could have dinner together. When the night arrived, I received a beautiful bouquet of red roses, with a card saying that he would pick me up in my dressing room at Covent Garden. When I was finished dancing, I was sitting in my dressing room and my dresser announced, "Sir Colville Barclay." And who walks in but my young man! "You!" I said. "Sir Colville Barclay?"

So Colville—"Collie," he was called—and I became friends. He was a member of the "white corps," the diplomatic elite, and the stepson of Lord Vansittart, the secretary of foreign affairs.

Everybody knew that war might be declared any day. After London, the Ballet Russe had a season in Paris. Collie was worried. Before I left, he said, "Choura, when I call you and say, 'Come to London,' that means you must do as I say, because the war will be declared."

Those last few weeks in Paris before the war were like the moments before a storm: you see the clouds and think, If I venture out, can I get home before the storm starts, or will I get caught? Paris was a bacchanale, with everybody intent on having a good time. *On a profité du temps.* Nobody wanted to miss anything, because tomorrow might be war.

One night, Collie telephoned and said, "Come to London," and I knew that I had to leave. That night I packed, and the next morning I took the last taxi to the station, where the last porter put me on the last train out of Paris, the Golden Arrow again. Collie met me in London. The next day, war was declared.

In Paris, gas masks had been distributed only to the French; in London, the police distributed gas masks to everybody. I felt that I was more or less prepared for whatever might happen—the Revolution in Russia had been my training in crisis. For my first air raid, I took along my nightgown, my new fur coat, and my passport, and then suddenly I realized that I had left behind what jewelry I owned. Well, that was stupid, I thought, so from then on I had a small suitcase packed and ready to go, and instead of my nightgown, I took my slacks—that's when women started to wear slacks, because they were more practical for spending the night in a church basement or a tube station.

The Ballet Russe had arranged for a tour of America. The company would continue, if only we could get there. In London, people stood in a queue for hours to get their passports stamped with permission to leave. Collie helped not only me to leave London but my friends, too—Alicia Markova, Anton Dolin, Paul Petroff, Irina Baronova, Gerry Sevastianov, a few others. We were about a dozen people. I gave Collie our passports, and he got them stamped. Once again, I packed all my belongings in a trunk and moved, like a turtle with my house on my back. The afternoon of our departure, Collie put us on the boat.

America had been working its way into my heart. With every tour I liked it more and more. I didn't identify with the people straightaway: it seemed to me that Americans had too much freedom, and that they didn't know what to do with it, whereas in Russia, we had less freedom and made better use of it. Nevertheless, America was somehow closer to what I remembered of Russia, because Russia is also a big country. In Europe, everything seemed to me so small and squeezed; the countries were living one on top of the other. But in America, there were open spaces. There was more room to breathe.

It was in America that Alicia and I renewed the friendship we had begun in the Diaghilev company. Since then, Alicia had grown up—I was struck by how elegant she seemed. We ate our meals together, went shopping together; we were always the last to leave the station together, stranded with our suitcases long after everybody else had gone, waiting for a porter to appear. Sometimes we shared a hotel room, talking and dancing until morning. Alicia would ask me about old ballets, and I would dance them for her, or talk to her about old ballerinas, telling her the stories that were told to me in the Theatre School. Sometimes, especially in the South, people didn't understand Alicia's British accent, and then I would translate for her. "These French girls," I would say, complaining to the waiter, "they just can't learn to speak good English."

Nearly every night, I received an invitation to supper. Americans were very hospitable. In every city, there were people asking us to their private clubs or to their homes. Some dancers would say they were too tired. But mostly, I would accept. Now, when people ask me what is the biggest difference between dancers in my time and dancers today, I tell them it's that when we were invited someplace, we would go. At parties and receptions, we cultivated our audience; we depended on them. When one of the clubs at Yale invited me to come and drink with them, I accepted the compliment and went. We drank from a loving cup filled with champagne and mint liqueur; the custom was to pass the cup without setting it down, until it was empty. Today, there are not many dancers who would do that. Their sense of responsibility to their audience ends when they step off the stage. They cut themselves off from everybody else and then complain because they stew all the time in their own juices. "Oh, I am so lonely," they say. They don't recognize that it is an honor to be asked into somebody's home and an insult to refuse.

There was always a man after me. Sometimes I was charmed, sometimes disappointed, but it was never anything serious. Gerry Sevastianov, Colonel de Basil's secretary, had been very much in love with me; I wasn't in love with him. I didn't run after men, and I wasn't looking to marry them. If you want a married life, you must be locked together with somebody, and both of you must work at it. But when you're a performer, it's very difficult. You must divide your life between your marriage and your art, and very often your art must come first. I was content to be unattached. There were always possibilities—I was never alone.

In 1941, when the company left for South America, Alicia and I shared a cabin. Arthur Rubinstein was on the same boat, with his family; we all became friends. And there also, to my astonishment, was Miss Twysden. Fortunately, I was traveling first class, and she was going tourist. Even so, I almost never managed to avoid her. If I would go out for a stroll around the deck or to the bar for a drink, she would follow me. Eventually, she made friends in the company—people who found her well educated, charming, and a good conversationalist.

At one of our first meals on board ship, Alicia and I were seated not far away from a table of naval officers. Suddenly, I saw that they were all drinking milk. I was astounded and horrified—grown men, drinking milk! One of the officers saw my expression and asked, "What's wrong?"

"Oh," I said, "you can lose the war drinking milk. You must drink vodka." So I called the head waiter and asked him, "Do you have a vodka?"

"Yes," he said.

"Serve it, please, to these officers at the next table." To their big amazement, the vodka arrived. They sent us a bottle of champagne, and so our friendship started.

They would invite us to the bridge after supper. When everyone else was going off to bed, the sailors would come and fetch us, and we would climb the stairs and enter the compartment with the steering wheel where the first officer was on duty. Alicia and I would sit on the floor, so that nobody could see us from the outside. One sailor was posted to keep watch, to warn us if the captain was coming. Another, whose duty it was to patrol the boat and make sure that all was well, would stop in every now and then to tell us about all the lovers he had surprised on his rounds. We would sit, talking and laughing, having a wonderful time into the middle of the night.

One evening, a few of our fellow passengers organized a costume ball. First prize for the best costume was awarded to Alicia, who went as a blackout, in a long black dress, with long sleeves and a high collar; on her head she wore a balloon, like the ones that filled the sky in London during the war.

En route to South America, the boat docked for an afternoon in

Trinidad. I wasn't allowed to go ashore, because I had then an Italian passport as a result of my marriage to Massera, but Alicia went.

"What can I bring you?" she asked. "What do you want?"

"Well," I said, "I have always heard about passion fruit, but I've never known what it was. So could you bring me some passion fruit."

A couple of hours later, Alicia came back with a basket full of little things that she had found on her shopping tour—English biscuits, English tea. "And here—" she said to me, "here is your passion fruit."

"My goodness," I said, inspecting it. "But how does one eat this fruit?"

Alicia wasn't altogether sure. "You know what the man told me?" she said. "He said to take off all your clothes, get into a nice warm bath, and eat the fruit."

"Okay," I said, following instructions. Well, I thought, this promises to be quite an experience. I got into the tub and, wondering what this exotic fruit would do to live up to its name, took my first bite. And sure enough, the man was right, but not for any of the reasons I was expecting. The juice went all over me.

In Rio de Janeiro, Alicia and I were together everywhere. Leaving the theatre at night, we would cling to each other, jumping with fright, because our fans who were waiting for us at the stage door would throw firecrackers at our feet as a way of showing their appreciation for our performances.

We visited the famous gardens, where we bought dozens of orchids for only three cents apiece. And there we saw for the first time tiny bluebirds that flap their wings very fast—they were such a beautiful blue. I think it was because of this bird that Alicia later changed the Bluebird pas de deux from *The Sleeping Beauty*. Traditionally, the man was the bird and the woman was a princess, enchanted by his song. But after South America, Alicia decided that she would become a bluebird herself, that they would be a pair of birds. And since then, many dancers have copied her.

One evening, I found Miss Twysden in Alicia's dressing room, acting as her dresser. Alicia took me aside and asked if I would help Miss Twysden financially by taking her on as my dresser, too. I said no at first, but Alicia pleaded Miss Twysden's cause, explaining that she could no longer get money from England now that the war was on.

After some hesitation, I relented. I spoke to Miss Twysden very clearly, explaining the terms—that there would be no lunches, no dinners, that she would be my dresser and nothing more. She agreed, and tried hard to be professional about her job. She became very friendly with Mme Pourmel, our wardrobe mistress, who gave her all kinds of odd jobs to do, and she did them quite well.

It wasn't long before Miss Twysden asked if she could speak with me—something very important. Right off, she told me that she had heard that I had been seeing Casimir Kokitch, a soloist in the company, and that she wanted to impress upon me that he was not for me. I was furious. "How dare you put your nose in my private life?" I said. "If ever again you dare to snoop in my affairs"—and I shook my fist—"I will ask the direction to throw you out of the theatre forever." She left in a hurry.

The rumors she had heard were true. In South America, I fell in love. Kokitch stayed at the same hotel as Alicia and I, and often in the evening he would come and sit on our terrace and watch the sun set over the bay, and we would talk. I was very lonely at the time. He had been romancing a young girl who I think perhaps didn't understand him very well, and so he began looking elsewhere. There is a time after thirty when your thoughts change and you want to be more settled. He would wait for Alicia and me after the performance, and the three of us would go to supper together—we always went out in groups. I suppose this seems like an unusual way to carry on a courtship, but we thought nothing of it. I didn't want to be always alone with him. Russians by nature love to live in company, not by themselves; a Russian family isn't just the husband and wife, it's also the grandmother, the aunts, all the poor relations. So in the Ballet Russe, we were quite accustomed to having people around.

Casimir was good company, amiable, beautifully built, good-looking, and dark of complexion—Yugoslavian. He was intelligent and sly and spoke both Russian and French. We called him "Koschka," which means "cat" in Russian, because he walked like a cat. He was a very capable artist, with a fair technique, good acting ability, and a commanding stage presence. He excelled in dramatic roles; nobody since has equaled him in *Rodeo*. But he was not ambitious. He didn't take class every day. Koschka had a reputation for being not such a very good guy—he played cards, he liked to go out dancing. But I liked all that—I thought that he was alive.

Back in America, the courtship continued. Nobody thought it would last. The other members of the company were shocked when we decided to get married, on tour in Los Angeles.

I think that I wasn't created to be a mother; I was created to be a dancer, to give pleasure to many people. But I also believe that every woman needs a man, and vice versa—that is the way the world is made. Maybe I was wrong before, I thought, marrying a businessman. I will try again with an artist, and maybe I will be happy.

The wedding was small, a civil ceremony at the city hall. Alicia was my maid of honor; Efrem Kurtz, our conductor, was Koschka's best man. The reception was held in Hollywood, at a Russian restaurant called Scheherazade run by a man named Gogi Chichinadze, who was a friend of mine and also of George Balanchine's. We had all met in Paris, where Gogi was dancing the *lezginka* in a nightclub to keep himself going, in the hope of paying for his studies at the university. But he was so good-looking and he danced so well that eventually he left his studies by the wayside, moved to America, and opened a nightclub of his own. Koschka and I invited twenty-five of our friends to the reception, but in the end a few hundred people turned out. The word got around, and people just came—well, it was California. Life there was very unceremonious. The press arrived to interview us. There were so many people I didn't even know. Each movie star brought his or her entourage. Jimmy Cagney was there—My goodness, I thought, how did he get here?

For our honeymoon, we bought a car and went to Florida—Koschka and I, with Igor Youskevitch and his wife, Mrs. Hurok's son Pepper, and Jeannette Lauret. It was six of us, driving all the way across the country, and we all stayed in the same hotels. We had a marvelous time, very gay.

When the United States entered the war, Koschka was taken into the army, along with six or seven other men from the company, including Youskevitch and Skibine. When Youskevitch left, I lost a partner—we had danced the Black Swan pas de deux, *Swan Lake* Act II, and a couple of *Giselles* together. Igor was very masculine and dramatic looking, handsome on the stage, but not very sensitive—it took a lot of coaching for him to learn all the artistic details of a role, and even then he wasn't one hundred percent inside the part. Somehow I don't think he ever liked dancing with me. There was a photograph of the two of us in *The Nutcracker*. I was posed on one knee and he was in mid-air, leaping over me. Igor had me erased from this picture, so that now where I used to be there is only the floor.

Most of the principal roles for men in the repertoire were taken over by the young Englishman Frederic Franklin, who was extremely capable. I had first seen him years before in the Markova-Dolin company and told Colonel de Basil about him, but by the time the colonel got around to seeing him dance, Freddie had already been signed by Massine. On the stage, Fred was very emotional, very musical—he played the piano very well by ear. All he needed was to hear a song once and he could play it for us. He had a good disposition and was willing to learn. By nature, he was a demi-caractère dancer, but during the war, with so many of the men gone, he was forced to take over the classical roles as well, and he danced them with honor. The shortage of premiers danseurs didn't affect me so much: besides Fred, I had two new partners—Leon Danielian, a pupil of Mordkin, a young soloist with a strong classical technique who came from Ballet Theatre; and Nicholas Magallanes, who was Mexican, a danseur noble trained at the School of American Ballet and a friend of Pavel Tchelitchev's, who liked to paint his Renaissance features. Nicky was a wonderful partner, and all the ballerinas adored him—he never quarreled with anybody. But mostly I danced with Massine, as before.

The Ballet Russe continued to tour. We danced more than ever, giving a lot of performances at USO camps all over the country. We loved performing for the servicemen. In San Francisco, where we used to stay for four weeks in the opera house, a friend of mine ran a courtesy club for officers. I told her that the boys could come to the ballet and stand in the wings. So every night there would be a group of them backstage, watching. They seemed to us young and very nervous—not knowing what would happen, where they would be tomorrow. "If you are still here," I would tell them, "do come again." And some of them would come back, others wouldn't, and that was how we knew that they had been sent overseas. Years later, when the war was over, some of these men came to see me in my dressing room and told me how glad they were to be home again; they brought their families to see the ballet.

On tour in Los Angeles we were often introduced to movie stars. Some of them I found slightly overdressed. The fashions in Hollywood were a little bit behind New York, and slightly exaggerated—if it was a narrow skirt, it would be a little too narrow; a wider skirt, a little too wide. But I admired many of the stars, and it was a thrill for me to meet them: Joan Crawford, Alexis Smith, Bette Davis, Greer Garson—one evening when we were dancing at the Hollywood Bowl, she came to visit, to sit in my dressing room. My dresser was God knows where, just when I needed to get ready to go onstage, and so Greer dressed me. Years later, when I was given the Capezio Award, she flew to New York to present it to me, at a luncheon at the St. Regis roof.

Balanchine had been struggling hard to establish ballet in America, but until the Ballet Russe came along, Americans didn't know what he was talking about. Our success paved the way for his. We introduced people to the ballet, and then they went to see more. If you go to the movies tonight and see a good film, you will go to the movies again next week. But if you see a bad film, you don't want to go back to the movies for months. In a way I regard American audiences as my children, because I helped to educate them. Every year the ballet audience was growing. Most of the big Broadway stars didn't want to go on tour; they thought that it was beneath their dignity. But we went all over the United States and Canada, bringing to Kalamazoo productions with beautiful scenery and modern music. That is why my name was so well known, because I spent so much time on trains, touring the country. Mothers brought their daughters, who then became mothers and brought their daughters—three generations came to see me dance. I didn't feel that it was a burden, so much touring—this was my life. It was only later, when we covered 102 towns in six or seven months, that it stopped being art and started to be what in Russia we call *baltura*, a gig.

But most of the time, I felt that our one-night stands in small towns were even more important than our seasons in the big cities. I have never danced for an audience that I thought was unworthy of my performance. In fact, never did an audience appreciate us more than in those small towns. Most great writers, philosophers, talented people of all kinds come from small towns, and I always thought that maybe there was some exceptional person in the audience who would go on to do something great, and that maybe I could inspire him or influence him, that I could introduce him to an art he didn't know anything about.

We were not really aware of what was going on in dance beyond the Ballet Russe. It was only later, when I read or heard about what had been happening at the time, that I understood how important the thirties and forties were for dance in America. But in those days, Martha Graham wasn't yet a success, and Ted Shawn I heard more about in Paris than in America. When finally I got around to seeing Martha Graham dance, I realized that she had achieved a breakthrough: before her, it seemed to me, modern dancers used to do a lot of movement with the hands, but Graham emphasized movement with the whole body. Even so, I felt no need to go off and study modern dance, the way Nini Theilade did, or the way many ballet dancers do today, because to my mind modern dancers weren't more modern than Fokine, and Balanchine was more modern than all of them together.

In the Ballet Russe de Monte Carlo, I again had the opportunity to work with Balanchine. His own company was not steady, and from time to time he worked as a guest choreographer for the Ballet Russe. One season, he joined us in California and made a new ballet, *Danses Concertantes*. Rehearsals were called for ten in the morning, very early, and my most vivid memory of them is of getting to the studio at such a peculiar hour and seeing on the piano the music, which was written in white notes on green paper.

The music was by Stravinsky—jazzy, very difficult, but wonderful. The dancing was also jazzy, but *sur les pointes*—very difficult, elegant, and syncopated. It was movement more with the body than with the feet—gay and playful. The tango, for example, is sexy, the waltz is a sexy dance; but jazz in its rhythms is playful. The jazz was in the rhythm of the movement, and also in the positions, which were a little different from classical ballet—the feet would go one way, the body would go the other. Years later, when Balanchine choreographed *Rubies* to Stravinsky's Capriccio, I thought of *Danses Concertantes*.

I danced with Freddie Franklin, and there were two girls, soloists—Mary Ellen Moylan and Maria Tallchief—with Nicky Magallanes. Balanchine took the cream of the company when he made this ballet. The beautiful costumes were by Eugene Berman, in shades of purple, green, pink, yellow, and black.

Balanchine also re-created for us his *Ballet Imperial*, originally made for Marie-Jeanne, a ballerina in his American Ballet Caravan. I wanted so much to dance this ballet, but I didn't; this second time he appointed Mary Ellen Moylan the leading lady. I was hurt that he didn't give it to me. "Don't be upset," he said. "I will do for you a beautiful ballet, *Mozartiana*." And he did.

Mozartiana was pearls of pure dancing, a long strand of beautiful steps strung together by the music, Tchaikovsky's orchestration of four pieces by Mozart. The choreography was very classical, rather coquettish, but there was no sex in this ballet, only the interpretation of the music.

Balanchine had choreographed this music before, for his company Les Ballets 1933 in Paris, and he choreographed it again later, for the New York City Ballet. But I think ours was the best version. Ours was more *vivace* than the first one, which was rather *triste*, to fit the mood of Paris at that time—*la tristesse* was in the air. In that first version, in the opening, which was set to the "Prayer" music, two men dressed in black, with plumes on their heads, came out carrying two poles on their shoulders, and on the poles was hanging a girl, all dressed in white, covered with tulle. They were a funeral procession, like the ones you could see in Paris at that time—a lonely coffin, covered with a veil and driven through the streets by two horses with plumes on their heads. All this, I remember, had a certain morbid expression to it; the music in this first section throbbed like a toothache.

The Ballet Russe version opened with the Gigue instead, danced by a boy wearing an eighteenth-century costume more or less the same as the one the boy wears in *Mozartiana* today, at the New York City Ballet, with one difference—the boy in ours wore a tricorne, which I miss, because it immediately transported you to the right period. The costumes Bébé Bérard designed for our *Mozartiana* were marvelous, very decorative. It was always a success because it had such a distinctive style.

The Prayer was danced by Lubov Rostova. Diaghilev believed that in his company there should be at least one beautiful woman, and he would present her. In this variation, Balanchine presented Lubov—she bourréed by herself.

Then came the Minuet, for six girls. They wore long scarves of tulle, attached to their headpieces and again to their hands, that floated beautifully when they moved their arms. *Mozartiana* was a very dressy ballet, and this section in particular was very formal, because the minuet is a rather pompous dance.

These first three sections were short. Then Freddie Franklin and I came out. I was dressed all in white, with a white plume on my head. We danced, then disappeared to change costumes for the adagio. When we returned, I was all in black, with a green wreath in my hair. The adagio was set to a violin solo, and it was always exciting, full of unusual movements that Balanchine never repeated. This was not a standard adagio; the steps were delicate, very light, and not uniformly legato— there was some allegro in it. There were développés with turns and twists, small lifts, a little jumping. My part was technically difficult, with everything on the toes.

A year later, Balanchine made for me another ballet, *Night Shadow*, which is now called *La Sonnambula*. There were two roles in it for women. Vittorio Rieti, who composed the music, wanted me to dance the Co-quette, but Balanchine wasn't sure. They were debating, back and forth, which part I would do. Finally, Balanchine said, "Well, let's ask Choura which part she wants to do—the Coquette or the dramatic role."

"Well," I said, "I always do coquettes, and for a change I would like to do the dramatic part."

"All right," Balanchine said, "then you will do it." And Maria Tall-chief, who always did dramatic roles, danced the Coquette.

I was the Sleepwalker, who falls in love with the Poet. Sleepwalk-ers are without fear, drawn along the edge of a building by the sight of the moon, passing directly through danger but never sensing it. I used to sleepwalk when I was a student at the Theatre School. Once I was following a light far off in the distance, and suddenly my best friend called me—"Choura!"—and woke me up: I was standing on top of a table in our dormitory room, facing the window. Now, whenever I see the full moon through the window, I draw the shade.

I worked hard on my role, on every step, because I wanted to transform myself, to be not just an ordinary woman walking but to move as if I were in a trance. Mr. B., when he rehearsed me, said, "Just go—go right to the audience, to the edge of the stage, and at the last moment, stop." I thought that I would fall into the orchestra, but even-tually I found a way to do what he asked, to walk as if the moon were pulling me forward. I tried to create an illusion, to seem to skim the floor. My role was almost entirely bourrées, on the toes, and Mr. B. worked with me quite a lot to get my steps smaller—if you do small bourrées, your weight doesn't rest for so long on the floor. At the Maryinsky Theatre, we grew up hearing the legend of Legnani's bourrées—she had one variation, in *Talisman*, in which she bourréed backward all the way across the stage, zigzagging from one side to the other.

In an ordinary pas de deux, the woman is somehow engaged by the man, and she goes toward him. But I was going toward the moon. And that attracts the Poet, because he can't make contact with this woman. That is the enigma of this ballet. He senses her understanding of his poetry and sees in her the unhappiness she feels at being married to a horrid man, someone she doesn't love. But the Poet knows that she belongs to the moon.

Night Shadow was mine, and the Sleepwalker came to be one of my signature roles. Even now, there are people who tell me that they cannot forget my performance in it. And now there is a legend about me—they say that at the moment when I took the dead Poet in my arms and carried him off, I went up on the toes and carried him off the stage on pointe. It isn't true, but I'm flattered that I gave that impression.

Together, Balanchine and I staged for the Ballet Russe a full-length production of *Raymonda*, a ballet we loved and remembered from the Maryinsky repertoire. The setting is medieval, and the story rather cumbersome, so foreign to American audiences that they didn't know what to make of it. But *Raymonda* contains marvelous dancing. For a ballerina, it's a wonderful opportunity to show every facet of your talent, with several variations in widely differing styles. There is a beautiful adagio in the first act, a beautiful trio in the second, and in the last, the Pas Hongrois, which is very dramatic. On tour, we took only the last act, the wedding, with all the divertissements, and this reduced version was more popular with our audiences. Balanchine later created three ballets for the New York City Ballet from Glazunov's music for this ballet: *Raymonda Variations, Pas de Dix*, and *Cortège Hongrois*.

By this time, the forties, my relationship with Balanchine was strictly professional. We saw each other occasionally at parties and had a good time. But mostly it was business and rehearsal; then he went his way and I went mine. I was always careful not to say or do anything that would be embarrassing. For his part, he was always kind and concerned for me. If we were leaving a party, he would ask, "Do you have anybody?" And if I said no, he would volunteer to see me home. There was no bitterness between us.

Now I realize that there were many different periods in George's life, and that for each of them he was a different man. I knew him during the early stages, but later, when, for example, the company he had built moved from the City Center to the New York State Theater, I could see that he was sure of his success, and his approach was different—his approach to art, his approach to his dancers. And I thought to myself, I don't know this man.

He seems, in retrospect, a loner. All his life he was creating ballets—he never really had a personal life apart from the theatre. His goal and his real love was art. I, too, had many loves, and my dedication was to my art, dancing. Many men asked me to marry and leave the stage, which I never could do—my art also came first. I consider myself very lucky that I always knew exactly what I wanted—a career as a ballerina. It's wonderful, belonging to art—it's always with you, whatever disasters you have to face. Your art stays by you, and in this George and I were alike: our dedication to our art was pure. We had this understanding, and it never changed.

Of all Mr. B.'s ballets that I danced, the one I adored most was *Serenade*. The music, Tchaikovsky's Serenade for Strings, is like a wave—I love to dance to this music, because it's very close to the Russian heart. Balanchine called *Serenade* a ballet that takes place by the light of the moon, and I've always thought this a marvelous idea, because the shine of the moon is so cold and disturbing, a little bit treacherous and very mystical. I danced the first girl, who enters at the beginning. She is a butterfly, having romances with everybody. And then along comes a married man with his wife: they walk, and in their path is this girl. The man has an attraction for her, they dance; but for him it isn't serious, and in the end he continues along the road with his wife. The girl is seeking, suffering, and then she is alone, turning to her friends. I asked Mr. B., and this was his explanation. And somehow, I think the part I danced—that girl was me.

Twelve

HE BALLET RUSSE spent most of the war years on tour, traveling by train from one town to the next in a long series of one- and two-night stands. Dancing the same program night after night, you get rather sloppy and very one-sided—suddenly, a choreographer demands something that you haven't been doing, and you find that you can't execute it. The days we spent traveling, we didn't have time for class in the morning; and on those rare days when we did have time for class, it was only practice, it wasn't real training.

In New York, I studied at Carnegie Hall, with Edward Caton, and at the School of American Ballet, Balanchine's school. The training at SAB was very good, I thought. Doubrovska was there, Vladimiroff, and Anatole Oboukhoff; Vladimiroff especially was a marvelous teacher. I knew that George was struggling to build a company, but he had no ballerina, no one with an extraordinary personality. The girls I saw taking class at his school didn't know what to give or how to behave. There was no tradition, no generation of dancers ahead of them that they could look to and copy. They learned by watching the ballerinas who came in to take class there, seeing how we behaved.

In Chicago, I always took lessons from Laurent Novikoff, a very good teacher who had been a first dancer at the Bolshoi Theatre in Moscow and later Anna Pavlova's partner. But otherwise, like everyone else, I looked after my own technique, which as a result of so much touring had deteriorated. I needed to advance, and there was nobody in America who could help me. So straightaway after the war, I went for one month back to Paris, to study again with Mme Egorova. I took a two-hour lesson every day. I couldn't afford private sessions, but it didn't matter—they didn't suit me. I preferred to work in a class, to see where I stood, to learn different approaches to the same movement, to find out what I could do and what others couldn't, and vice versa. Ballerinas generally want to work alone, so that no one will discover what they can't do; but I was never shy in that way.

I had decided to make America my home. David Lichine bought a big house in the country, a hunting lodge near Lakewood, New Jersey, and he persuaded me to do the same. "Buy a house near me," he said, "so that when we get old, we'll be able to visit each other and have dinners together." But no sooner had I bought a house than Lichine moved to Hollywood. I stayed in my house and for the next twenty-five years spent my free time there. Two doors away, Doubrovska and Vladimiroff moved in, then Mme Pourmel, in the same neighborhood, and Igor Youskevitch—there were five or six dancers who settled in that area, and we were all quite friendly.

In 1946, I became an American citizen. The Ballet Russe, exiled from Europe during the war, had changed. Most of the new girls we had taken into the company were American, and even the Russians had become Americanized. No one had any desire to move back to Europe. We had our success, our friends—everything was here.

After ten years of Miss Twysden's intrusions, I had finally come to accept her, and she had changed toward me—she had stopped her adolescent adoration. She would spend weekends with me at my house in New Jersey, and I found her quite intelligent. She was writing a book about me. Miss Twysden had come from one of the oldest noble families in England. Her brother, Sir William Twysden, who lived in London and Bournemouth, was very displeased with Elizabeth's behavior, the idea of her taking up and traveling with a ballet company. For many years, they weren't on speaking terms. But after the war, he came to see her in New York, and peace was restored.

As for my own sister, Elena, ever since I had joined the Ballet

Russe, she had been writing to me in care of Sol Hurok. She sent me news of her family. When she was in her late twenties, she had married an officer in the Red Guard, and I had two nephews. And then, toward the end of the war, the letters stopped. I think that she and her family must have all been killed during the siege of Leningrad. I never heard from her again, and there was no way for me to trace her.

Koschka returned from the service, and we got reacquainted, spending as much time as possible at my house. He had what in Russian we call "golden hands"; he built shelves and a new entrance to the kitchen; he laid the carpet and painted the walls; he poured concrete for the terrace. One day, Miss Twysden and I argued for such a long time over how to cut the dining room curtains that finally he lost his patience, snatched the material out of my hands, and cut the curtains himself—beautifully.

Before the war, Koschka didn't drink hard liquor, but when he came back, he started drinking, and it became a terrible problem. When he was sober, he was charming, as before; but when he was drunk, he was sullen and mean, and there was nothing I could do with him. For a long time, I didn't take his drinking seriously, because I assumed the war had brought it on, and now that the war was over, his drinking would go away. But gradually, I understood that the real cause of his drinking was his jealousy of my success.

For example, we bought a car, and at the garage in New York City, even though I registered our names as "Mr. and Mrs. Kokitch," one of the attendants discovered that I was the famous dancer Danilova. So whenever we came to pick up the car, they would always call out: "Danilova's car!" There were press conferences at which nobody paid Koschka any attention, in spite of my saying, "Here is my husband."

After seven years together, after many long talks and many tears, we separated—just in time, I think. If I had stuck with him, I doubt if he would have ever stopped drinking. Koschka joined Alcoholics Anonymous and pulled himself together, married a pretty, charming Broadway star named Iva Withers, who is today one of my closest friends, had two children, and lived happily ever after.

I resigned myself to our divorce. When I fell in love with a man, I always built him up in my fantasies. I was never realistic; I expected him to be better, stronger, wiser than he could be. And so once again I was disappointed.

Nevertheless, I am very thankful for all the things I learned from Casimir. He insisted that I put some money aside—otherwise, he said, you will spend it all on furs. And therefore I was able to buy my house. So in spite of the fact that it wasn't a happy marriage, I can now remember only his kindness.

When Massine and Denham originally formed the Ballet Russe de Monte Carlo, the strict condition was that Massine would be the artistic director and Denham would be the business manager. But as time went on, Denham started making suggestions that had to do with the dancing, and Massine couldn't stand it. In the beginning, his ballets had dominated the repertoire; but by the time he left, in 1942, it was much more varied.

There were ballets by David Lichine and Marc Platoff that didn't turn the pages of history but were charming nonetheless. And we maintained several of Fokine's ballets. I danced *Schéhérazade* for a time. I had hurt my back and while I was recuperating, Mr. Denham asked if I would do the role of Schéhérazade, because my name was specified in the contract between the company and the theatres—I had to do something. The ballet is set in a harem, so nobody goes on pointe. Actually, Schéhérazade is a role for a première danseuse. For me, after being a ballerina, I felt as if there were practically nothing to do. But it seems that I was good in it, and I performed it until I was well enough to dance again. Then I went to Mr. Denham and said, "Please, take it back."

One day, Mr. Denham asked my advice. The company was engaged to dance in *Song of Norway* with the Civic Light Opera in Los Angeles, and he was trying to decide whom to hire to choreograph it, Balanchine or David Lichine. "How can you compare them?" I asked. "It should be Balanchine, of course." So George was hired.

It was a very happy time for the company, rehearsing in California in the summer. The show was about Edvard Grieg, the Norweigan composer, and there was a lot of dancing in it. I did the concerto—my solo was his fantasy as he was composing. I did the ball, "Peer Gynt," and the variations. I was an Italian ballerina, with a little scene of my own and a few lines to speak. And then, at the end, I was an allegorical figure, a maiden personifying Norway. The show was an enormous success, and we had a lot of fun dancing in it. The run was extended.

Unfortunately, the Ballet Russe had already been scheduled to open two weeks later in New York, so *Song of Norway* continued without us. Nobody wanted to leave.

Some people today talk as if ballet choreography has been traditionally a man's domain, but in my day, in the Ballet Russe, there were many women who were respectable choreographers: Antonia Cobos, who did for us *Madroños*; Ruthanna Boris; Ruth Page; Agnes de Mille; Valerie Bettis, whose work was always interesting, always intelligent. It seems to me that there were then more women choreographing ballets than there are today.

Alexandra Fedorova, who was married to Michel Fokine's brother, Alexander, staged the Black Swan and the Sugar Plum Fairy pas de deux for us. She had been a soloist at the Maryinsky, trained at the Theatre School, but her husband managed the Troitzky Theatre in Leningrad, and she went occasionally to work for him, staging little tableaux for variety acts and sometimes appearing herself. She was quite well known, and I thought she did a brilliant job staging these classical divertissements and the full-length *Nutcracker*, which we took with us in a one-act version—the second act—on tour.

In 1949, I myself staged *Paquita*. We needed a classical ballet to close the program, so I pieced together what I remembered of Petipa's choreography from the Maryinsky production and filled in the holes. Eugene Berman designed the set, and Castillo the costumes, so we were beautifully dressed. *Paquita* contains a number of interesting variations and divertissements; I danced in it myself, with Oleg Tupine.

One evening, during one of our seasons at the City Center, I was in the audience watching and suddenly I was summoned backstage by one of the other dancers. "Come quickly," she said, "Lord and Lady Keynes are asking for you." So I rushed to my dressing room and there was Lidia Lopukhova—Lady Keynes—trying on my shoes and trying to stand on her toes. She and her husband invited Mr. B. and me to tea at their suite at the Waldorf. The telephone would ring, and Lord Keynes's secretary would come and interrupt us: "The White House, sir," or "Lord Halifax calling." And then Lidia would say, "No, no, Maynard, come here—Choura is telling us about how she dances *Coppélia*." She was so cute, I thought, wanting to know all about what was happening with the ballet, treating us as if we were her long-lost relations.

In spite of the fact that the Ballet Russe had become more and more American, it was still Russian in spirit. Beginning with Diaghilev, a great wave of Russian art swept across all Europe, and the Americans we took into the Ballet Russe—Danielian, Sono Osato, Nana Gollner, Marc Platoff—were swept by that same wave. We taught them how to dress, how to spend their money, what to bring along on tour, how to be a member of the company, and they adapted; in the end, they were absolutely Russian.

There is something in the Russian character, I believe, an inclination to art, that shows itself in the way Russians fill their everyday lives. Think of the long winters—Russian women look at their windows full of snow and copy the design of the snowflakes in their embroidery. Russians dance without being taught. This can also be said of Americans, I think, and maybe that is why the Ballet Russe felt so much at home in the United States.

But only Russians have the dedication required to carry on the ballet as we did. There was a group of us who stayed with the company year in and year out, in all kinds of weather, and we made the Ballet Russe de Monte Carlo strong. The Marquis de Cuevas asked me to join his company. Ballet Theatre offered me a contract when it was just getting organized. But I didn't want to leave the Ballet Russe, because it was Russian. My security was there. Our company was ballet's family—Massine, Balanchine, everybody came and worked with us.

So when Alicia Markova, Anton Dolin, and Igor Youskevitch left for Ballet Theatre, it was hard to swallow, somehow defeating. They were stars, and they had given us a higher standard. Losing the premiers was not only hard on the company's morale, it was hard on its business, because each time somebody left, there were fewer stars on the roster. Sol Hurok, after twenty years representing the Ballet Russe, dropped us and took on Ballet Theatre, because it was a newer company, with more big names to attract the public. Balanchine took Maria Tallchief and Nicholas Magallanes for his own company. The Ballet Russe was growing weaker and weaker.

Without Massine, Denham was free to act as artistic director. At the time he was patronizing a dancer by the name of Nina Novak, who was also ambitious. She had received her training in Poland, where she had married an American GI; she came to New York and joined the

Ballet Russe. Diaghilev once said of a girl in his company that she was "first in the second division," and that he preferred that she stay there than that she be "second in the first." The same, I thought, applied to Nina Novak.

Her influence grew. Little by little, she took over the casting, rehearsals, everything. She wanted to be artistic director, and she tried to get rid of those of us who had been the backbone of the company, because we knew more about ballet than she did. I saw her performances; I saw the way she was changing *Les Sylphides* in rehearsals. Here and there, she would put her paw into it. Well, to change such a classic—I think it's a pity. It is not permissible, from my point of view. I decided that this was no longer my kind of company and gave Mr. Denham one year's notice.

My last performance as a member of the Ballet Russe de Monte Carlo was in Houston, in December 1951, in *Gaîté Parisienne*, a ballet that had been with me since my first season in the company. Saying my goodbyes, I felt an enormous sadness. Americans, I find, are always looking for an opportunity to move upward, to find something a little better, to improve their position. But Russians, once they get into a company, never budge, and it was this unity that made the Ballet Russe last so long. We had been happy, and with one happiness in hand, one doesn't go seeking another. Mr. Denham often talked about the glory of Russian art; we had spent years showing Russian ballet to the world, and its success, the astonishment and enthusiasm of our audiences, was our reward.

When six years later Denham asked me to return to the Ballet Russe as a guest for its season in New York at the Met, I agreed and asked that he put my name in the publicity so that people would know when I was scheduled to perform. He refused. One night, in the middle of the can-can in *Gaîté Parisienne*, the curtain came down. We were still dancing; the ballet wasn't yet over. But it seems that the evening had run late; and beyond eleven-thirty, Denham had to pay the stagehands and orchestra overtime. So he simply halted the performance. Again I said my goodbyes, disgusted and glad that I was no longer dependent on the company. My life had already taken a more interesting turn.

Thirteen

WHEN I LEFT the Ballet Russe de Monte Carlo in 1951, I didn't just dive—I had invitations from other companies to appear as a guest artist, and an offer to teach. I still loved London, and the affection was mutual—the ballet audience there still cared for me. With pleasure I went to dance with the Festival Ballet, which was then being run by Anton Dolin and Alicia Markova. I found the situation in London changed since the days before the war, when the only real ballet that English audiences knew was what we brought them in the Ballet Russe. By 1951, London had well-established ballet companies of its own. Ninette de Valois had built the Sadler's Wells Ballet into a national institution, and in 1949, while I was still with the Ballet Russe, I had accepted her invitation to appear with the company as a guest artist. There were some fine dancers, I thought; but to the management's way of thinking, there was only one—Margot Fonteyn. Moira Shearer was also a beautiful dancer and a beautiful woman. But Fonteyn became the first truly English ballerina, the first to be classically trained completely in what we now think of as the English tradition.

The English style at that time struck me as indifferent. Now, I think, the English are more expressive in their dancing; back then they restrained themselves in order to be correct. It was as if they were not entirely sure what they were doing, so they were afraid to express themselves. Well, Americans did that in the beginning, too.

To the Festival Ballet, at their request, I brought *Mademoiselle Fifi*, by Zachary Solov. It's a short ballet, with a cast of only three, and a silly plot: both the young man and his papa fall in love with Mademoiselle Fifi. Anton Dolin danced the role of the papa, and Michael Maule danced the young man. Anton and Alicia Markova had returned to London after their years at Ballet Theatre, and it was a great pleasure to see them again. Alicia I found, if I may say so, a little bit swollen-headed. Not with me, but with other people she could be quite difficult. But we had known each other for such a long time that our friendship was not affected.

In 1952, Freddie Franklin and Mia Slavenska had formed their own company in New York—twenty-one dancers in all—and they invited me to appear with them. The Slavenska-Franklin Ballet opened in December 1952, at the New Century Theatre, where we danced for two weeks. On the program was a ballet called *Ballerina*, which Mia choreographed; I danced in it with her. Our season also included Valerie Bettis's *A Streetcar Named Desire*, the pas de deux from *Don Quixote*, Slavenska's *Symphonic Variations* to the music of César Franck, an excerpt from *The Nutcracker*, and *Mademoiselle Fifi*. When our New York season was over, we went out on the road.

Once again, Miss Twysden served as my dresser. The big event in the world at that time was Queen Elizabeth's coronation, which was televised. All the dressers gathered around a TV backstage to watch it. At one point in the ceremony inside Westminster Abbey, a dozen or so representatives of the oldest noble lineages in England rose to their feet, and the camera panned slowly along the row. Miss Twysden looked up from her mending. "Oh," she said, "there's my brother."

Our repertoire in the Slavenska-Franklin Company was good, but the budget was limited, too small to make the productions look chic. People had seen the Ballet Russe and Ballet Theatre, and then along came our little group—well, we couldn't compete. The company lasted a little more than a year, through a tour of Japan and the Philippines. Beyond that, Mia and Freddie couldn't hold it together.

In the meantime, I had accepted an offer to go to Dallas, to teach in a school run by Edith James, a former Denishawn dancer. She had a big studio, but it was only for children, and she wanted to expand it, to offer professional classes. All right, I thought to myself, why not? What is the difference where I am? I had always been interested in teaching, not simply as a job to fall back on but as an extension of my dancing, and I accepted Edith's offer with enthusiasm. Always in the-atrical circles in Russia they say that it isn't the part that makes you, that you make the part, and that was my approach to my position in Dallas: I thought, Well, I will establish a reputation for this school; I will make people come to Dallas. Edith and I worked together well, and in the three seasons I spent there, the studio was very successful.

We made our pupils appear everywhere—at charity functions and debutante balls, at receptions and department stores and museums. There are always opportunities, here and there, for little numbers, and we saw to it that we danced wherever we could, as often as possible.

I always think that in life there must be a goal, something you are working toward—not off somewhere in the future, in the distance, but something on the horizon, close enough that you can see it. The goal I set for my students was a scholarship in New York. I went to John Rosenfield, a dance and film critic for the Dallas *News* who was very well liked and well respected, and asked his help in raising money so that some of my students could go in the summer to study at the School of American Ballet. Each scholarship required five hundred dollars, to cover tuition and living expenses. John got on the phone, called a few of his friends, and in ten minutes he raised several thousand dollars. That summer and every summer for the next four years, we sent two girls to New York, and this boosted the prestige of the school.

In Tokyo, on tour with the Slavenska-Franklin company, I had met a woman by the name of Mme Tachibana. She liked me and liked my dancing, and she said that she wanted me to teach her little girl, that she would send her daughter to Texas to study with me. I didn't pay much attention at the time, because so many mothers come backstage and promise to send their daughters to lessons, and then they don't— it's just *une façon de parler*. But when I arrived in Dallas, I told this story to Edith James and she said, "Choura, you will see. She is Japanese. If she said she will send her daughter, she will." And sure enough, a few months later we received from the consul in Dallas a message: Would we sponsor this little Japanese girl in America? Yes, certainly, we replied. It was wonderful publicity for the school: here I was, having just come from Japan, and now here was a young Japanese dancer sent to study with me. In Dallas, it was a sensation. The girl's name was Asami Maki, and she stayed for two years.

My years in Dallas were happy. I lived in a furnished apartment near the studio, and the girls who had cars would take turns driving me to and from classes. I wasn't worried about performing, but I still thought of myself as a dancer—I practiced every day so that I would be prepared to perform whenever the opportunity came my way again. I met fascinating people. Every Sunday, I went to the symphony, and after the concert people would generally come back to my apartment or to Edith's for supper. It is the same everywhere, I think: a dance studio acts as a magnet for musicians and painters, the most interesting society of any town. People who were just passing through always stopped in to say hello—Salvador Dali, Ernest Ansermet. Dallas was absolutely astounded that I knew all these people.

During the summers, I came back east, home to New York and to my house in New Jersey. On one of those summer trips, my friend P. W. Manchester from *Dance News* invited me to dinner. "Choura, you must come back to New York," she said. "You mustn't bury yourself in Texas." Well, I thought, perhaps it is time for a change.

Alicia and Anton Dolin had gone all over the world with their own little concert group, and then dropped their touring to go back to England and form their own company, the Markova-Dolin Ballet, which became Festival Ballet, with Beryl Grey. I asked my manager, Alfred Katz, for his advice on forming a concert group of my own—I wanted to get a few dancers together and go to the Far East, all over the world, anywhere. The major companies—Ballet Theatre and the Ballet Russe de Monte Carlo—made a regular circuit of cities and towns all over America, and it seemed to me that to go directly to the places they didn't visit would look like an admission on my part that I was now a second-class dancer. So, I thought, why not go where people have never seen ballet and perform works that were suitable for me and my friends? Mr. Katz had the right connections. In 1956, I formed a small troupe, called "Great Moments of Ballet," and he got us our first engagements.

We were only four people—Roman Jasinski and his wife, Mosce-lyne Larkin, Michael Maule, and me. Kurt Neiman, Mia Slavenska's husband, was our stage manager; he also drove the car, a giant-size station wagon.

At the end of our first tour, Hurok asked us to join his series, and then the company changed. Roman and Moscelyne left to settle down in Tulsa, Oklahoma; and Michael Maule came down with hepatitis. So I engaged in their places Bobby Lindgren and his wife, Sonja Taanila, and Freddie Franklin—and off we went.

Freddie and I were great friends, but sometimes we quarreled. Back in the Ballet Russe de Monte Carlo, when Balanchine and I were doing *Raymonda*, I asked Fred if he would dance the principal role with me and he suddenly replied thank you very much, but he was sick and tired of carrying me around the stage. Once, also in the Ballet Russe, he and I were dancing *The Red Poppy*, and I was practicing my pirouettes on the stage before the curtain went up, trying out the floor. And while I was turning, with Fred supporting me, somebody walked across the stage so close to me that I got frightened, jerked my arm, and hit Fred in the mouth, knocking out a tooth. What a drama it was! When Fred went to have the tooth replaced, his dentist couldn't believe that I had done it. "But she's so lovely, so romantic, so ethereal," he said. "How could she do such a thing?" It was incidents like these that over the years brought us close. In every friendship, I think, there are ups and downs, and when Fred joined my company and we started to dance together again, our friendship revived.

We toured all over America and Canada, and abroad to South Africa, South America, the Philippines, Hawaii, and Japan. Our reper-toire varied, but always the program followed the same pattern: we opened with a ballet or divertissement for all four of us, then a solo for each of us, two pas de deux (one for each pair), then something for three, and last, again, something for four. Well, by the end of the evening, no one could believe there were only four of us—"Where is the rest of the company?" they would ask, because our program was so well designed and the repertoire was excellent. We did excerpts from *Les Sylphides* and *Swan Lake*, and the *Sleeping Beauty* pas de deux, the waltz from *Le Beau Danube* and the pas de deux from *Gaîté Parisienne*, which, though they were both waltzes, were completely different in mood— one was Viennese, the other French. I asked Job Saunders, a Dutch dancer I knew from the Ballet Russe de Monte Carlo, to make a ballet for four, and he created *Twilight*, set to Fauré's *Dolly Suite*. I asked Balanchine to adjust *Mozartiana* for a cast of four, and he obliged. We did a slightly rearranged version, without the minuet. We also did his Hands of Fate pas de deux from *Cotillon*. I was touched by George's generosity: he gave us his choreography and refused to take any money for it.

One thing I understood was that the production, no matter how small the scale, had to be first class, so I insisted on live music and engaged William McDermott to be our conductor and travel with us when we went abroad, because we usually performed with an orchestra. In the United States, if the town where we were playing was too small for him to gather an orchestra, we had two pianists to play arrangements of all our music.

In our first year, I earned twenty thousand dollars, which I immediately spent on costumes. To some, this might sound extravagant, especially today, when so many ballets are danced in leotards and tights. A lot of Balanchine's ballets don't demand costumes, because one would lose the movement in them or because the double work is so important and the skirt would get in the way. Also, I think, costumes were sometimes too expensive for the New York City Ballet in its early years. But before Balanchine, costumes were part of the choreography—we would run and our skirts would flow behind us, giving our running an ethereal quality. In a leotard, that same running looks different; often, a leotard obliges you to move differently. I understand why Balanchine didn't "dress" many of his ballets, and I think he was right, but I get lonesome for beautiful costumes. I am always so happy to see Roland Petit's company or some of the other European companies, because they are always so well dressed on stage.

In my own career, I learned the importance of good scenery and costumes. Diaghilev spent a fortune for them. The curtain would go up, and the audience would gasp. If the first thing they see is a letdown, you must fight against that bad impression for the rest of the evening. I knew from experience that costumes provide enchantment, and so I ordered ours—for all of us, even the boys—from Karinska, at a price of about a thousand dollars each. My tutu alone, I remember, cost nearly five hundred dollars. But whatever the difference in price between my tutu and a skimpy little skirt, the effect on the stage was worth every penny. I was grateful that Karinska agreed to dress us, because there was no one better—in her work, she combined an understanding of movement and the mind of a couturier.

Over the course of my career I paid a lot of attention to costumes and how they changed. I think back on the leotards Tchelitchev gave us for *Ode* and laugh when I remember how naked we felt—so naked that we wore our dressing gowns over our costumes until the moment before the curtain went up.

The first real change in the cut of a tutu that I can recall was in Russia, for Kchessinskaya, who commissioned Prince Tchervachidze to make her a costume that would disguise the fact that her legs were short. At that time, all tutus were in the shape of a lampshade, gathered at the waist, like a dirndl skirt. Prince Tchervachidze invented a tutu with a short yoke, slightly lower in the waist. Later, Karinska improved on its cut, making it much lighter and smaller, in the shape of a flower, with layers of many different lengths. In the Ballet Russe de Monte Carlo, she made a special tutu for every ballerina, so that they were not all the same measure—for this one, shorter; for that one, a little longer.

Bébé Bérard, for Massine's *Seventh Symphony* of Beethoven, gave us chiffon dresses, and he mixed the colors—pink, yellow, and blue together—so that the picture was of the sky at sunset. Each dress was in two or three different shades, swirled together, and this idea was later adopted in Paris by the couture, for evening gowns. The skirts literally floated, and this was thanks to Karinska's genius: at the hem, she sewed horsehair, so that the bottom of the skirt didn't cling to our legs.

Karinska made my black tutu for *Mozartiana*, and it was ingenious—not all black tarlatan, because solid black would be too opaque and would "cut" the line of the legs. Instead, she made it in alternating layers, black and pink, so that the effect was still dark but softer.

Miss Twysden had stayed with me and with the wardrobe department during my years in the Ballet Russe. When I formed my own little troupe, I asked her to come along, since she had by that time so much experience in taking care of costumes. Everyone was impressed by the quality of our wardrobe mistress. We had enormous success everywhere, all over the world. My only regret was that I had stayed so long with the Ballet Russe de Monte Carlo and hadn't organized a group of my own sooner.

The time at last arrived when I had to say goodbye to my public and to dancing. My farewell performance was in September 1957, in Japan. Asami's mother, Mme Tachibana, upon her daughter's return home, had founded a company there, and my group went and mixed with hers. I staged for her *Coppélia*, *Swan Lake*, *Paquita*, and taught classes. We stayed together almost three months—one month to rehearse, another two to tour the country. For my farewell, I danced *Raymonda* in Tokyo. At the final curtain, there were flowers, confetti, and tears.

In Russia, we were taught never to touch our knees to the floor when taking a bow unless there was royalty in the house; we were to go on our knees only to royalty or to God. Otherwise, your audience thinks, I conquered her—I made her go on her knees. I think it is more dignified to bow low, in deep révérence. I notice that today ballerinas go on their knees all the time—I suppose they think of it as a gesture of humility. But to my way of thinking, it looks like abject gratitude; it is too much, it's like talking all the time in superlatives—the most, the greatest, the best. And before long, the mediocre is called the best, and the best is nothing special, because there is no longer any name for it; the highest distinction has already been spent. I tell my pupils that they must save their superlatives. In the Theatre School, we had a highest grade of twelve—twelve was perfection. I think in my time only two pupils, Spessivtseva and Doubrovska, finished with a grade of twelve. The rest of us, no matter how good we were, were given eleven, or ten, or nine. After the Revolution, this scale was eliminated completely. But often I think back on it, because it reserved a place in our minds for the utmost. At the end of my last performance, taking my final curtain calls, I spread the flowers I had been sent at my feet, to flatter the senders; and as a gesture of thanks for the support and devotion I had received over the course of my career, I went down on my knee to my audience.

Fourteen

I WAS SAD to finish dancing, but not frightened—I never felt as if the earth were crumbling under my feet. I continued to give myself a class every morning. I knew that I would never leave the ballet, that I would always be connected somehow, through teaching or staging. A teacher performs when she demonstrates for her pupils, especially in a variations class. I perform for my students. I have never stopped performing. I am sorry only that no film exists as a record of my dancing at the peak of my career. Apart from *Spanish Fiesta,* in which my role was very small, there is only one variation, the Sugar Plum Fairy's from the last act of *The Nutcracker,* filmed in South Africa for a cigarette commercial. I saw this years ago and liked it.

The transition from a life lived on the stage to a life lived off the stage was difficult, but the difficulty was primarily social. I lost a lot of friends, because I was no longer a star. My true friends, of course, stayed with me. Financially, I started to run into trouble. I reassured myself that all through my life, whenever the future looked uncertain, something fortunate had happened. But I wasn't relying on an act of God, blindly thinking that He would take care of me. I used my common sense. I knew that if I couldn't find a teaching position in New York, I would have to go to the provinces.

When I left the Ballet Russe, I had sublet an apartment from some friends, the first in a long string of short-term furnished apartments. It was more than ten years before I had a home of my own, apart from my house in the country. I moved here and there, and in between I stayed at the Devon Hotel, on Fifty-sixth Street. From there, I went regularly to practice in one of the studios in Carnegie Hall, and on my way, every day at the same time, I used to run into a gentleman who would nod at me and smile as we passed. Finally, as we had met so many times, one day he bowed and introduced himself: he was Fyodor Lensky, and he had a studio himself in Carnegie Hall, the International Ballet Studio; if one day I would like to teach again, he said, he would be delighted if I would teach for him. "How nice," I said. "Thank you very much," and we parted.

Again I ran into him. "What are you doing?" he asked.

"Oh, nothing," I said.

"Wouldn't you like to teach at my studio?" I wasn't sure. "Come and see it." And he offered to enlarge the studio if I would teach for him. That was a nice gesture, I thought, and finally I agreed. I taught in his studio for two years. We had a very cordial arrangement.

I had left the ballet stage, but I still had a big name, so I was hired to appear in a musical, *Oh, Captain!*, produced by Dan Coleman, Melissa Hayden's husband, and directed by José Ferrer. The captain, played by Tony Randall, had two wives—one in England, one in Paris. He went to visit his French wife, and when he crossed the Channel and reached the Normandy shore, he was greeted by a French girl selling flowers—that was me. I had a few lines; we had a little dance, most of it in pantomime, about going out on the town together. He opened the door, I got in the car, we went to a nightclub, we sat down. Then we danced a little can-can; he said goodbye and went on his way. His French wife was played by Abbe Lane, a nightclub singer appearing in her first big role on Broadway.

We went to Philadelphia for previews, and there the show was cut—every day a little more, because it was too long. One day I was cut—José Ferrer thought that maybe I wasn't necessary. But without me, the captain had to go straight to his French wife—there was no transition, no little scene to let the audience know that he was now on French ground. So the next day I was reinstated.

On opening night, February 4, 1958, I received from Nora Kaye a "gypsy robe," sewn with little good-luck charms from all the Broadway gypsies who had worn it over the years. I had to put it on and run into every dressing room, wishing the entire cast good luck—this was the tradition, a rite of initiation for a dancer appearing for the first time on Broadway. I carried out my duties and, after our opening night, sewed a flower on the robe, then passed it along to another friend from the ballet, who was making her Broadway debut.

Actually, I had been on Broadway twice before. Once, in *The Great Waltz*, the American version of *Waltzes from Vienna*. My part in it in America was a flop—I did the same waltz I had done in London, but here for some reason nobody cared, and I left the show to go back to join the Ballets Russes in Europe. I had also spent two weeks on Broadway in *Song of Norway*, in which the entire Ballet Russe de Monte Carlo participated under Balanchine's direction. It was a magnificent production, a tremendous success, and at the end of our commitment none of us wanted to leave and go back to dancing *Swan Lake*.

This time, my stay on Broadway was much longer, eight months, and I was glad to be in *Oh, Captain!*, to be performing every night—it didn't matter to me that the routine was always the same, though I found Broadway a much less disciplined world than the ballet. I was shocked to see that some of the girls in the chorus used to run from their dressing rooms directly onto the stage, without pausing in the wings to collect themselves or concentrate on what they were about to do. And what was even more extraordinary, we would see each other every night, coming and going, at the stage door, in the corridor, and they would never say "good evening" or "hi" or "boo"—nothing, *nichevo*. The theatre might as well have been a railway station.

I received good reviews for my part in *Oh, Captain!*, and I waited one year for something to follow. Teaching at Lensky's studio, I earned fifty dollars a week, sometimes less. I was having a hard time making ends meet. My bank account was melting fast. One day, I was sitting in my drawing room thinking, What on earth shall I do? when suddenly the telephone rang—it was John Gutman, from the Metropolitan Opera, one of Rudolf Bing's assistant managers, who said, "I am here with

Antony Tudor and we are wondering if you would choreograph the ballet in *La Gioconda* for us."

"How wonderful!" I said. "I would love to do that."

We arranged a time when I would go and see him the following day. And then, when I hung up the telephone, I realized: Ah, *La Gioconda*, the Dance of the Hours—that awful old beaten-up piece of music. I must find an angle, I thought, and I began my research, to see if there was anything in Greek mythology or anywhere that might be useful. But nothing came to me. Finally, I called Miss Twysden and asked her to help. That evening, we met for dinner and discussed the possibilities. She told me about a poem "To Night," by Shelley, in which the Night falls in love with the Day. Perfect, I thought, and I used this poem as the basis for the ballet. It began with the day, with the entrance of Bruce Marks as the Sun, attended by four boys—he entered and immediately did grand pirouette. And then came the Night, who was Lupe Serrano, and they joined each other for the adagio. We stopped the show at every performance. Soon, the Met invited me back to stage the ballets for other operas. I choreographed the "Emperor Waltz" in *The Gypsy Baron* for Violette Verdy and James Mitchell, the polonaise in *Boris Godunov*, the ballets in *La Périchole* and *Adriana Lecouvreur*. They were all successes—in two seasons, I had no failures. I was waiting to be invited to return the next year, and then suddenly I read that the Met had invited Alicia Markova in my place. I was amazed and hurt. If only they had written me a letter, I thought, or called to say, "Thank you very much, such a nice relationship, we are sorry"—anything. But nothing. It was hard to swallow.

I had made new friends who helped me through these times. Miss Twysden had gone to work at B. Altman in the book department, and there she met a salesman, Don Smith, who shared her passion for books and also, they soon discovered, for ballet. Don and I became friends, and when he went to work for Abercrombie & Fitch, he introduced me to Eugene Fraccia, the buyer in the clothing department there. One afternoon a few days before Christmas, Don and Gene called to ask if they could come by. Minutes later, they were at my door, their arms full of packages. "So here you are," I said, "distributing your gifts to all your friends." "Yes," they said, "this one is for you." I opened it. "And this one." I opened that. "And this one. . . ." And so it went. All the packages were for me. There were dresses, a pants suit, a dressing gown—they outfitted me from head to foot, at a time when I couldn't afford to buy anything for myself.

It was through Don and Gene that I met their friend Lermond Dean, a dancer who had studied at the School of American Ballet, danced on Broadway, and switched to dress designing when he injured his knee—he had a degree from Parsons School of Design and today has his own business on Seventh Avenue. Together, these three friends helped me to maintain my image now that I was no longer on the stage.

Lewis Ufland, my manager, also stood by me. I had met him as a young man, in Alfred Katz's office. Katz had trained him, but Lewis by that time was trying to open his own agency. "Well, then," Katz said, "here is Choura, your first client." To Lewis I owe my second career. When I finished dancing with the Ballet Russe, he suggested that I give lectures about ballet, about how it was in Russia, about Diaghilev and my career in America. I wrote the lecture with Miss Twysden's help, and through Columbia Artists I received some engagements, mostly in women's clubs in the Midwest and the South. Lewis came to hear me speak; he made corrections and suggestions and gave me the encouragement I needed. I continued to lecture on occasion for several years.

But whatever money I made slipped quickly away. I had no savings. At the end of my years with the Ballet Russe de Monte Carlo, as a prima ballerina, I received $350 a week, which was considered a big salary for a dancer. By that time we had a union, and it provided for us to be paid extra for extra rehearsals and established a higher scale for our wages—before that, for most of my career, I earned $200 or so a week. There was never enough to put anything aside. I was sitting in a boat with many holes in it—I owed money here and there, and it seemed that I would never pay it back. I would plug one hole only to discover that another was leaking. One day, I ran into Balanchine—as usual, on the street. "What are you doing?" he asked me.

I said, "Nothing. I really needed something, so I'm teaching."

"Why don't you come and teach the variations you remember?"

"What variations?" I asked, rather stunned.

"You think and tell me," he said, and he turned on his heel and walked off, leaving me standing there with my mouth open.

I went home and cried a little bit, made myself a drink, and then took myself in hand. Sit down, I said to myself, and think what you can do. *Coppélia, Raymonda*, several old ballets came to mind. So I called Balanchine, and soon I was teaching at the School of American Ballet.

First, I did excerpts from *Coppélia*—the *padrugi*, or friends, and the adagio, and then some variations. My pupils worked hard. When after a few weeks I thought that the time had come for the other teachers to have a look, I invited them to my class. "Come and see what I do, how you like it," I said. And everybody looked startled that I would ask. Nobody came. They weren't interested. They were busy teaching their own classes.

I taught for a month, and Mr. B. didn't come, didn't come, until finally I picked up the telephone and said, "I am working and I don't know if I am on the right path. Will you please look? Tomorrow." He came then and looked and said, "Yes, you are on the right path." And then I could proceed. I was at the time teaching both for Lensky and for Balanchine. I wasn't on the faculty at SAB, I was just teaching this one variations class. After a year, in 1964, Balanchine found me a place on the faculty, and then I left Lensky and his studio at Carnegie Hall to devote myself to my new position.

Opportunities to perform still came my way from time to time. I was asked to do some Chinese role at a musical theatre in Connecticut, but I refused. I always refused, unless I was asked to play the part of a dancer, something I understood. I was invited by Harold Prince to go back on Broadway, to appear with Alexis Smith in a show called *Follies*. I couldn't decide whether to do it or not, so finally I called George, to ask his advice. "If you need the money badly," he said, "then go. All they want is your name." By that time, I had some security. I no longer needed to accept every offer for the money it paid. And, in spite of the fact that I was still in good form, it seemed to me that my career on the stage was finished. To perform, you must be on the stage continually, otherwise you develop bad nerves and your stage presence disappears—before long, your personality doesn't come across anymore. I knew that it would take a couple of months to get my bearings back, and that the public would expect to see me as they remembered me. To come back, I thought, is always a disappointment, for everybody. And so I said no. When I went to see the show, I was glad—I saw that I would have returned in the role of an old lady with a past, which is not very flattering.

In 1976, I was asked by Herbert Ross to appear in a movie, *The Turning Point*, which he was directing. I knew him through the ballet—he was a former dancer and choreographer, the husband of Nora Kaye, and this movie was to be about ballet. In it, I played myself—a Russian teacher, a former prima ballerina coaching a young dancer in my roles. We were never allowed to see daily rushes during the filming—Herb said that some people get very upset watching themselves, and it spoils their performance. So I first saw myself at a screening, just before the movie opened. Well, they say that when you see yourself on film you're always at first shocked and disappointed. Maybe the problem is that we think we're prettier and cleverer than we really are. In any case, I didn't recognize myself. I know your profile, and you know mine, but we don't know our own. I saw myself on the screen and thought, Who is that woman? That woman is saying my lines!

No, I wasn't about to pack my bag and leave for Hollywood. By this time, teaching at the School of American Ballet had become my life. Over the years, Balanchine asked me to stage excerpts from *Paquita*, *Le Pavillon d'Armide*, *The Sleeping Beauty*, *Swan Lake*, *Raymonda*—the ballets we were brought up on in Russia. I would teach the choreography as I remembered it, then Mr. B. would come to a rehearsal and okay what I had done or give the finishing touches, suggest that I do this instead of that.

Students today have trouble dancing in the classical style—it is different from what they are used to, the movement is more tightly framed. But also, I think, they don't always understand what these ballets are about. A ballet like *The Sleeping Beauty*, for example, is a souvenir from an era when the world was a different place. It is late-nineteenth-century Russia looking back over its shoulder at eighteenth-century France; it is a picture of the Sun King's court painted by Petipa and Tchaikovsky. Most young dancers today approach *The Sleeping Beauty* as if it were an antique, too fragile to touch—they tiptoe gingerly around it. I try to explain the ballet to them in the terms of the world we live in today. *The Sleeping Beauty*, I tell my pupils, is like the royal wedding of Prince Charles and Lady Diana. The pas de deux is not a love story—it is purely ceremonial, very elegant and cool, for the benefit of society. There is no flirtation, no kissing; it is a public dance by the princess and her fiancé.

The variations in the Prologue need deciphering for dancers today. The fairies bestow their gifts on the newborn princes, and I explain to my students what each variation stands for. One fairy brings prosperity, symbolized by breadcrumbs—our daily bread. Another brings beauty, symbolized by flowers. The songbird fairy gives to the princess a lovely, musical voice. The so-called "finger variation" is about fate, which pushes you first here, then there, the fingers always pointing. The version of this variation I teach was choreographed by Nijinska. There was a finger variation in Russia—she modernized it and added a few things, and her version became standard in the Diaghilev repertoire.

I love *The Sleeping Beauty*, and if I were twenty years younger, I would stage the entire ballet and set it in New Orleans during Mardi Gras. The Prologue would be a big reunion, in a beautiful mansion. In the last act, the party would include variations by people dressed for Carnival as fairy-tale characters, and by the Precious Stones, who embody the qualities of different gems. (It was these variations, I think, that gave Balanchine the idea, on a larger scale, for his ballet *Jewels*.)

Together, Balanchine and I staged *Coppélia* for the New York City Ballet, in 1974. The ballerina role is a marvelous opportunity for a dancer to display her personality—there is a lot of dancing, with variations in several different moods. I worked with Patricia McBride, who I thought looked perfect for the part, exactly like a doll. I would show her the steps, and then Balanchine would come in at the end of our rehearsal and add a little, finishing up what I had started. I did the first two acts and he did the last. In my acts, the choreography remained basically the same as before, but sometimes we found it too simple—there were empty places, and Balanchine filled them in. He made the dancing a little more up-to-date and complicated the movement, mostly in the variations and parts of the adagio. The dances between Swanilda and her friends and the business with Coppélius and the doll he didn't touch.

Around 1938, when I was with Denham.

In the Denham *Swan Lake*.

In *Saratoga*, with
Freddie Franklin.

In *The Red Poppy.*

With the Slavenska-
Franklin company in
Mademoiselle Fifi.

3

With Oleg Tupine in
the Denham *Paquita*.

My own touring group:
Moscelyne Larkin is seated;
Michael Maule is on my
left; Roman Jasinski is on
my right.

In the Denham *Beau Danube* with Igor Youskevitch.

At my country place in New Jersey with Freddie Franklin,
in the early forties.

Getting married in Los Angeles in 1941. Left to right, David Libidins, me,
Koschka, Efrem Kurtz, Alicia Markova, Mrs. Libidins.

Above, making up for
Sonnambula; left, in my
Snow Queen costume
from *Nutcracker,* with
Freddie Franklin.

Left, with Leon Danelian in *Danses Concertantes*; below, in an early version of *Serenade* with Freddie Franklin.

Opposite, in *La Sonnambula* (then called *Night Shadow*) with Freddie Franklin.

Above, in *Song of Norway*; opposite, in
Mozartiana.

With Zulu warriors in South Africa.

About to go on safari in Kenya.

South America, on our way to Bogotá.

On the beach at Monte Carlo.
Above, with Alicia Markova, Anton
Dolin, Freddie Franklin; right, all alone.

Life with Alicia: top, on tour in America in the forties; center left, in Paris together, after the war; center right, picking flowers in New Jersey; bottom, together just two years ago at the Ballets Russes reunion in Houston.

Left, in Japan for the first time; below, in a teaching convention in Chicago in the fifties; opposite top, working with Misha Baryshnikov in Hamburg in 1976; opposite bottom, helping Mr. B. re-create *Coppélia*. The dancers are Helgi Tomasson and Patty McBride. Seated are Lincoln Kirstein, Mr. B., and myself. Overleaf, my farewell performance in Tokyo. Rose petals fall from the rafters.

In the third act, everything was Balanchine's idea—all the movements were new, but of course in the classical style.

It is ironic, I suppose, that for most of my career I appeared in new ballets, by choreographers who were avant-garde, and now, in my teaching, I have become a guardian of the classical style. Well, I have simply done what was needed for the advancement of my art. When I was young, the classics were safely enshrined in the Maryinsky repertoire; it was fresh air, innovation, a new language of movement that we needed. But now, I think, it is a solid understanding of the classics that is lacking, especially here in America, and I direct my energies toward that.

A few years ago, I was at a dinner party attended by Natalia Makarova, and after dinner she asked me to show her a variation from Fokine's *Le Pavillon d'Armide.* "Oh, how awful, just dreadful!" she said. "It's so old-fashioned." And I became furious. "Natasha," I scolded her, "I think you with your dancing are much more old-fashioned than Mr. Fokine." I can see in the Soviet style an extension of the way I was trained, but I think what happened here in ballet in our century is much more interesting than what happened there. The capital of the ballet world has in my lifetime moved from St. Petersburg to New York City, and I have been one of the few to witness every stage of the shift. Somehow, in Russia, ballet has become the exhibition of dancing. Soviet dancers no longer want to show the story or the mood so much as they want to show their technique—this one can turn three times in the air, lifting both his legs, and that one can do something else. But it's no longer expression; it's exhibitionism.

The best of what goes on in ballet here is to my way of thinking better than what goes on anywhere else in the world, but I would never go so far as to say that everything is marvelous. Sometimes, I wonder what will become of ballet in the hands of the next generation. Twyla Tharp, for instance—people tell me how inventive she is, but I don't see it. What did she invent? She made a ballet with Jerome Robbins for the New York City Ballet, and to me it is chaos. There is no design. One person does one thing, another person does another, a third person does a third—apparently, there are people who find all this activity going on at once exhilarating, but I am not excited by it. It makes me mad. The dancers were not partnered; they were dragged around the stage by the armpits. I watch and think to myself, Is it worth it to do battements tendus and perspire every day in order to be able to do this? I think break dancers on the street are often more interesting, because they at least have their own style.

After Miss Twysden died, in 1978, I sold my house in the country. Every weekend for years, she and I had gone there together and entertained my friends. Once, on a trip to London, I met her family, who were all charming. They couldn't understand why she didn't want to live in England, and frankly neither could I, except that she loved Russians so much—our art, our music, our way of living. She knew Russian history and literature better than most of us who were born in Russia. I think she felt more at home with us than with the English.

At the end of her life, she thanked me for the wonderful times we had had together. The terrible thing is, I never loved her. She was so devoted to me—blindly, I thought—that it annoyed me. How can you respect someone who gives up her own life and moves in on yours? Friends used to say that she was secretly in love with me; but if so, she knew enough to keep it a secret. I found her bossy, possessive, and often jealous. She lived in one small room in the Wellington Hotel, a block from my apartment, and would always insist on coming over to cook for me, or if I was going out, to help me dress. But despite her good intentions, she was never any help. "Miss Twysden does everything for me," I used to tell my friends, "—badly." She brought out something mean in me, a part of myself I dislike. Even so, it's true that she taught me a lot—about history and nature, about the philosophy of life, for which I am very grateful. Being brought up during the Bolshevik era in Russia, I had only one point of view, one narrow angle, because that was the way we were taught to think, that was what the Party dictated; I was very limited. But Miss Twysden showed me that other people could have different points of view, and she taught me to respect their opinions.

When you have no relatives, other people in your life come to take the place of family—Miss Twysden, for one, and Balanchine. When I had an important decision to make, when I sold my house and bought myself an apartment, I talked to George and took his advice. I always knew that if something tragic happened, I could go to him and he would help me. In the years since I began teaching for him at SAB, we saw more of each other, but only on matters of ballet, strictly business.

Even so, there was a bond between us; we shared a past that stretched all the way back, beyond Diaghilev, to the Theatre School and our youth.

Most of our conversations took place in passing—on the street, in the corridors. Two years before he died, we met one day at the school and he said, "No more romances for me, no *mariages*, thank you very much," and he bowed. "I am interested only in art." And we laughed at the effects of our old age. For most of his career, I think, art and romance were all wrapped up together—there was no distinguishing between them. There was about the roles he made for women something special. Each woman is a little fascinating, somehow complex, and Balanchine liked to discover that enigma in each of us. In every ballet, there was that romantic thread, spun in the choreography and extending from him to his ballerina. This is true, I find, even in ballets that have nothing to do with romance, like *Kammermusik No. 2*, which is like an IBM machine.

A year before he died, George organized a festival in honor of Tchaikovsky at the New York City Ballet. It was then, I think, that he began to prepare himself to leave this life. In all Tchaikovsky's music there is that tragic note, and Balanchine seemed to hear that aspect more clearly than before. He must have had some premonitions about his death. His thoughts, I found, had already moved beyond the concerns of this world. He was no longer with us.

He spent his last few months in the hospital, where I went to visit him twice. The first time, he looked at me: Who is she? Ah, Choura. And what to say? Nothing, really. It was difficult. We talked about when he first went to Switzerland, when I accompanied him to the sanatorium there, and about how beautiful the mountains were. He wanted to go to Switzerland again, this time to stay, he said. He wanted to look at the mountains again, to be with nature. The second time I went to visit, it was to say goodbye. But he was asleep, and I didn't want to wake him. Two weeks later, he died.

I thought of all that we had shared and of all the times when we would be in situations that brought back some person we had known, some incident we had lived through, some joke we shared, and I would say to him, "You see? Remember that?" When he died, I realized that I have nobody to say that to anymore. There is nobody left.

Fifteen

ONE HAS TO HAVE a talent for teaching—a separate talent, different from the kind that makes a great performer. The greatest performers don't always make the greatest teachers, and certainly the greatest teachers have not always been great performers themselves. For instance, Preobrajenskaya in her time was an interesting ballerina—she was innovative, and she was an actress. But she couldn't pirouette very well. Later, when she became a teacher with her own studio in Paris, she became famous for her ability to teach her pupils to turn; Irina Baronova, Tamara Toumanova, all the girls she taught could pirouette exceptionally well. And Egorova was certainly a better teacher than she was a dancer. At the Maryinsky, she danced mainly *Swan Lake* because she had such beautiful arms, but she was not really a prima ballerina, though she later became a first-class teacher. So I don't think it's necessary to have been a great dancer to be a great teacher, but it does help; it adds something. A great ballerina, if she is willing and has a gift for teaching, has more to offer her students—she can coach them not only in technique but in actual roles, telling them, "Here you must rest," or "Before this step you must pull yourself together and concentrate," or "Here you must stop thinking and just go." There are certain tricks that only a ballerina knows. By teaching, you hand down the secrets of your trade to the next generation of dancers, who can profit by them.

I was lucky enough to study with the best teachers of my time. Traveling and dancing all over the world, I could compare one teacher's method with another's and borrow from them all. When I teach, I give my pupils combinations I learned from Mme Egorova, from M. Legat, from Mme Nijinska, from M. Fokine, from Mme Vaganova and the rest of my teachers at the Theatre School. When I was a student myself, I noticed that some teachers were knowledgeable but very dull, and my classmates and I didn't dance our best for them. Other teachers who were perhaps not so expert impressed us with their energy and made us work harder. There were teachers who somehow communicated to us that they cared; there were others who seemed indifferent. The best had patience, which I think is essential.

Students can always sense which teachers care about them and which do not. I love my pupils and try to show them understanding. Some are shy and need encouragement; others are what I call "blue jays"—they think well of themselves and go all the time to the front row, where they will be seen. I tell my pupils, "You must come forward and fight for your place. You must not be soft. The angels do not come down and get you. You must step forward and nominate yourself."

There must be a thread of good will, a feeling of warmth and fondness, that extends from me, the teacher, to each student. It is important that they know that I care about them, not because I tell them so but by the way I work with them. I don't hesitate to criticize my pupils, but I never insult them. Sometimes I scream at them, but always with love.

I dislike teachers who try to work their way into the souls of their pupils and become their friends. A good teacher should not be afraid of being unpopular. If there is a step your pupils are afraid of, you must give it to them over and over again, until finally they say to themselves, Oh, this teacher annoys me so, I will do the step, just to make her stop. I believe that there should be a respectful distance between a teacher and her pupils, but the respect should not be founded on fear. The teacher who inspires fear in her pupils is working against herself, because her students, if they are scared, will be too tense to dance well. Instead, I think, a teacher must win the respect of her pupils—you must prove to them during the course of the lesson that you know more than they do, that they have something to gain from you, and once you have done that, they are yours. If you have a pupil who can't do two pirouettes, you must tell her what to do in order to turn. "All right," you say, "your way isn't working, so now please try it my way." And if you help her, if she does two pirouettes correctly, she will place her confidence in you from then on.

Class begins at the barre. When I began to teach, Mr. Vladimiroff told me, "The human body is a delicate mechanism, like a racing car—you must warm it up carefully and thoroughly before you race it." It is at the barre that you warm your muscles and get your bearings. You find your balance there—you can concentrate on certain movements, to get the feel of doing them correctly, before you stand on your own two feet in the middle of the floor. The barre gives you a third leg—you begin class with three legs and then you finish with two.

Even though the exercises follow the same pattern every day, I watch my pupils carefully when they are at the barre to make certain that they are executing the basic movements and positions correctly. Each day, I begin with half pliés in first and second position, then deep pliés: grand plié, port de bras, grand plié, balance. First, second, fourth, and fifth positions—one side, then turn the other way. Next I do battements tendus, first with pliés, then without pliés, then quick battements tendus—always varied, never set. These are followed by battements tendus jetés.

At the School of American Ballet, we don't insist that the children turn out the legs too much the first year, because if you force the turnout before they have the strength to maintain it, they roll over on their feet. But in the second year, we demand more and more turnout, particularly at the barre. At the barre, where you are more or less stationary, you can work more turned out than in the center—you don't need to maintain your turnout in motion, and you have the help of your "third leg" for support. So beginning in the second year, we require that our students turn out more than is comfortable for them, until finally they reach a perfect fifth position—the toe of each foot exactly even with the heel of the other.

Some people disagree and say that the second year is too early to ask for a perfect fifth position, that the children are too young. It's true that in the beginning, fifth position is difficult for them. But children are soft—you can take their legs in your hands and just turn them—and I give them exercises that turn out the heel, the thigh, the whole leg. For instance, I do battements tendus with a plié in fourth position, then relevé, to develop the turnout in the thigh. I demand good turn-out as soon as possible, because if dancers acquire it early on, it stays with them. For the rest of their lives, a perfect fifth position comes automatically.

I teach classical exercises, and I demand that they be done exactly as they should be done. If students want to be serious, the teacher must pay close attention to details, because in classical ballet if a fifth position isn't right, it's wrong—there is no room for interpretation. But if people want to do popular dancing—to go on Broadway, for example—then it doesn't matter so much how their fifth position goes. (Lately, it has become fashionable among the older students and some members of the company, the New York City Ballet, to exaggerate the fifth position and overcross the feet—I call this "tenth position," and I refuse to accept it in my classes.) It is up to my pupils after they finish school how they do the movements, how they execute fifth position; but during my class, they must do it precisely right.

After battements tendus, I give ronds de jambe—first, par terre; then grands ronds de jambe en l'air. This is the movement—développé and carry the leg all the way around, from the front to the side to the back—that develops height in extension. I proved this to myself when I was teaching in Dallas. I ran an experiment in my classes: we did grands ronds de jambe regularly, and my pupils all had big extensions.

When I was growing up in the Theatre School, a high extension was considered vulgar, and even Margot Fonteyn never raised her leg higher than her waist. It is only because of Balanchine, who wanted the leg higher, that dancers have begun to develop their extensions, and I personally agree with Mr. B. The leg in développé should not be stopped; if it is, the movement becomes stiff and mechanical. Instead, I think the leg should just go, reaching upward; the movement must be free if it is to be graceful.

Most dancers today think that a high extension comes from

stretching, and they stretch and stretch—they tear their muscles, stretching them farther than they have the strength to support. This stretching has become an obsession—just because Mary can stretch her legs behind her ears, so must everybody else in the class! My students come to class and first thing, they do hard stretches. I warn them constantly: "If you want to stretch, do it after exercises at the barre, when your muscles are warm and limber." I say this over and over, I bang my head against the wall, but they don't listen. They tear their legs apart. I see them sitting between rehearsals in grand écart, in a split, and say, "Why don't you do your two pirouettes that are not so hot instead? Why don't you work on something that is important? How high can you do développé? Higher than your head?" It becomes ridiculous.

Instead of so much stretching, I give my pupils exercises that concentrate on the muscle at the top of the thigh, to control the leg—slow ronds de jambe, or grands battements. A grand battement by itself is not enough, because you can kick the leg and never hold it. I make my pupils hold the leg at the top, to build strength at the height of their extensions.

These are exercises that must be done correctly and with care; otherwise they can overdevelop the muscles of the thigh. Looking back, I realize that many of the girls I grew up with at the Theatre School had big calves and thighs, overdeveloped because they had overworked those particular muscles. Mr. B., when he taught, was always very conscious of which muscles he was working and was careful not to abuse them. Sometimes, for example, he would make us do sixty-four battements tendus, but he would break them up—sixteen on one side, sixteen on the other side, sixteen and sixteen, or variations, not all the same and not all in one gulp. I don't allow my pupils to "sit" in any position or to abuse their legs with harsh accents. "Don't force the movement," I tell them. "Just do it gently." The movement should always be soft and very elastic.

After fondus and frappés, I do adagio and then petits battements sur le coup de pied, to warm up the knees, then ronds de jambe en l'air, which I save for last because they require a highly complicated use of the knee and you must be very warmed up in order to do them correctly. I give rond de jambe en l'air en dehors, en dedans, with a plié, sometimes with a jump—everything, always different.

I take teaching very seriously, and I like to sit in on other teachers' classes to see how they go about things differently. Many teachers become famous for their methods—Cecchetti, for instance—structuring their lessons a certain way or giving the same sequence of exercises every Wednesday one way, every Monday the same. But to my way of thinking, it's a mistake for a teacher to settle on a system like that. The exercises at the barre are like the Bible, more or less the same wherever you go. But the exercises in the center of the floor vary greatly from one teacher to the next, and that is where the true art of teaching lies. In the center, you must get your student on balance, make her turn, make her jump, make her graceful, make her dance.

In the center, I begin with adagio, then battements tendus and fondus, usually in combinations with some sort of fancy pirouettes. There are students who are afraid to turn—for their benefit, I lead up to pirouettes gradually. I structure my class in such a way that they are prepared to turn. "What is a turn but a balance?" I tell my classes. It is all in the placement, which is very important—only dancers and flamingos stand so much on one leg.

I give my pupils the opportunity to practice their balance first at the barre, by ending nearly every exercise combination with a balance. This is the way we were taught in Russia, where good balance was admired to the same extent that a high jump, for example, is admired today. Anna Pavlova used to take a position and stay by herself, unsupported—that was one of her tricks, and ballerinas everywhere copied her until eventually it became boring. Somebody once described to me another ballerina's performance. "You must see her to believe it," he told me. "She stays so long on one toe!" Well, I thought, so what? I am too busy dancing. These long balances that used to bring down the house and bring the performance to a halt are out of fashion now, no longer in good taste; but dancers must still learn how to hold a long balance, for the sake of their pirouettes. I was taught by Mme Egorova and M. Legat to do balances at the barre and half-turns to practice my placement, and I do the same for my pupils, so that full pirouettes, doubles, triples, and turns in sequence come more easily in the center.

But to be a really good teacher, one must be also a psychologist, able to build in your pupils the confidence they need to dance without hesitation or holding back, to help them overcome their fears, to soothe their minds. They are anxious because they are not sure that they will do the turn, and already they doom themselves. "If you fall," I say, telling them what Mme Vaganova told me, "you will sit on the floor—it is right underneath you. It won't be like falling from the second story."

I teach my students to take the preparation, the plié before the pirouette—or before the jump or any big movement—very quickly, to disguise it as best they can so that the turns seem to come out of nowhere. In Russia, we are told that the preparation shouldn't be seen, because if you prepare and prepare, the audience begins to expect a miracle and then, when you do your two or three pirouettes, no matter how nicely, the audience is disappointed.

There are different schools of thought on the subject of the proper position for pirouettes. At the Royal Ballet, for instance, they place the foot lower than we do. Here, in general, we turn with the foot at the knee—just under the knee, not above, because from there the knee can come forward and stop your momentum. The toes should be below the knee in front or in back, but never directly to the side, which looks crablike and not at all pretty.

Balanchine insisted that his dancers relevé by rolling up and down through the foot, instead of hopping onto pointe, all in one movement. I respect his thinking, of course, but in my classes I teach relevé as I learned it in Russia—not rolling through the foot but using the knee and pushing with the heel; this enables you to make the transition to pointe more quickly. For a relevé that travels, they have to jump onto pointe. So it is necessary for dancers today to know both ways.

The one "trick" that I pass along to my students to help them in pirouettes is that they must think of closing two arms, not just one. From the usual preparation—right arm forward and left arm out to the side—one begins the turn by opening the right arm and closing the left. But this leaves some dancers lopsided and off-balance—they close one arm and forget all about the other, as long as it is hanging there in place. "You look like invalids," I tell them. "You are healthy people, you have two arms. Please use them both." And then, somehow, they are straighter and in balance.

After turns, I do allegro, exercises designed to get my pupils to move fast. Again, I use psychology: I make them go one way, then the other—jeté to the right, turn to the left, moving constantly with all sorts of changes of direction, so that their muscles can never settle into some comfortable position or predict where they are going next. Dancers get sluggish when they are fed a diet of combinations that are familiar to them. Ah yes, they think, here it will be plié, now it will be jump. Their reaction time gets slower. I try continually to surprise my students, to catch them off their guard. Just at the moment when they think they will do a plié, that is where I make them jump instead.

When they jump, I tell my students that however the foot departs from the floor, that is how the foot must land, so that they come down by rolling through the foot, with the knee turned out. Otherwise, they can hurt themselves.

The way dancers use their feet has changed tremendously since I was a student, and I think that Balanchine helped to bring about the change. When I danced *Mozartiana*, or any of his ballets, I used to do my exercises faster, particularly battements tendus, to make my feet quicker. But Mme Egorova was also going along with the time, speeding up the standard for allegro and making us work more lightly on our feet on pointe, so that our weight didn't sink into our shoes. Massine's ballets demanded a lot of dancing on the toes, much more than the old classics we were raised to dance in Russia. Today, the girls in the New York City Ballet work much more on the toes than we did, taking class on pointe, rehearsing, performing—as a result, they have steel pointes.

At the end of the lesson, pupils should want to do more. That is what my teacher M. Legat told me. Some dancers say, "Oh, we had such a marvelous class, I can't move." Well, from my point of view, that is a very bad class. Class is for teaching people how to do things; the idea is not to exhaust them and leave them with their tongues hanging out, like dogs who have been taken for a run around the block. A good class is one that seems too short. "Ah, what a pity," you say. "The lesson is finished already."

Most of the dancers I teach are very capable: they fall short mainly in the way they use their arms, and sometimes they forget to use them at all. Arm positions to these dancers are an afterthought, to be added only when the legs and feet are perfect. When these dancers do decide to use their arms, the position is usually dreadful, not precise and often not pretty. In second position, for instance, we were taught—and I teach my students—that the arms should always be slightly lower than the shoulder, not at the same height; otherwise, you look like a scarecrow. This is a difference of at most a few inches, but it matters a great deal in the way you present yourself to your audience.

In other countries—in England, Denmark, and still in Russia—dancers are more careful with their arms. At the Royal Ballet, for instance, they dance with their fingers together, which I have always thought makes their hands look like spoons. The English port de bras is a little bit Victorian, slightly affected. In Balanchine's choreography, the arms are freer. As a result, our girls have a tendency to throw their arm positions away, and so when they are given something classical to dance, they don't know where the arms should be in relation to the feet. I teach my students classical variations that force them to think all the time about the whole body. I want them to understand that arms are more than decoration, that arms are like violins, for expression.

The classical port de bras is full of gestures outward. I tell my girls, "It's like the Oriental greeting—you touch your fingertips to your forehead, to your lips, to your heart, and then make a small bow, meaning, 'My thoughts, my speech, my heart are yours.' " When you bourrée, I tell them, unfolding your arms, you give your heart. Fifth position, arms overhead, framing the face, should be automatic, like a soldier's salute: "Attention!"

Many dancers harbor tension in their hands. I tell them what Yeichi Nimura, the famous Japanese dancer, said to me. I was dancing *Swan Lake*, and I thought my arms weren't very good, not soft enough. So I asked his advice. "Make a fist," he said, "then let it go." In this way, the fingers relax and soften.

Americans are hard-working, ambitious, and impatient. They want to get better faster. Already, the training that took seven years in Russia we have condensed to five. Russians are maybe more perfectionist. To my way of thinking, six years would be better than five; but generally speaking, for somebody very talented, five is enough. Some students, however, make up their minds that instead of taking class once a day every day they will take class three times a day and make progress three times as fast. They dance too much. I think it's terrible—they ruin their legs, they get overblown muscles in their calves and thighs, and in class their legs are so tired that they can't work correctly. Dancers need rest, as much as they need exercise.

They must learn to measure their energy. After they are taken into the company, the demands on their bodies are even greater and it is easier for them to overwork, because they are trying to make an impression and advance. After class in the morning, they have rehearsal, which is the equivalent of another class, and then usually a performance in the evening. Many dancers when they get tired simply stop going to class. They are called for rehearsal, they must perform, they need their sleep. Or perhaps they think that because they have roles to dance, because they are a success on the stage, they no longer need to struggle with themselves in class. They are mistaken. I tell them that this is the most important time of all to take class, when they are tired. They must go and do only the exercises at the barre—not relax and sleep—and then relax the next day; this is according to Mme Vazem, who was our famous coach in Russia, and Pierina Legnani, who was a remarkable technician. Their advice was never to miss class. It is in class that you place yourself, you purify your technique; it is by performing that you become stronger. A dancer's life must consist of both, class and performance, or else it cannot go forward.

At the other extreme, there are dancers who are better in the studio than they are on the stage—they are what we call "classroom performers." There are some in every company. These dancers, no matter how proficient they may be, are not real artists. A real artist is awakened on the stage.

In technique classes, I teach my pupils how to execute classical movements; in variations classes, they must interpret those movements. It is by dancing great choreography that they learn style. For instance, I teach them a variation from *Swan Lake*. "Don't forget that your arms are no longer arms, they are wings," I tell my pupils. This is exercise for the imagination. In class, of course, arms are always arms, nothing else. Many girls dance very well but have no attack. I tell them that they must announce themselves; they must arrive nicely and say to the audience, "Here I am."

I teach variations from *Paquita* and *Coppélia*; from the Kingdom of the Shades scene in *La Bayadère*; from *Les Sylphides*; from *The Sleeping Beauty*, including all the fairies' variations and the ballerina's from the first and last acts; variations for the ballerina and the soloists from the first-act dream scene and the Pas Hongrois from *Raymonda*. The style is always purely classical, but there are different flavors—Hungarian, Oriental,

Spanish. I look and see what my students are lacking: if this class needs relevés, I give them the variation with sixteen relevés at the end. If that class's pirouettes are not so good, I give them a variation with lots of turns.

Each day, I prepare them for the next lesson. We start out doing one-third of the variation; tomorrow we will do a little more than we did today. In this way, they develop their endurance. Classical variations are difficult because they provide no opportunities for relaxation. All the time you must carry yourself, you can never for a moment let go. "You start a variation and you must finish it," Mr. B. told me, and I tell my pupils the same. In class, you do the assigned combination and then you go aside and rest. But a variation consists of many combinations, without stopping, and by dancing it straight through, you grow strong enough to go on the stage.

For this reason, because it is the most rigorous, classical ballet is still the best method of training. If you can dance classical ballet, you can dance anything; but the reverse doesn't work, it isn't true. The laws that govern classical dancing are strict: there are five positions of the arms and feet and nothing in between. All classical choreography is based on those five positions, and when you dance, they must be clear and absolutely correct. First position, we were taught in Russia, is arms directly opposite your soul—rounded in a circle in front of you. Your soul lives here, in your chest, in the hollow at the base of your ribs, in the region called the solar plexus. That's first position, and in classical ballet, it is the gate to all other positions. Everything classical passes through first position: wherever you're going, on your way to arabesque or développé à la seconde or sous-sous, your arms must pass through the gate.

Mr. Balanchine in his choreography invented a lot of movements, but always he kept the five classical positions as a base, and so we call his choreography "neoclassical." If Petipa would have you lift one leg slowly, Balanchine would in the same measure have you lift the leg twice or move the arms twice as fast. Even when he was restaging the old ballets, in the classical style, Balanchine adjusted certain movements to make them more interesting for our time. The life that we live now bears almost no resemblance to life as we lived it when I was a child: now we live faster, travel faster, so it makes sense that dancing should be faster. Ballet has changed to keep up with the tempo of life.

Mostly I would say that the slight revisions Balanchine introduced involve speeding up the movement or syncopating movements that in classical dancing are rhythmically very even. Pas de bourrée, for instance, in Petipa would be: one, two, three. But in Balanchine's choreography, it would be slightly different: for example, one-and-two, hold three—the first two steps are faster, so that you get where you're going more quickly. Or, another instance, the old way of doing pas de chat is to lift one leg, then the other—one at a time. But Balanchine sped up the timing so that the second leg immediately follows the first and you see a clear position—both legs up—in the air. Balanchine took classical ballet steps and sharpened the focus, so that you see a perfect fifth position or a jump at its height, and the time it takes the dancer to get from one position to the next is shorter, because she moves faster in between.

When I began teaching, Balanchine told me, "Do whatever you want." We agreed on the basics of the technique, of course, because we came from the same school. I think I am very lucky to have been brought up in Russia at a time when the Theatre School was the best in the world, raised by teachers who were all qualified in the classical style, the Petipa style—it is Petipa by whom we swore in Russia. For the Danes, it is Bournonville; and for America now I think it will be Balanchine. Certain things I do as a teacher I learned myself, in my own career; certain other things I learned by watching Balanchine teach; and a lot of what I do I acquired by going to see his ballets, to see what he was asking from his dancers on the stage and what they needed to develop in their technique.

I give my pupils the pure classical technique as I learned it, according to Petipa, for their foundation, but I also try to keep up-to-date with the way the technique is changing. The emphasis shifts, the rhythm alters. When I teach classical variations, I try to adapt them to the way we dance today, because that was what Balanchine wanted, and I am preparing my pupils to dance his repertoire.

Dancers have been changing, too—my pupils are different from the way my friends and I were when we were girls. I was young for my age: at seventeen, I looked fifteen. (Partly, I think now, this was due to the lack of food.) The girls today seem to me old for their age. Looking at so much television, they see a broader piece of life, they see the way other people live. This is information that when I was young could be obtained only by reading books. All we knew of the world then was as much of it as we saw reflected in our families. Things would happen, we would find ourselves in some difficult or awkward situation, and we wouldn't know how to handle it because it was outside the scope of our experience; it was beyond what we had seen.

But despite their grown-up poise, Americans are, I find, rather timid in their dancing, too shy to show their emotions. In Russia, we were shy in life and abandoned on the stage, but here it is vice versa. When I am working with my pupils in the studio on a love scene, I find that I have to coax and squeeze. They don't understand that if they act passionate about someone on the stage, they are under no obligation to act that way in life. They are afraid that the man will think it is their real emotion. But we were always told in Russia that on the stage you can do anything and then walk away from it—your actions on the stage don't carry over into your life. My pupils are sometimes afraid to pretend.

American girls are also built differently from the way we were in Russia. The Russian woman is rather voluptuous; Americans are more sportive. Russians don't do sports, they eat; but American girls are always aware of their figures, of how many calories they're taking in. We didn't think about these things.

In Russia, dancers were not conscious of their looks. We didn't have the notion that a ballerina should be slender and good looking, not too small. At the Maryinsky, there was no ideal. A pretty face was the main requirement. Karsavina was pretty and also slender. Vaganova was a big technician but never had a great career as a ballerina, because she was rather ugly. Looking back now, I see that there were many girls at the Maryinsky who were not such good dancers but were kept on for their beauty.

No one talked then about losing weight—that started later, with Olga Spessivtseva. We had always considered her beautiful; but when she went away to dance with the Diaghilev company, she lost weight, and when she returned to Russia, she looked ravishing. In our minds, she became the image of a ballerina. Even so, I don't think we made a decision to aspire to that image until later, after we left Russia and went to Europe. When I came to Diaghilev from Germany and was told that I had to lose weight, I was astounded—it had never occurred to me to think of the picture I was presenting. Our awareness changed. It was Balanchine, I think, who gave us the ideal image of a ballerina, who in his choreography made us realize how much more beautiful movement looks on a body that is streamlined. And now this streamlined silhouette has become the norm: it is what a dancer is supposed to look like.

I don't think it is without exceptions: real talent can make us forget that a dancer is not quite according to our specifications. For instance, I tell my pupils, "If you are small, you must pay for it on the stage and do more—you must be better than the dancer who is taller."

Americans are raised to believe that everyone is created equal; but ballet—even in America—is not so fair. Still, I think a good dancer, one who is talented, has more opportunity here than in Russia, where roles are distributed according to the policy called *emploi*. Dancers in Russia are cast according to type: you are designated classical or soubrette or demi-caractère from the start, and for the length of your career you dance only the parts that are within that type—the roles that would come most naturally to you, that your temperament and physique are ideally suited for. Well, when there are two hundred and fifty dancers employed in a company, the directors can afford to be so choosy: you are too short to dance the prince; you are blond and so can't dance the Spanish variation. I find our policy here in America better, because it leaves room for surprises. Sometimes a dancer who is not by nature suited to a role triumphs in it and enlarges our thinking, giving us some new understanding of the ballet. After all, our notion of a role is mostly based on our memories of the people who have danced it in the past.

Russians take art very seriously. For them, ballet along with opera and drama is on the highest plane, to be treated with reverence. This has its advantages: when I was in the Theatre School, we felt that what we were doing was important to society, especially after the Revolution, when we were called on to give performances for the unions and factory workers. This conviction gave us an incentive: we shared a certain ambition that was larger than ourselves, that went beyond stardom. Young dancers in America are missing that, I think. Ballet is not so much at the center of our culture. Most students here are looking to make their way to establish a place for themselves in a company, to make their living dancing. They work hard when they are in school so that when they get out they will be hired by a good company and given the opportunity to dance good choreography. Apart from the New York City Ballet, I think, most American companies dance a rather dull repertoire. There is no sense of taking part in something creative and exciting; ballet today seems to me to be rather still water.

When I first came to America, there was no ballet company here. Now there are ballet companies all over the country, in every small town. I think this is a mistake. Many of the people who dance in these companies aren't talented, and the quality of their productions is not very high. It would be much healthier for ballet, I think, if there were only several large companies to which everybody would come.

People often say that in our time dancing has become more athletic. I disagree. To me it seems that just the opposite is true: ballet was more athletic at the end of the nineteenth century, with Pierina Legnani commanding the stage like a fire engine, doing her forty-eight fouettés. That way of dancing was, from my point of view, ugly and uninspired. Today it's different. A dancer who comes out and displays her technique so brazenly, without any real purpose in the ballet, we would consider tasteless. Soviet technique is of course different, much more acrobatic than ours. Acrobatics is interesting and often thrilling to watch, but we are dancers, not acrobats, and ballet is an art, not a sport. I think Soviet dancers sometimes overstep that line. But we don't, thanks to Balanchine and Jerome Robbins; the repertoire they created keeps us on the right path.

I think an artist should go to see everything. I tell my pupils to go to museums, to concerts, to the opera, to the theatre—drama is very important if they are going to dance dramatic ballets. Athletes narrow their view: they must concentrate only on their sport, to the exclusion of all others. But dancers, I believe, should have a working knowledge of the other arts; they should be exposed to everything.

During the Revolution, when the times were so difficult in Russia, Feodor Lopukhov insisted that we go to concerts and museums, to get out and learn about the world instead of sitting at home and feeling sorry for ourselves. Later, with Diaghilev, we were constantly surrounded by painters, composers, writers, all sorts of people pushing us to think in new directions. For the sake of our art, we taught ourselves to be curious, and that curiosity stayed with us; it is still in my blood. When I hear people talking about some new show or exhibition, I think to myself, My goodness, I am already behind the times, and I rush right out to see it. I think there is nothing to take the place of this sort of knowledge: the more you know, the more cultured you are, the more it shows in everything—in your walk, in your talk, in your art. I see young dancers today go to class and then go home. They are so tired, they say. They are not living. Sometimes they go to the ballet, but I don't see them at the opera, at the symphony, at a film. Of course, there are a few exceptions, but in general I find that dancers today restrict themselves.

The school is, I think, partly at fault. We should have courses in the history of art and the history of dance, the history of costume, music, and theatre. These were subjects that were part of our curriculum in Russia. The history of costume, for example, was for us a fascinating subject, a survey of how styles changed, which is important for a performer and especially for a choreographer, because in different costumes you must behave differently. Ladies wearing hoop skirts couldn't run, couldn't perform certain duties; they developed a way to maneuver their hoops, to climb a flight of stairs or sit down gracefully. Now, in our century, girls are wearing slacks and they have a different way of carrying themselves as a result. Along with costumes, we studied the history of manners: in medieval times, the men and ladies when they danced didn't clasp hands—that would have been considered too daring. Instead, the women rested their hands on top of their partners' for support, the way we would rest our hands on a table. From the beginning, the School of American Ballet was patterned on the Theatre School because, as we knew it, the Theatre School was the best school for ballet in the world. Unfortunately, at the School of American Ballet we don't have room for academic classes—we have only four rooms on the third floor of the Juilliard School building, four studios that are constantly in use, and we need at least four more.

Ideally, a ballet dancer's education should include classes in other kinds of dancing—mime, folk, character, and modern. Mime is, I think, old-fashioned but still necessary because it helps to create a character or to indicate the style of a specific century. Mime is to classical ballet training what Latin is to a university education—a course that can help you in all your other subjects. In mime, young dancers learn the significance of gesture. I think that they should be required to see the films of Charlie Chaplin.

They should study folk and character dances—the polonaise, the tarantella, the mazurka, the czardas, and the waltz, Viennese style—for expression. If you think about it, our movement, the basic classical vocabulary, comes from folk dancing. Port de bras and jump—every nation has its own routines that are not very different in principle from what we do. Stravinsky in his violin concerto uses Russian melodies; Balanchine in his *Square Dance* uses American folk-dance steps. Even if a dancer never has occasion to perform folk dances except in these distilled versions, I think it is important that she know them, that she have command of them, first-hand; they broaden her range. Spanish dancing is particularly useful for young dancers because it's very beautiful, complicated in its rhythms, and completely foreign in its style. I encourage my pupils to study it, to get them to move more freely.

I also encourage them to study modern dance; I think it opens their eyes and helps to unwind their bodies, because classical dancers sometimes get stiff trying to hold themselves for pirouettes, always supporting their own weight. For me, the classical dancer is like a rose, a flower that blooms by opening outward, reaching upward, and the modern dancer is like wisteria, a flower that droops and bends, not denying gravity but cooperating with it. Modern dancers move terre-à-terre, and unlike most classical dancers, they know how to collapse very gracefully; they make excellent use of the floor.

Men are by nature rather earthbound, and women, according to their physique, much more ethereal. There is a certain roundness to a woman's body and the way she moves; a man's body is a triangle—wide shoulders, small waist, small hips—and the way he moves, his lines and positions, must be angular. Men of course have a different jump, using much stronger muscles; they have more force behind their takeoff. And they don't do so much développé, because they don't need it; if a man does a high développé, it looks acrobatic. I am in favor of separate classes for men and women, because the technique for each of them is completely different, and so is the style. In the beginning, for little children, the training is all the same, but as soon as they cross the line into adolescence, they should be given a different approach. Then, I think, they should be taught by someone of the same sex. A male teacher can give girls the fundamentals, but later, when the time comes to refine the arm positions and add the finishing touches, I think the training should be woman-to-woman and man-to-man.

If I am training a boy and I see, for instance, that he is dancing with an overly feminine accent, I tell him to look at Michelangelo's statue of David, to look to sculpture for examples of figures and poses that are both graceful and manly. In sculpture, men don't generally stand in first position, with their weight equally on both feet; they stand on one leg, in a position that is more asymmetrical, more angular.

Most teachers today, I know, are content if their pupils execute the steps: perhaps they feel that these issues of femininity and masculinity are related to sexual preference and so are nobody's business. But what goes on the stage I consider my business, and a male dancer who is not a manly dancer is less effective. In our ballet, men are men and women are women on the stage, and that has nothing to do with how they choose to behave in their private lives. These differences are important and they must be preserved on the stage, because they provide more opportunities for drama. One season not long ago, I went to see *Romeo and Juliet*, with a lovely girl as Juliet and, as Romeo, a young man who danced in a feminine style and made no effort to convince us that he liked Juliet. He would look matter-of-factly every now and then at his beloved, the way one might look at a clock to see what time it is. Well, I thought, this is an outrage but probably not poor Romeo's fault. He thinks that the choreography is the role's only requirement, that the character will somehow emerge from the steps themselves, and no one has taken the trouble to tell him otherwise.

It is the performer, not the audience, who must imagine an entire world in the theatre, a world more vivid than the one we live in every day. It is the artist's responsibility to envision that world and then to bring it into being, so that it is concrete: it exists on the stage and actual events take place in it. I tell my pupils to make a list of facts and to run through that list, like a litany, just before the curtain goes up, as I did when I danced *Gaîté Parisienne*. You must know where you are, on earth or in heaven. On earth—then where? In Paris. You must know what time of day it is. Say, five o'clock. You must know who you are. Not me, Choura, but a French girl, a glove seller. You settle all of this in your imagination, and then you can begin.

I impart to my pupils the standards that were imparted to me, standards that they must never compromise, not even for a moment. When I traveled with the Ballet Russe de Monte Carlo, dancing in small towns, in high school auditoriums, I behaved no differently than I would have if I had been dancing at the Metropolitan Opera. I made all the usual demands on myself. Every night, I arrived at the theatre by six o'clock, in time to run through a full class and put on my makeup. Claudia Cassidy, a reviewer in Chicago, once criticized me for not taking off my red nail polish to dance *Swan Lake*, and I realized that she was right. From then on, no matter where we were dancing, even in the middle of nowhere, I always powdered my shoulders and back with white talc for the second act and put on silver nail polish. Many other ballerinas didn't go to all this trouble, but to my way of thinking they cheapened their own performances. I found their attitude appalling, full of disrespect for the theatre and for their audience.

I try to teach my students by example. To explain to them how to sparkle is impossible; you must sparkle yourself, and then they can copy you. I think it's important for children to see women who are well dressed if they are going to develop good taste. My pupils can see that I am very strict with myself, and so they don't balk when I am very strict with them. American children, I find, take to discipline well—they love it. Children need—they want—to be told what to do, where to go. Unfortunately, at the School of American Ballet, we have no facilities for boarding students; so even though our school is modeled on the Theatre School, there is this one important difference. If you are a boarding student, you obey the laws of the school—there is no maybe. If you disobey, you are punished. This is the way I was brought up in Russia, and I think we were much happier for it, because we knew what we could do and what we couldn't, and that knowledge gave us a sense of security. We were busy, on a schedule; we wore uniforms; we got up at the same time every day. These things were never questioned. And I think they made the path smoother for us as adults, because already we accepted certain patterns as a matter of course: when the sun gets up, I must get up, too.

I do not tolerate laziness or excuses, from myself or from my pupils. I tell them, "You decide one afternoon to skip the lesson and from then on you will have to struggle with yourself. What used to be automatic will then be open to question. If today you are too tired, you don't come, then why not tomorrow or another day, too? You will be tired again." And this way of thinking is the beginning of the end.

"Don't cheat yourself," I tell them. "I want entrechat six, not royale." It's exactly the same. Because once you allow yourself not to do entrechat six, then soon you will stop doing two pirouettes, then next stop doing pirouettes on pointe, and eventually you will stop doing anything at all. Goodbye, dancing.

I tell them that if something goes wrong during a performance, they must immediately practice it when the curtain goes down, as soon as the applause is ended. They must not leave the stage before practicing that particular step, in order to overcome their fear of doing it again.

The satisfaction of being a teacher is in your students' progress. They come to your class unable to do the variation, and at the end they do it very well. But it is amazing, I find, that people go constantly to teachers who are bad. That I noticed when I taught for Lensky. Sometimes I would have so many new students who couldn't do two pirouettes, and I would ask them, "How long did you study?" "Ten years," they would say. "You study ten years and you can't do anything—can't do two pirouettes, can't do entrechat six. Did it occur to you that your teacher must be lousy?" "Oh no," they would say. "My teacher is marvelous, I love my teacher." Well, but who has this teacher created? Nobody. There are people who teach for twenty years and they don't create anybody. This is to my way of thinking all the proof anybody could want that they are bad teachers and not to be patronized.

Much of what a dancer needs to be good, I think, can be developed. I saw this proven many times in Russia: there were children who were in the beginning absolutely incapable, yet by working hard, by working everything—their extensions, their toes, their coup de pied—they developed. I watched some of the most untalented people become soloists and some of the most talented grow up to stay "near the water," because they were lazy and not interested.

The signs of promise you can see at the beginning. When a dancer is twelve years old, already her features are starting to mold. And you are afraid: Oh, this one will be too tall, or that one doesn't have such a nice expression—it all counts. Or, this one has everything she needs, but she just admires herself in the mirror. She is blond, she is pretty, and she thinks that's quite enough. Like any teacher, I concentrate on the ones who have talent, but I try not to let them know that I think they are special. I work my pupils hard to develop the physical attributes they will need, to compensate for what they are lacking. Most of all, I work to develop their musicality. Without it, I tell them, they are nothing. Their timing must be perfection, the dancing right on the music, and only then can they give the impression of interpreting the music.

Many teachers believe that musicality is rare and God-given, beyond their power to shape, but I disagree. I think that for any dancer it is a necessity, and I know that it can be cultivated because I cultivate it in my students. I teach them to associate music with movement, to listen hard, so that they learn to sense immediately the places where the choreography fits the score. In the waltz variation I teach from *Raymonda*, for instance, there is a sequence of arabesques fondus, and in them the leg in arabesque moves with the melody. I give my pupils exercises in which I vary the accent—one day, battements tendus with the accent out; the next day, the same with the accent in. Most of the time, in classical ballet, the accent is up. I explain to my pupils that they must learn to accent everything, and then the rhythm will help them. I demand that all my pupils, even little children, be right on the beat. For everyone, the temptation is to be a little bit sluggish and to lag slightly behind the beat. I tell my students, "If you dance for three hours like that, you will be off by three bars."

Good dancers are made every day, by good teachers; but great dancers are born. A great dancer has something extra—I think it's personality. She isn't just a dummy who waves her hands in time to the music; her movements have meaning. If a dancer is great, you look from the audience and say, "Who is that girl?" She is somebody you notice, not because she doesn't keep her place in the line, but because she has about her dancing what I call perfume, something that caresses you.

I think to be a dancer, it's a calling. It is not commercial. This is the Russian point of view. Commercial artists, to my way of thinking, have no place in the theatre. This is not to say that dancers shouldn't earn a lot of money, or that they shouldn't go to work, for instance, on Broadway, which is commercial, but that they shouldn't look to money to reward them for their dancing. Because money alone will never be enough.

Balanchine always said that dancers are aristocrats, that we were born into the ranks of a nobility that is based on art, and I agree. In any society, the truly privileged class is made up of artists, who are chosen people. Their talent is God-given, and it sets them apart. It sustains and comforts them; it gives them a purpose. This has been my lifelong conviction, and I pass it along to my students, just as my teachers instilled in me as part of my training a sense of dignity and pride.

I finish every class with a révérence, which I consider important practice, but practice of a kind that has nothing to do with technique. Unfortunately, most dancers today execute révérence as if it were just another combination, without stopping to realize that it is a gesture and that, as a gesture, it must mean something. A dancer must charm her audience—by holding the pose at the end of a variation, which is difficult; by bowing to them when she comes on the stage. Révérence is an expression of humility, a dancer's way of thanking her audience for their applause. I teach my pupils that we dancers have much to be grateful for.

Sixteen

I HAVE BEEN a prima ballerina and a celebrity, inducted into halls of fame, given numerous awards and the keys to dozens of cities, and even made an honorary Sagamore Indian. And yet, I don't think so highly of myself. For one thing, I am stubborn. Being passed around, changing hands so much as a child, I became very difficult, a little liar. To punish me, my aunt would put me in the corner. "If you don't apologize," she would tell me, "you will stay forever." And I would think to myself, Well, I will stay forever. I am also selfish, short tempered, and impatient—I don't suffer fools very easily, and I hate people who complain. If someone who has known me well were to draw up a list of my faults, none of them would come as a surprise to me.

But though I may not be a great human being, I have lived up to the standards I set for myself. Being an orphan, I think now, must have shaped my personality, because I couldn't count on anybody. I learned to rely on myself. My discipline has been my security.

A woman—any woman, not only a ballerina—should make herself beautiful. I think that if you don't bring beauty into the world, you are living a rather low, animal-like existence. A woman should wear what suits her, not the current style if the current style doesn't flatter her features. This is what I learned in Paris, and it's a lesson that has stayed with me. I try to dress elegantly whenever I go out. I'm not saying that I wear my evening gown in swimming, but if I'm going downstairs to the laundry room, I put on a nice pair of slacks and a blouse; I try not to look as if I just got out of bed—not because I think somebody will recognize me but because I think I owe it to the people I encounter to look presentable.

The dancer's duties go beyond the stage. If you are a ballerina, you are a public figure. I am shocked at the way many dancers today neglect the responsibilities that come with their position. I see them on the street, on their way to buy groceries, wearing a T-shirt and an old pair of blue jeans when the night before they were on the stage looking gorgeous. I think they resent being so much in the public eye, always on view, but they have no right to: I find their attitude arrogant. When you are a star, your name becomes a household word. Your image and your private life become the property of your admirers. This is part of the unwritten, unspoken agreement you make with your audience; this is the price you must pay in exchange for your fame. And if your fans come to worship you, if you become the object of their fantasies, if they form in their minds a picture of you that has nothing to do with who you really are, that is none of your business. You must not contradict or disappoint them.

As a dancer, I was often cast as a flirt, and I suppose I am flirtatious. I am an optimist by nature, very gay, and when I meet people, especially men, I convey this, by making conversation that is lively and lighthearted.

Today, of course, there is no romance. Not long ago, I saw *Gaîté Parisienne* revived at Ballet Theatre. The dancers didn't understand the ballet, and I don't think anybody explained it to them. Because Paris when we knew it was really something— a city with love in the air, like a perfume. Everywhere, there was some flirtation—that was the way people passed the time.

Now a man drags you to the bed—or vice versa—and that's that. It used to be that there was so much suspense. You would meet a man. He would say, "May I have your telephone number?" And you would think, Well, is he worth it or not? You would give him your number

. . . and then wait. The telephone would ring—maybe it's him. All right, it *is* him. "What are you doing today?" he would say. "Would you like to come and have a drink with me?" So you would go and the two of you would start to know each other. Then he would bring you home. "What are you doing Friday?" he would ask. "Can we have lunch or dinner?" And if it would be dinner, then maybe he would kiss you—kiss you in the taxi or kiss you good night. Well, the first couple of times, he would just be interested to know all about you. And then he would say, "Come and see how I live and we will have a drink." And here you had to be careful. But it would be up to you, whether you had an affair with him or not. The first kiss meant a lot then—more than it does today, I think. Now everybody is in such a hurry, they want to get down to business right away and skip all the preliminaries. Nobody today understands how much fun the preliminaries used to be.

But times change, and if you don't change with them, you are left behind. I enjoy the company of young people because they provoke me to think, to re-examine the way I have always looked at the world. We have in Russia a proverb: "Tell me who your friends are, and I'll tell you who you are." My friends are for the most part younger than I am, and thanks to them, my outlook is not *démodé*. I feel as much a part of the world today as I did when I was twenty.

The world, as far as I'm concerned, still divides clearly into right and wrong, black and white—there is little if any grey. I think that talent and excellence are always recognized in the long run, if not straight away. Life seems to me fair, though sometimes when you are in the midst of tribulation, it seems horribly unfair. But at the end of the road, you can look back and see that even the worst experiences brought with them a lesson or prepared the way for something good. You tally both columns, the pluses and the minuses, and they balance.

We have another proverb in Russia: "You make your own happiness"—and I believe it. Life brings to everyone difficult situations; in this, we have no choice. But we can choose whether to accept those situations graciously or to rail against them. The people who quarrel with fate turn bitter. They harm themselves; their attitude is unattractive, and it eats away at the stamina they need to get through life. Whereas the people who accept their destinies graciously grow stronger instead of weaker. They are the ones who in the long run survive.

So much of what I know, not only about dancing but also about life, I learned from Balanchine. One season, when we were in the Diaghilev company, the time had come to sign new contracts, and I began asking around to find out how much money the other dancers were making. How much is *she* paid, I wondered—I want more than she gets. And how much does that one receive? I want exactly the same. But no one would tell me her salary. So finally I asked George. He told me, "Sit down and think how much money you want. You must decide for yourself, and then be satisfied. Because there will always be better dancers and worse dancers than you, people who are prettier and people not as attractive—you will always have your own good qualities, and your faults will always be with you. You can't spend your life trying to catch up to somebody else." I realized that he was right; and from then on, the only contract that really mattered to me was the one between me and my dancing.

Sometimes I think how nice it would be to return to Leningrad and see again the white nights I remember so vividly. For two weeks every year all life was suffused with a pale blue light different from the light at any other season. I know that I will never go back (though I'm told that I could if I chose to), because my home now—even my spiritual home—is America. I sacrificed marriage, children, and country to be a ballerina, and there was never any misunderstanding on my part—I knew the price. I put my dancing first, before my allegiances to friends and lovers, even husbands; before my home. It is possible to be a ballerina and give only fifty or seventy-five percent of yourself to your art, to conserve the rest and make of it a life for yourself, apart from the stage. But that was not for me. I gave one hundred percent of myself to my art, and my art has repaid me.

A Note on the Type

The text of this book was set in Weiss, a type face designed in Germany by Emil Rudolf Weis (1875–1942). The design of the roman was completed in 1928 and that of the italic in 1931. Both are well-balanced and even in color, and both reflect the subtle skill of a fine calligrapher. Designed by Iris Weinstein.

OTHER FROMM PAPERBACKS:

FLAUBERT & TURGENEV
A FRIENDSHIP IN LETTERS
edited and translated
by Barbara Beaumont

SECRETS OF MARIE ANTOINETTE
A COLLECTION OF LETTERS
edited by Olivier Bernier

KALLOCAIN
A NOVEL
by Karin Boye

TALLEYRAND
A BIOGRAPHY
by Duff Cooper

VIRTUE UNDER FIRE
HOW WORLD WAR II CHANGED OUR
SOCIAL AND SEXUAL ATTITUDES
by John Costello

PIAF
by Margaret Crosland

BEFORE THE DELUGE
A PORTRAIT OF BERLIN IN THE 1920's
by Otto Friedrich

THE END OF THE WORLD
A HISTORY
by Otto Friedrich

J. ROBERT OPPENHEIMER
SHATTERER OF WORLDS
by Peter Goodchild

THE ENTHUSIAST
A LIFE OF THORNTON WILDER
by Gilbert A. Harrison

INDIAN SUMMER
A NOVEL
by William Dean Howells

A CRACK IN THE WALL
GROWING UP UNDER HITLER
by Horst Krüger

EDITH WHARTON
A BIOGRAPHY
by R.W.B. Lewis

THE CONQUEST OF MOROCCO
by Douglas Porch

THE CONQUEST OF THE SAHARA
by Douglas Porch

HENRY VIII
THE POLITICS OF TYRANNY
by Jasper Ridley

INTIMATE STRANGERS
THE CULTURE OF CELEBRITY
by Richard Schickel

BONE GAMES
ONE MAN'S SEARCH FOR THE
ULTIMATE ATHLETIC HIGH
by Rob Schultheis

KENNETH CLARK
A BIOGRAPHY
by Meryle Secrest

THE HERMIT OF PEKING
THE HIDDEN LIFE OF SIR EDMUND
BACKHOUSE
by Hugh Trevor-Roper

ALEXANDER OF RUSSIA
NAPOLEON'S CONQUEROR
by Henri Troyat

MARY TODD LINCOLN
HER LIFE AND LETTERS
edited by Justin G. Turner
and Linda Levitt Turner